# The Everyday Language of White Racism

Linguistic anthropology evolved in the twentieth century in an environment that tended to reify language and culture. A recognition of the dynamics of discourse as a sociocultural process has since emerged as researchers have used new methods and theories to examine the reproduction and transformation of people, institutions, and communities through linguistic practices. This transformation of linguistic anthropology itself heralds a new era for publishing as well. **Blackwell Studies in Discourse and Culture** aims to represent and foster this new approach to discourse and culture by producing books that focus on the dynamics that can be obscured by such broad and diffuse terms as "language." This series is committed to the ethnographic approach to language and discourse: ethnographic works deeply informed by theory, as well as more theoretical works that are deeply grounded in ethnography. The books are aimed at scholars in the sociology and anthropology of language, anthropological linguistics, sociolinguistics, and socioculturally informed psycholinguistics. It is our hope that all books in the series will be widely adopted for a variety of courses.

### Series Editor

**James M. Wilce** (PhD University of California, Los Angeles) is Professor of Anthropology at Northern Arizona University. He serves on the editorial board of American Anthropologist and the Journal of Linguistic Anthropology. He has published a number of articles and is the author of *Eloquence in Trouble: The Poetics and Politics of Complaint in Rural Bangladesh* (1998), *Language and Emotion* (forthcoming), and *Crying Shame: Metaculture, Modernity, and the Exaggerated Death of Lament* (forthcoming), and editor of *Social and Cultural Lives of Immune Systems* (2003).

### Editorial Board

Richard Bauman – Indiana University
Eve Danziger – University of Virginia
Patrick Eisenlohr – Washington University in St. Louis
Per-Anders Forstorp – Royal Institute of Technology, Stockholm
Elizabeth Keating – UT Austin
Paul Kroskrity – UCLA
Norma Mendoza-Denton – University of Arizona
Susan Philips – University of Arizona
Bambi Schieffelin – NYU
Lukas Tsitsipis – University of Thessaloniki, Greece

### In the Series

1. *The Hidden Life of Girls*, by Marjorie Harness Goodwin
2. *We Share Walls: Language, Land, and Gender in Berber Morocco*, by Katherine E. Hoffman
3. *The Everyday Language of White Racism*, by Jane H. Hill

### Forthcoming

*Living Memory: The Social Aesthetics of Language*, by Jillian R. Cavanaugh

# The Everyday Language of White Racism

Jane H. Hill

⊛ WILEY-BLACKWELL

A John Wiley & Sons, Ltd., Publication

Blackwell Publishing was acquired by John Wiley & Sons in February 2007. Blackwell's publishing program has been merged with Wiley's global Scientific, Technical, and Medical business to form Wiley-Blackwell.

*Registered Office*
John Wiley & Sons Ltd, The Atrium, Southern Gate, Chichester, West Sussex, PO19 8SQ, United Kingdom

*Editorial Offices*
350 Main Street, Malden, MA 02148-5020, USA
9600 Garsington Road, Oxford, OX4 2DQ, UK
The Atrium, Southern Gate, Chichester, West Sussex, PO19 8SQ, UK

For details of our global editorial offices, for customer services, and for information about how to apply for permission to reuse the copyright material in this book please see our website at www.wiley.com/wiley-blackwell.

*Library of Congress Cataloging-in-Publication Data*

Hill, Jane H.
    The everyday language of white racism / Jane H. Hill.
        p. cm. – (Blackwell studies in discourse and culture)
    Includes bibliographical references and index.
    ISBN 978-1-4051-8453-3 (pbk. : alk. paper) – ISBN 978-1-4051-8454-0 (hardcover : alk. paper)  1. Racism in language.   2. Racism–United States.   3. Discourse analysis–Social aspects–United States.   I. Title.
    P120.R32H55 2008
    306.44089–dc22

                                                                                2008013078

A catalogue record for this book is available from the British Library.

# Contents

# Preface and Acknowledgments

Some members of audiences for talks about the topics I treat in this book have accused me of presenting an overly negative view of the state of race relations in the United States. I do insist that racism remains an active force in White American culture in the twenty-first century. However, I write this in my 69th year. I grew up in segregated schools and neighborhoods, listening to the frankly racist talk of friends and family members. My dear grandmother and grandfather, my beloved father and his three brothers and their wives, my delightful aunts, all of them (except a couple of the aunts) highly educated, could hardly be together for half an hour without the conversation turning to "the jigs" – their preferred epithet for African Americans. My mother and my husband and my sister and brothers and I dreaded these offensive conversations and we did our best to steer the talk toward harmless topics, but it often seemed that no theme existed that did not provide new openings to return to their obsession. While my life is still spent almost entirely among other White people, I rarely hear that kind of talk today. And I have found that White Americans are today relatively honest in talking and thinking about the place of race and racism in their own lives, compared to people of similar class and status in many other countries I have visited. Furthermore, people of color now encounter opportunities in the United States, including positions at the very highest levels of power and visibility in government, business, and the professions, that were unthinkable 25 or 30 years ago, and that would be unlikely in most White-dominant countries today, even in Europe. So there has been positive change. But every serious study shows that White racism continues to be a deadening and oppressive fact of life for the vast majority of people of color in the United States. This book is an effort to understand why this is so. Why does racism persist in so many forms in a country where to call a person "racist" is a deep insult, and where "equal opportunity" is a universally articulated value? In this book I use the tools of my trade – linguistic anthropology – to try to understand this puzzle. Linguistic anthropologists believe that to use language – to speak, to write, to sing, to joke, to listen, to read – is the most important way that human beings make the world, and make it meaningful. So everyday talk and text should be the single most important way that White Americans come to understand the world in terms of race, to practice racism, and to learn to tolerate its effects, sometimes in full consciousness of what they are doing, and sometimes in reduced consciousness or denial. So I focus on the ways that White racism is, as anthropological jargon has it, "produced and reproduced" through everyday talk and text. Many examples in this book come from language in mass media, but, given the way that American lives are utterly saturated with talk and text from such media, I insist that media language must count as yet another form of "everyday language."

This book is about White racism, for two reasons. The first is that I live in a White world, and I have not undertaken formal fieldwork in order to observe everyday discourse about race among Americans of color. I have benefited enormously from conversations with colleagues who can offer insight into White racism from a non-White perspective, and from writing by anthropologists of color, from W. E. B. Du Bois to Audrey Smedley, Faye Harrison, and Ana Celia Zentella, who have made significant contributions to theorizing racism. The second reason is that I believe that the (understandable) distrust and even hatred that many non-White Americans feel when they think of or interact with White Americans, sometimes called "racism," is not very important in the great scheme of things. Of course this distrust and hatred is painful for Whites at an individual level. Like most White Americans, I can think of times when I or my children have suffered pain in interactions with people of color who disliked and distrusted us, or even abused us, just because we were White. But these experiences have been both few and ephemeral. They have occasioned no enduring withdrawals of privilege, no consequences beyond a moment of hurt and anger. These experiences cut deep, and I continue to remember a few with some pain. But they have very limited structural consequences. When a White person chooses to avoid a "bad neighborhood," this choice has few costs for her. In contrast, should a person of color choose to avoid all of the environments where she is likely to be hurt emotionally or even physically, the costs would be devastating, since these environments – the admissions office of a school, the reading room of a library, the human resources department of a corporation, the aisles of a discount store, the sidewalks of a neighborhood – will include nearly all of the sites where significant symbolic and material resources are distributed in our society. And, since she cannot possibly avoid these, the moments of painfully unjust rejection – like those that sometimes trouble me, even though they were minor incidents that occurred years ago – are multiplied and multiplied into an endless and acute source of stress that it is difficult for any White person to imagine. I try to think about how I would feel, about what kind of person I would be, if the half-dozen very negative experiences in my entire long life that happened because I am White were multiplied into threats that would loom for me every single day. When we consider this, we are required to conclude that, among the many appalling consequences of life in a racist society, the occasional discomforts and restrictions felt by Whites because they are stereotyped by people of color surely rank very low. And we must also be struck by the extraordinary toughness, courage, and fundamental strength of character that must be shared by the vast majority of people of color.

Because I have not conducted research on racism in other countries, this book is about White racism in the United States. Furthermore, I will focus here on the way it plays out among the people I know best – middle- and upper-middle-class White professionals, the kinds of people who read newspapers and use the Internet, and who produce the kind of talk and text that might be heard or read beyond the sphere of immediate family and neighbors. For want of a better term, I will refer to these people as White elites, even though only a very few of them are movers and shakers at the highest level. While the comparative literature shows that there are many kinds of racism, I believe that elite White racism in the United States is the most important and influential form of racism in the world. The global power of elite White Americans means that everyone in the world must reckon with what they think and do. The forms of racism that they accomplish – and, indeed, their forms of anti-racist practice – influence how people think and act around the globe.

White American racism is an inspiration for racists globally, but it is also one of the great puzzles for people in other countries. Most White American anthropologists who have worked outside the United States have been asked about it, in tones ranging from the accusatory to the merely curious, by interlocutors at all levels of society. Doing fieldwork in Mexico, I have had conversations about *racismo norteamericano* with interlocutors ranging from illiterate peasants to distinguished professors (working-class Mexicans, who have to navigate White racism as part of the trick of coming to the United States as undocumented migrants, are especially knowledgeable and aware about it). I speculate that around the world White American racism is considered to be at least as typical a feature of life in the United States as is American wealth. People in other countries measure their own local experiences of racism against what they believe to be American patterns, deplore the global influence of American racism, and wonder how it is that American life can encompass such a contradictory combination of the best and worst in human nature.

Regrettably, this book does not treat anti-Semitism, which is obviously closely linked to racism, shares much of its logic, and figures in the prejudices of most racists. Anti-Semitism around the world is apparently on the rise, and must be carefully watched. But this is a vast subject in its own right, and falls beyond the scope of this book.

One last warning. In speaking, I do not use racist epithets. As a teacher, I have learned that uttering them, even when they are carefully framed as examples, may cause great pain to students. However, writing and reading are a different kind of context. I am concerned that the moment of collusion between writer and reader when the reader encounters "k..e" or "n....r" may be an even more powerful site for the reproduction of racializing practice than is the moment of shock when the reader encounters the words spelled out. With the ellipses, both writer and reader share a false comfort – we are not the sort of people who would ever spell these words out – that is immediately contradicted by what is silenced in a deep presupposition – we both know these words. So racist epithets, spelled out, will appear in this book. I prefer the shock, the confrontation with ugliness, the recognition that these words and what they mean are in our world. I have thought carefully about the fact that writing the words out may be, at a deep level of self-construction for me, a moment of shamefully pleasurable catharsis, as much as it is a conscious choice made on theoretical grounds; I accept that responsibility. I also accept responsibility for the pain that seeing these words will bring some readers, and I apologize.

I owe thanks to many people for helping me develop the ideas in this book. I thank the many students, including especially Laura Cummings, Elizabeth Krause, Jacqueline Messing, Andrea Smith, Gayle Shuck, Elea Aguirre, Barbara Meek, Adam Schwartz, and Elise DuBord, who have found these ideas exciting and have encouraged me to work on them, and who have themselves contributed both new materials and exacting criticism. Among colleagues to whom I owe special gratitude are Ana Alonso, Barbara Babcock, Charles Briggs, José Cobas, Gloria Ladson-Billings, Norma Mendoza-Denton, Susan Philips, Jennifer Roth-Gordon, Carlos Vélez Ibáñez, Kathryn Woolard, and Ana Celia Zentella. Other colleagues and students, too numerous to mention, have sent me e-mails and clippings for my collection of materials, and I thank them all. I should especially mention Greg Stoltz, Luis Barragan, and Lori Labotka, who have checked bibliography and transcribed interviews, and Dan Goldstein, who did most of the interviews cited in Chapter 5.

My husband, Kenneth C. Hill, and my sons Eric and Harold, have as always contributed sustaining love and patience. I thank especially the Center for Advanced Studies in the Behavioral Sciences for a residential fellowship in 2003–04, and the University of Arizona for granting me sabbatical leave during that year, permitting me to pull together the many scraps of more than a decade of attention to the questions developed in this book.

# Chapter 1

# The Persistence of White Racism

## Introduction: Racism, Race, and Racial Disparities

I began to write this chapter in the early months of 2004, 140 years after the abolition of slavery in the United States in 1864, 80 years out from the establishment of citizenship for Native Americans in 1924, and during the 50th anniversary of the US Supreme Court's great decision of 1954, *Brown v. Board of Education*, which ended official segregation in US public schools. The US Civil Rights Act of 1964, which proscribed racial discrimination in broad areas of American life, was 40 years old.

The people who made these landmarks live in daguerreotypes, in flickering black and white film, in reunions of graying veterans of the Civil Rights movement. Today most Whites see White racism as a part of the American past, and anti-racist struggle as largely completed. Yet people of color – African Americans, Native Americans, Americans of Latin American or Asian or Middle Eastern ancestry – consistently report that they experience racism (Alter 2004; Bobo 2001; Feagin and Sykes 1994). These reports are not the product of oversensitivity or paranoia. Instead, they may even understate the impact that White racism has on the everyday lives of people of color (Bonilla-Silva 2003; Feagin and Vera 1995).

While American workplaces and public institutions are increasingly integrated, very few Whites have social friends among people of color (Bonilla-Silva 2003:107–111). White isolation makes it easy for them to dismiss the complaints of people of color as "whining" and "playing the race card." Whites do not themselves experience harassment for "driving while Black," or the stony inattention encountered when "ordering a restaurant meal while Indian." Their conversations with family and friends are never interrupted by perfect strangers telling them to "Speak English! This is America!" Nobody has ever tried to seduce them by confessing that they've "always wanted to make it with a hot Asian chick." And they don't have the kinds of conversations with people of color where they would hear about such incidents, which are so frequent as to be stereotypical. Everyday moments of discrimination are only part of the picture, though. Statistics for a wide range of indicators stratified by three major racial groups in the United States, shown in Table 1, reveal a consistent picture of gross disparities.[1]

The numbers in Table 1 capture quantitatively what is obvious to anyone who drives through an American city, attends a college graduation, visits a corporate headquarters, sits in a hospital emergency room, or accomplishes any other kind of everyday engagement with the world. What might explain these vivid inequalities? Brown et al. (2003) argue that they result from two opposing dynamics, "accumulation" that favors Whites, and "disaccumulation" that continues to disadvantage people of color. Yet we know that ordinary White people do not feel that they enjoy any benefit due to their race. Nor do they believe that people of color continue to face disadvantage. So, how do White people explain these numbers, and the visible evidence that they quantify, given that they think that racism has ended in the United States?

**Table 1**  Disparities in economic, health, and social indicators by "race" in the United States[2]

| Indicator type | Statistic | Hispanic | African American | White |
|---|---|---|---|---|
| Economic | Per capita income (2004) | 14,106 | 16,035 | 25,203 |
| | Median family income (2004) | 35,401 | 35,158 | 56,700 |
| | Household net worth (2000)[3] | 9,750 | 7,500 | 79,400 |
| | Home ownership[4] | 49.5% | 48.2% | 72.7% |
| | Unemployment (2005, with high school degree, no college) | 4.5% | 8.5% | 4.0% |
| | Poverty rate | 21.9% | 24.7% | 10.8% |
| Health | Private health insurance (under 65)[5] | 41.7% | 53.9 | 71.4 |
| | Life expectancy[6] | 79.5 (2001)[7] | 73.3 | 78.3 |
| | Infant mortality | 4.00/1,000 | 13.65/1,000 | 5.65/1,000 |
| Social | Married | 57.0% | 41.0% | 61.0% |
| | Female-headed family with children under 18 | 25.0% | 52.0% | 18.0% |
| | Women never married | 25.6% | 39.5% | 18.7% |
| | High school degree | 58.5% | 81.1% | 85.7 |
| | B.A. degree | 12.0% | 17.6% | 28.0% |
| | Incarceration per 100,000[8] | 742 | 2,290 | 412 |

Most White Americans do admit that isolated pockets of White racism persist – perhaps in northern Idaho, or southern Georgia. However, the disparities charted in Table 1, which are consistent across every region of the United States, are unlikely to result from the actions of those very few members of the White community – openly declared White supremacists – that all Whites categorize as "racists." A few thousand Ku Kluxers can hardly claim responsibility for the fact that the average household net worth of African Americans is less than one-tenth that of White households.[9]

Since common sense requires White Americans to reject the idea that these racial disparities are due to racism as they understand it – that is, as overt expression of White supremacy – they often conclude that they result from some fault of those who suffer. So they are credulous when the long-discredited idea that there might be a biologically based difference in intelligence among the races was revived in the last years of the twentieth century, in the bestseller *The Bell Curve* (Herrnstein and Murray 1994). However, while differential intelligence might explain the disparities in educational accomplishment seen in Table 1, it hardly accounts for the twofold disparity in figures for unemployment. Surely the labor market offers enough grunt jobs that this difference should be no more than 11 percent or so, as predicted by *The Bell Curve*'s figures for differential intelligence.[10] Instead, the table shows a 100 percent disparity, with African American unemployment twice that of Whites. Nor can the alleged average difference in IQ explain an African American infant mortality rate two and a half times that of Whites. The Hispanic figures contradict such an association: Hispanics have rates of school completion similar to those of African Americans, and yet exhibit lower rates of infant mortality even than Whites.[11]

A White American trying to account for these statistics might turn to ideas about cultural differences among ethnic groups, believing, for instance, that Hispanics typically enjoy large, close-knit extended families that provide good support for expectant mothers, explaining their low figures for infant mortality. Or they might believe that African Americans do not value higher education, but seek success in fields like sports and popular music, thus explaining their low rate of completion of bachelor's degrees. But, as we shall see below, these ideas about "culture" do not survive critical attention from an anthropological point of view.

Of course we cannot ignore the weight of history. African Americans were never compensated for their exclusion as slaves from the wealth of the nation built with their labor, for being terrorized by Whites out of such small property as they might accumulate in the dark years of Jim Crow, for their formal exclusion from resources distributed by twentieth-century government programs such as the GI Bill, FHA mortgage assistance, aid to small businesses, and support for farmers, through the mid-1960s and even later (Lipsitz 1998). Disparities in household net worth, or life expectancy, might be a residue of this history. But "history" does not explain differences in short-range phenomena such as median per capita income, unemployment, college graduation, or incarceration. If discrimination has been largely vanquished for the last 40 years, two generations, the racial stratification of these factors should surely have disappeared.

Along with many other scholars who have investigated the question, I suggest that what does account for these numbers is the persistent culture of White racism in the United States. White racism is not just part of American history. Instead, White racist culture today organizes racist practices in White-dominated institutions such as schools and health-care facilities, and everyday choices and behaviors by the vast majority of Whites operating as individuals. White racist culture is shaped by a "White racial frame," "an organized set of racialized ideas, stereotypes, emotions, and inclinations to discriminate" (Feagin 2006:27), along with interpretations that rationalize the discrimination against people of color that is indeed old (dating back to the earliest stages of the oppression of people of African descent by Whites in the New World), but continues as a vivid fact of life in the contemporary United States. The impacts shown in Table 1 are of such generality, and such a magnitude, as to suggest strongly that racism must be practiced in some way by a very substantial number of Whites, at every level of class and status. To render their practices invisible, and to tolerate or to discount their effects, Whites must share negative stereotypes of people of color, permitting them to blame these victims. How are such stereotypes produced and reproduced among people who deny that they are racist and who claim to abhor racism in word and deed (Bonilla-Silva 2003; Feagin and Vera 1995)? How does White racism actually work today?[12] This book aims at a partial answer to these questions by examining how White Americans produce and reproduce the culture of White racism through their use of language, from high literary text, to language in every sort of mass media, to everyday talk and text produced by ordinary people.

Before turning to my main topic, the reproduction of White racism in language, I want to introduce the theories that anthropologists and other scholars today find most productive in thinking about race, and about White racism. These critical theories challenge what I call the "folk theory" of racism. The folk theory is an interpretation, a way of thinking about racism, that is crucial to the perpetuation of White racist culture. Since for most White people the folk theory is undeniable common sense, ideas that contradict it require careful discussion. The folk theory interacts with the linguistic ideologies discussed in Chapter 2 in intricate ways that make possible the simultaneous reproduction and denial of White racism. Since one of the goals of this book is to show how this works, we need to know what the folk theory of racism is, and why it is inadequate to explain racial disparities in American society today. And we need to understand the critical theory of White racism as culture, which underlies the ideas presented in this book.

## Two Theories of Race and Racism: Folk Theory and Critical Theory

Cognitive anthropologists (e.g. D'Andrade 1995) use the term "folk theory" or "folk model" to label the everyday understandings of the world, found in all societies, that are revealed by ethnographic analysis. Folk theories influence scientific theories, and vice versa. But real differences exist between folk theorizing and the theories developed by scholars and scientists. Folk theoreticians are not unreflective, but they have not been trained in the tough discipline of searching for contrary evidence. Instead, folk theoreticians often handle contradictions by "erasure" (Gal and Irvine 1995), a kind of inattention that makes contradictory evidence invisible. Consider a sentence invented by the sociologist Stanley Lieberson: "Americans are still prejudiced against blacks." Lieberson found that, even though about 12 percent of Americans *are* Black, Whites seldom notice the contradiction in this statement. This is erasure. In contrast, Lieberson's respondents were startled by another sentence: "Americans still make less money than do whites" (Lieberson 1985:128). For these subjects, "Whites" could stand metonymically for "Americans," but "Blacks" could not.

Folk theorizing uses what scholars call "ad hoc" or "stipulative" explanations for contradictory evidence. For instance, Bashkow (2006) found that Orokaiva people in New Guinea were acquainted with White people who did not match their stereotypes of "Whitemen" (for instance, as very soft-skinned, or as never doing hard physical labor). But they did not conclude from this evidence that their stereotypes were mistaken. Instead, they decided that these White people were simply untypical. Some Orokaiva said that they were probably not real "Whitemen," but reincarnations of dead Orokaiva relatives, returned in disguise.

People use folk theories to interpret the world without a second thought. They are a part of everyday common sense. But they are also more than this. Since common sense is valued, folk theories and categories are not only taken for granted, they are the objects of considerable intellectual and affective investment. I have found on many occasions, in teaching and lecturing, that to question the folk theory of racism elicits from my fellow White Americans a defense of it that is acutely felt and even angry. To challenge this common sense is to become an oddball or a divisive radical.

The folk theory of race and racism

While anthropologists usually prefer to emphasize diversity, my research suggests that most White Americans share a single set of folk ideas about race and racism. These ideas, which I refer to as the "folk theory of race and racism," attend to so much that is irrelevant, erase so much that is important, and create so many traps and pitfalls that it is probably impossible to develop anti-racist projects within their framework. The folk theory shows up in the talk and text that I will analyze in later chapters. Even more importantly, it shows up in classes and courtrooms, in the deliberations of legislative bodies, in programming on television. Most White readers of this book, and their friends and families, will have invoked it in their own talk and text. It is ubiquitous, and it is taken for granted. So I outline the folk theory here in order that readers can learn to recognize and critique its terms.

The first part of the folk theory holds that "race" is a basic category of human biological variation, and that each human being can be assigned to a race, or, sometimes, to a mixture of races. The folk theory holds that these races are biologically real, the obvious trace of the origins of the American population in historically and biologically distinct geographical populations formed in human evolution. Folk theoreticians do argue that these races may not be permanent, because intermarriage and biological mixing will gradually erase their differences. Thus racism will disappear by itself, since there will be no differences left for racists to notice.

In contrast, most human biologists and social scientists find that the everyday-language category of "race" labels a sociopolitical phenomenon, not the dimensions of human biological diversity that are revealed by research in human genetics and related fields. The everyday-language "races," as products of history and culture, are very real, and they can even have biological effects. But categories like "White" and "Black" are not categories of biological evolution.

The second part of the folk theory holds that racism is entirely a matter of individual beliefs, intentions, and actions. In the folk theory, a racist is a person who believes that people of color are biologically inferior to Whites, so that White privilege is deserved and must be defended. Racism is what this kind of White supremacist thinks and does. The folk theory holds that such people are anachronisms, who are ignorant, vicious, and remote from the mainstream. Their ignorance can be cured by education. Their viciousness can be addressed by helping them to enjoy new advantages, so that they can gain self-esteem and will not have to look down on others. Since education and general well-being are increasing, racism should soon disappear entirely, except as a sign of mental derangement or disability.

One of the most difficult exercises that this book recommends is to move away from thinking of racism as entirely a matter of individual beliefs and psychological states. White Americans generally agree that things happen in the world because individuals, with beliefs, emotions, and intentions, cause them to happen. They consider this understanding to be the most obvious kind of common sense. Yet not everyone approaches the world from this perspective, and it is very interesting to try to think about racism from outside the framework that it imposes. Critical theorists do not deny that individual beliefs figure in racism. But we prefer to emphasize its collective, cultural dimensions, and to avoid singling out individuals and trying to decide whether they are racists or not. Furthermore, critical theorists insist that ordinary people who do not share White supremacist beliefs can still talk and behave in ways that advance the projects of White racism. I will try to show, in chapters to come, how racist effects can be produced in interaction, in an intersubjective space of discourse, without any single person in the interaction intending discrimination.

These first two parts of the folk theory predict optimistically that racism should disappear because intermarriage will blur racial differences, and because better education and advances in human well-being should eliminate the conditions that produce White supremacists. The third major premise of the folk theory, however, is not optimistic. It holds that prejudice is natural to the human condition. All people are thought to make invidious distinctions and "to prefer to be with their own kind." Certainly anthropologists have documented that people around the world make invidious distinctions about every possible dimension of human difference, and the individual and cultural preferences and prejudices shared by many White Americans are no different. But for critical theorists, what is interesting about White racism is not so much its system of invidious distinctions. Instead, of most interest is how Whites are able to use these to distort the allocation of resources among different kinds of people. The magnitude of White power, and the enormity of this distortion, makes White racism a very distinctive phenomenon. Furthermore, critical theorists see that this part of the folk theory, the idea that prejudice is natural, invites Whites to focus, not on their own practices, but on those of their victims. Whites often point out that non-Whites prefer to be with one another. A stereotyped example is self-segregation by seating patterns in school cafeterias, where, it is said, African American students all sit at the same tables by preference. The folk theory locates this behavior on exactly the same moral plane as the preference by all White students to sit together at other tables, and permits Whites to speak of "Black racism" as if it were exactly like White racism. Whites are very fond also of the idea that African Americans often discriminate among one another by color, valuing light skin and wavy hair. Similarly, the political conflict between African Americans and Latinos receives a great deal of attention in White-dominated media. Clearly reflection on such conflicts is important and satisfying for White Americans, since it relieves them of any distinctive guilt or responsibility.

We can see the folk theory at work in an opinion piece by a young White journalist that was published in the *Arizona Daily Wildcat*, the student newspaper of the University of Arizona (Buchheit 1997). The essay, titled "People even more ignorant than I," was a strongly worded attack on racism as "bunk," which all intelligent people have rejected and only ignorant people have sustained. The author claims to have known three examples of "racists": "Crazy Running Bear, a.k.a.: Scott," a Native American, who "hates the white race," "Nip," a "Korean White Supremacist" (the author assures us that "Nip" really is the nickname of this person and is not intended as a slur), and "mindless, inbred-to-keep-that-white-Aryan-purity-surviving, ignorant skinheads." These examples are contrasted with a "Mexican-American" who is "proud of his heritage, and who he is," but who does not "feel superior to other races" or hate them. These examples illustrate the folk-theory view that racism is a matter of belief held by ignorant people, as well as the idea that anyone can be a racist. The idea of the biological reality of race that will disappear with mixing is presented at the climax of the essay as an argument against the logic of racism: If every racist individual looks into their genealogy, the author writes, "I GUARANTEE that you will find at least one example of some 'inferior' blood line infecting your system, turning you into all that you hate" (Buchheit 1997:5).

This author clearly desires an end to racism, and wants to educate "those few with good hearts, and bad rearing, who are just a bit confused and need a push in some direction." However, the folk theory does not provide him any purchase toward this goal. Instead, it leads him to miss almost completely the ways that racism really works in his world. The essay is notable for its exclusive focus on individual hatreds as opposed to institutional racism and its obvious effects. For instance, the University of Arizona had in 1997 (and unfortunately still has) very small numbers of students of color, especially given the demography of its region. Yet two out of three of the supposed racists mentioned in the essay are people of color, who in real life are much more likely to be the victims of racism than they are to function effectively in advancing racist projects. The only White racists mentioned are "ignorant skinheads." But the University of Arizona is plagued with racist behavior by ordinary White students, not "ignorant skinheads." In the Spring of 2007, a scandal erupted on campus when students posted on their Facebook pages pictures of a party celebrating Martin Luther King Day, where guests came as their favorite Black person. The preferred costume was a "pimp" or "gangsta" outfit, or, for women, to come as a "ho." Members of the African American Student Association (only 2.8 percent of students at the university are Black) protested, and concerned university administrators convened workshops and forums to reflect on the incident (Smith 2007).

While an undergraduate essay might be expected to be a bit naive, ideas that are identical to those in Mr. Buchheit's *Arizona Daily Wildcat* contribution dominate nearly all public discourse about racism in the United States. The folk theory is deeply embedded in American law (Crenshaw et al. eds. 1995). A 2004 US Supreme Court decision, *Grutter v. Bollinger*, demonstrates that the folk theory is held at the very highest levels of the justice system. In this decision the Court ruled that the University of Michigan could continue to practice certain forms of race-based affirmative action. Justice O'Connor wrote for the majority that "The Court expects that 25 years from now, the use of racial preferences will no longer be necessary to favor the interest approved today" (*Grutter v. Bollinger et al.*, 2003). The "interest" mentioned by Justice O'Connor is the desire of American institutions for "diversity." Urciuoli (2003) has shown that "diversity" is often merely a glib label for a form of corporate accommodation to a globalizing world, and has little to do with redressing any history of discrimination. Justice O'Connor's wording clearly reflects the folk-theory idea that education of recalcitrant racists, and racial mixing in "diverse" institutions, will bring the end of racism, and within 25 years at that.[13]

## Race is a Social and Political Fact, Not a Fact of Human Biology

With the folk theory now sketched out, let us develop in more detail some examples of how it works, and how it contrasts with critical and scientific theories of race and racism. First, recall that in the folk theory race is a biological fact of human nature. Most White Americans think that anyone who opposes this idea is simply blind to the obvious. However, human biologists and human geneticists almost universally agree that the "races" and "ethnic groups" – Black or African American, Hispanic or Latino/a, Asian – that are not only salient in everyday language, but are the categories used by US government agencies going about their official purposes, are not biological units in any ordinary sense.

The word "race" first appears in English in the seventeenth century, and is probably borrowed from the Spanish word *raza*, of uncertain etymology (Smedley 1993:37). *Raza* first appeared in Spanish-language discourses that distinguished Christians of "pure blood," *sangre limpia*, from persecuted descendants of converted Jews and Muslims (Smedley 1993:38; Fredrickson

2002). That is, the word expressed Christian ascendancy, and had little to do with skin color and the other external signs that define race for American English speakers today.

The use of these external signs in folk thinking about race today preserves the scientific biology and anthropology of 50 to 100 years ago. Through the 1960s even university textbooks in biological anthropology labeled the human races with words like Caucasoid, Mongoloid, Negroid, and Australoid. Many Americans still use the scientific-sounding racial terms found in these antiquated sources. Thus Jacobson (1998) points out that the novelist Philip Roth, with a keen ear for American talk, could invent a White woman who insists on the difference between a "Semitic" versus a "Caucasian" race.

Racial typology has not completely disappeared from biological anthropology. Many forensic anthropologists, who are often asked by law enforcement officials to identify human skeletal remains by folk-racial categories (which continue to live in the law), believe that the old racial types are useful in this task and that the malleability of skeletal dimensions under changing environments has been exaggerated.[14] Some African American leaders worry that claims that there is no scientific basis for the idea of race will undermine their arguments for race-based social programs aimed at redressing discrimination. Scholars and scientists who still use the old racial typologies are, however, few and far between. As the mapping of the human genome has revealed more and more sites of human variation, scientists consistently find that this variability never maps neatly onto any of the systems of racial typology that were once taken so seriously.[15] From a biological point of view, humanity has evolved as a single lineage (Templeton 1998).

While biological anthropologists and human geneticists have agreed for at least 30 years that the folk theory of race has no scientific foundation, this consensus is repeatedly presented in the mass media as if it were astonishing breaking news. For instance, *Scientific American*, the leading popular science magazine in the United States, headlined its December 2003 report on the results of the recently completed Human Genome Project with "Science has the answer: Does race exist? Genetic results may surprise you." This line captioned a colorful montage of "morphed" female faces, with skin color graded but facial features identical (a classic iconic representation of the folk idea that race mixing is eroding racial difference).

Not only is this venerable scientific consensus presented in the press as an astonishing novelty, when it is proposed, it is strongly resisted. Many people remain convinced that racial differences, in the folk-theory sense, are important for scientific medicine. Those who advance this view argue that "political correctness" in the form of the denial of the biological reality of race will damage efforts to improve public health and to cure disease in individuals. The idea that the biological reality of race must be recognized because of the racial association of certain diseases is very robust, in spite of the fact that many human biologists find it controversial or simplistic. In one of the many ironies and contradictions that are the hallmark of the folk theory, this idea was invoked in California during 2003 by anti-racist opponents of Proposition 54, the Racial Privacy Initiative. Proposition 54 would have amended the state constitution to make any reference to race, ethnicity, color, or national origin illegal in regulations governing education, public contracts, or public employment. It was authored by California's foremost advocate of colorblind public policy, Ward Connerly, a prominent African American businessman, who also composed the state constitutional amendment of 1996 that successfully ended affirmative action in public higher education in his state. Connerly believes that any attention to racial differences, as by affirmative action policy, simply perpetuates racism and racist injustice.[16] The argument against his colorblind initiative that found the most purchase with the general public, and that almost certainly was the most important factor in its defeat by a substantial majority of California voters in the election of November 2003, was that it was, as one advertising slogan proposed, "an attack on our health-care system": the proposed amendment would prevent physicians from paying attention to associations between race and disease. This episode strongly reasserted the robust folk idea that race is biologically grounded.

Robert Sussman and Alan Templeton, human biologists at Washington University in St. Louis, sharply disagreed with this position (Hesman 2003). They pointed out that associations between race and disease are merely statistical, so they are of little use in the diagnosis of individual cases. Furthermore, these associations have at least as much to do with poverty and stress – that is, with race as a social and political category – as they do with genetic variation. American racial categories have so little connection with human variation as understood in biology that the contribution to diagnostic precision of "knowing a patient's race" is almost certainly far less significant than the contribution of such "knowledge" to well-documented medical neglect (Brown et al. 2003). People of color, as Templeton noted, deserve the same kind of individualized diagnostic attention that Whites receive: "If you're an individual and you're sick, you don't really care about the averages" (Hesman 2003:A1).

Some scholars argue that racism today is a "New Racism" based on cultural, not biological, discrimination (Balibar and Wallerstein 1991; Stolcke 1995). But there is much evidence that the idea of "race" among American Whites remains firmly grounded in folk ideas about biology. For instance, the so-called one-drop rule – that one drop of African blood makes a person Black – remains vigorous. In December 2003, six months after the death at the age of 100 of Strom Thurmond, Republican of South

Carolina and one of the strongest segregationist voices in the United States Senate of the 1940s through the 1960s, his 78-year-old daughter Essie Mae Washington-Williams, a light-skinned woman who strongly resembles her father, announced her paternity. In the extensive news coverage, Mrs. Washington-Williams was frequently referred to, in a one-drop-rule locution, as "Senator Thurmond's Black daughter." Out of 75 documents on the Lexis-Nexis database that referred to Mrs. Washington-Williams by race, 24 called her "Black." The others all used folk-racial language, calling her "mixed-race," "bi-racial," or "half and half." Mrs. Washington-Williams's mother, Carrie Butler, was always referred to as "Black" (with lower-case "b" in the original sources).[17] Ms. Butler's exact lineage is unknown to me, but if she was like most African Americans of her generation, she probably had White ancestors. Senator Barack Obama, Democrat of Illinois, is often described as "the only Black member of the United States Senate." Senator Obama is the child of a White American mother and a father from Kenya. Sometimes he, like Mrs. Washington-Williams, is called a "mixed-race" person. But the expression "mixed-race" presupposes the basic integrity of typological races and echoes old ideas of hybridization and miscegenation.

These examples also illustrate the excessive concern on the part of journalists that people of color (but not Whites) be properly labeled by race. American Whites obsess about racial labels (and take that obsession for granted as natural) because they make choices about how to think about other people based on racial categorization. Racial labels shape fundamental perceptions. In a famous study, Rubin (1992; Rubin and Smith 1990) studied how college students respond to the race of instructors. Rubin used a method called a "matched guise." A White female, a native speaker of American English, recorded a four-minute classroom lecture, which was played to groups of randomly selected White students. One group was shown a picture of a White woman, and told that this was the speaker. A second group was shown a picture of a woman with East Asian features, and informed that this woman had recorded the lecture. The two photographs were made in the same setting, and the women were dressed very similarly and were judged to be equal in attractiveness. The students in the "Asian speaker" condition reported that the speaker on the tape had a foreign accent, and, astonishingly, did significantly less well on a follow-up test over the four minutes of material than the students who were told they were hearing a White speaker! The problem could not possibly have been foreign accent – which many White college students feel strongly compromises their ability to learn (Shuck 2004) – since all the students heard exactly the same White American female voice. What Rubin demonstrated was that students will hear a foreign accent even when there cannot possibly be one, simply on the basis of a speaker's appearance, and that this mistaken perception will affect how much they understand and remember of what is said.

We can see clearly, then, that the folk category of race is much more than a mystification and distortion that has made many people understand historical processes of discrimination and differentiation as simple "biology." The folk theory creates the reality in which Americans live. Understanding it is a requirement for a person who wants to function effectively in American society, where it organizes interactions at all levels. And it can be a life-and-death matter. As Gloria Ladson-Billings (personal communication, January 2004) likes to point out, "Your race is what you are when the cops pull you over at two o'clock in the morning."

Folk categories of race create cultural effects. Members of groups classified as non-White strongly feel the sense of community that results from sharing ways somehow to live with oppression. Cultural formations specific to these groups, which include some of the world's most exciting and admired art, music, and literature, have developed within these communities. Furthermore, social and political race even creates biological effects. The selective pressures on African Americans, who suffer an infant mortality rate of 13.65 per thousand, are different from those on Whites, with a rate of 5.65. Elevated frequencies of hypertension and diabetes among African Americans probably trace partly to the stress of constant exposure to discrimination and partly to the biological consequences of the discrimination-shaped poverty, with its substandard housing, unhealthy diets, and inadequate medical care.


## Whiteness and the indeterminacy of racial categories

The great majority of anthropologists believe that what most people call "race" is best understood as a social and political reality, and not a biological fact. One reason that they take this view is the evidence of the great flexibility of American racial categories, both official and unofficial, even in recent history. The ways in which people are assigned to a race, even in the official recording of birth certificates and categorization in the United States Census, have changed frequently (Dominguez 1986; Menchaca 1993). Official documents of the US Census are extensively footnoted with cautions that statistics by race are not comparable across the decades, because the racial and ethnic categories in the Census have changed.

When scholars first began to look for evidence that racial categories in the United States are social and political constructions, not biological reality, they often focused on the phenomenon of "passing," cases where light-skinned African Americans successfully lived as Whites. Passing shows that racial categorization is unreliable. More recently, changing ideas of

Whiteness have attracted much attention (Delgado and Stefancic, eds. 1997; McDermott and Samson 2005; Rasmussen et al., eds. 2001). The definition of who is "White" has frequently shifted during US history. In the early years of the American republic, Benjamin Franklin could write that "In Europe the Spaniards, Italians, French, Russians, and Swedes are generally of what we call a swarthy complexion; as are the Germans also, the Saxons only excepted, who, with the English, make the principal body of white people on the face of the earth. I could wish their numbers were increased" (quoted in Jacobson 1998:40). Franklin wrote long before a famous tract of scientific racism, Madison Grant's *Passing of the Great Race* of 1916, popularized the idea of the Nordic peoples as the prototypical Whites. American Whites today can hardly imagine how Franklin could have seen Swedes and Germans as "swarthy." This example shows how what seem to us today like fundamental perceptions may be of very recent historical origin, in this case, ideas of Whiteness centered on Grant's Nordic stereotype. Contemporary White Americans can no longer see "swarthiness" among Swedes, and find it astonishing that anyone ever did so.

Some ethnic groups thought of as indisputably White today once faced considerable discrimination. Roediger (1991) and Ignatiev (1995) have recorded the "whitening" of Americans of Irish ancestry. Brodkin (1998) described "How Jews became White folks." Jacobson (1998) illustrates the "manufacture of Caucasians" out of the diversity of European "races" in everyday interactions and in the workings of national institutions during the twentieth century. However, Jacobson points out that while European immigrants, such as the Irish and people from eastern Europe and the Mediterranean, often faced discrimination (and, in the case of Jewish immigrants, anti-Semitism), they were always recognized as White in legal terms under the Naturalization Act of 1790, which admitted "free white persons" to American citizenship. The Naturalization Act of 1870 extended the right of citizenship to "aliens of African nativity . . . and persons of African descent" (Jacobson 1998:227). Jacobson documents a complex give and take throughout the first half of the twentieth century as applicants for citizenship who did not fall clearly into the categories defined in these laws, such as Mexicans, Japanese, Syrians, and South Asians, petitioned the courts to be recognized as White. Menchaca (1993, 2001) reviews the dilemmas faced after the Mexican War of 1848 by Mexicans in the newly conquered American territories. Many of them had African and Native American ancestors, so the full US citizenship rights supposedly guaranteed to Mexicans in the 1848 Treaty of Guadalupe Hidalgo were withheld from them. Citizenship was not extended to Native Americans until the American Indian Citizenship Act of 1924.

The boundary between Whiteness and Color is always actively contested, as people use diverse means, from "passing" to cultural conformity to legal confrontation, to become recognized as White. In-between categories are constantly emerging, from the mixed-race categories permitted in the 2000 US Census to local labels like "Melungeon," adopted by people in Appalachia who could identify as "White" but who want to honor their African ancestry (McDermott 2004). The old category of "Creole," long established in southern Louisiana, did not employ the one-drop rule (Dominguez 1986). The diaspora after Hurricane Katrina in 2005 has greatly disrupted identities for this population, because New Orleanians who were "Creole" in the pre-Katrina city are simply "Black" in Houston or Atlanta.

The reverse of "becoming White folks" is racialization into Color, a process today affecting Americans of Middle Eastern ancestry. When I taught at Wayne State University in Detroit from 1968 to 1983, I learned that Arab Americans were known in the region by the racist epithet "sand niggers." A Supreme Court decision of 1981, *Saint Francis College v. Al-Khazraji*, ruled that Arab Americans had standing as complainants against "racial" discrimination (Haney Lopez 2000:167). However, Morsy (1994) argued that Arab Americans had experienced a period of at least tentative assignment as "honorary Whites." The 2000 US Census includes people of Middle Eastern origin in the category "White." This status surely ended, at least unofficially, in the aftermath of the attack on the World Trade Center in New York City on September 11, 2001. The small Arab American population in the United States, which includes many highly educated professionals and business people, now finds itself firmly relocated within the zone of Color, and instances of discrimination against Americans of Middle Eastern ancestry, including violence, are today commonplace.

While students of Whiteness emphasize diverse ways of being White (Hartigan 1999, 2005), official US government policy does not acknowledge this. Instead, the US Census homogenizes Whites, but divides people of color into multiple subgroups. Goldberg (1993:78) suggested that this policy is part of a long history of White-dominated institutions using racial taxonomies to "divide and conquer." The 1990 US Census included four non-White possibilities: Black, Hispanic, Asian-Pacific Islander, and American Indian-Alaska Native. The Census of 2000 distinguished "race" from "Hispanic origin," permitted respondents to check more than one box for race, and allowed write-in mixed-race labels like "Irish-Salvadoran-African American." A category "some other race" was also made available, and answers included labels like "Moroccan" and "Belizean." The 2000 Census divided "Asian" into five subcategories, and "Pacific Islander" into three. "Spanish/Hispanic/Latino" was divided into Mexican/Mexican American/ Chicano, Puerto Rican, and Cuban. The category "Black or African American" was not subdivided, a choice which ignores the social salience of some subgroups of the Black population, such as West Indians (immigrants from

the English-speaking Caribbean), Dominicans and Puerto Ricans categorized as "Black" in the United States, and Haitians.

While the folk theory is optimistic that racial mixing will bring the end
of racism, 98 percent of respondents to the 2000 US Census checked only
one race.[18] Of the slightly more than 6 million people who checked two
or more, over a million were Whites claiming to be partly American
Indian/Alaska Native. Such a choice by Whites has become a way of
staking a romantic claim to American authenticity rather than the revelation
of an embarrassing non-White ancestry. Today, it may also advance a claim
on new wealth that tribes and bands who have built gambling casinos share
among enrolled members.[19] The results of the 2000 Census cannot, of
course, be compared to the results of earlier censuses where mixed-race
categories were not available to respondents. However, they make clear
that only a small minority of Americans choose to be seen officially as
mixed-race people.

In contrast to the elaborate subdivisions of people of color seen in the
US Census, in many contexts a single social contrast between Color and
Whiteness accounts for the ways that White racism plays out in the United
States. To make this observation is to take a controversial position, since
it moves away from the "Black–White binary" (Perea 1998) and "Black
exceptionalism" (Espinoza and Harris 2000): the idea that African Americans were uniquely damaged by economic loss and social-psychological
degradations under slavery and Jim Crow, and that African Americans are
uniquely centered in White racist imagination as prototypical Others.[20]
Much evidence does support Black exceptionalism. Everyday White racism
of the type that Davis (2000) calls "micro-aggression" is probably felt most
acutely by African Americans. Only African Americans are categorized by
the "one-drop rule" (Harrison 1995:60). African Americans exhibit a
uniquely low level of intermarriage with Whites (Sanjek 1994; although
apparently tolerance for intermarriage is increasing, as noted by Bobo 2001).
However, other non-White populations have also suffered a heavy burden
of discrimination. American Indians constitute less than 1 percent of the
population of the United States. Most Whites never encounter them, and
many share positive, albeit essentializing and romanticizing, ideas about
Indians. However, Indians were devastated by genocidal attacks that continued into the early twentieth century in some parts of the United States,
and by the nearly total expropriation of their land and wealth which continues to this day. Indians encounter every kind of discrimination including
stereotyping, ostracism and exclusion, and violence. The adoption of casino
gambling as a tribal business on some reservations has led to racist backlash,
often led by White gambling interests such as the race-track industry, who
encourage Whites to see casino profits as ill-gotten gains, undeserved privileges that Indians in no way deserve to enjoy.

Latinos and Asian Americans are especially likely to be stereotyped as "foreigners" (Lee 2000), but also suffer every other kind of discrimination. The expropriation of property from Mexican Americans by Whites occurred everywhere between 1848 and the end of the twentieth century (Briggs and Van Ness, eds. 1987; Menchaca 1995; Sheridan 1986, 2006). Asian Americans as well suffered the taking of property, as when Japanese Americans were forced to sell their homes, land, and businesses at panic prices when they were removed by force from the West Coast during World War II. Asian Americans encounter "glass ceilings" in business and the professions, even since becoming the "model minority" in the 1980s and 1990s. And Asian Americans also encounter racist violence. The White murderers of Vincent Chin in Detroit in 1982 and Yoshiro Hattori in Baton Rouge in 1992 either received very light prison sentences (in the case of the Chin murder) or were let off without penalty (in the Hattori case). In Spring 2004, as I began to write this chapter, the Asian community of San Jose, California, was mourning the death of Cau Bich Tran and seeking justice for her. Tran was a tiny 25-year-old Vietnamese immigrant mother of two who was killed in her own home on July 13, 2003, by a San Jose police officer. She had called the police for help in opening a locked door. When the officer entered the home, she was holding a Vietnamese-style vegetable peeler, with a six-inch blade, trying to use it to jimmy the door. Since she did not understand English well, she did not drop the peeler when the officer ordered her to do so. He shot her dead, claiming later that the shot had been in self-defense. A grand jury refused to indict the officer for what is widely considered in the local Asian community to have been an act of, if not flat-out murder, at best a manslaughter, a profound error of judgment rooted in racist stereotyping.

Marable (1995) finds that all people of color in the United States confront very similar structural contexts and have very similar experiences with racism. He argues that this circumstance makes obvious the need for political alliances across superficially diverse racial groups. Delgado and Stefancic (2000:226) report that in museum collections of racial memorabilia, "We found striking parallels among the stigma-pictures that society disseminated of the four groups [Mexicans, African Americans, Asians, and Native Americans]. The stock characters may have different names and appear at different times, but they bear remarkable likenesses and seem to serve similar purposes for the majority culture."

Carey McWilliams (1943) saw many historical and sociological connections among the experiences of people of color. The confrontation with Native Americans by the first colonists shaped the way that their descendants understood Africans brought as slaves. After the Civil War, California politicians anxious to crush the ambitions of Chinese immigrants worked closely with politicians from the Deep South who were forging Jim Crow segregation. Mexican Americans in the US Southwest, argued McWilliams, filled for Whites a political–economic and ideological site that elsewhere was occupied by African Americans, and were treated accordingly.

Like Marable, Delgado and Stefancic, and McWilliams, I have noticed that there are few differences among kinds of stereotypes that Whites assign to non-White groups. Of course new stereotypes do emerge from time to time, such as the idea that Asian Americans are especially intelligent. As recently as the early 1970s the driving concern of the Chinese community in San Francisco was very similar to that of other US minorities, that public schools were failing their children. *Lau v. Nichols*, a 1972 decision of the US Supreme Court, held that children of Chinese ancestry should have access to bilingual education in Chinese and English to improve their chances of school success. Yet today's media representations of Chinese Americans reflect nothing of this very recent history. To quote a teenaged character in a 2004 film, *The Perfect Score*, the highest scores on the Scholastic Aptitude Test (SAT), used to evaluate potential for success in tertiary education by most US colleges and universities, are earned by "Chinese girls who never watch television." (The message of the film was that other young people are best advised to cheat.)

This new stereotype of high Asian intelligence would seem to be a positive development. Yet when Whites act on it, the result is often discrimination. In 2002 the University of California announced a de-emphasis on SAT scores. This was one of many responses by the university that were said to be aimed at mitigating the drop in matriculation by African American and Latino/a students that followed the passage of a 1996 amendment to the State Constitution that prohibited using race as a criterion for admission. But many Asian Americans believe that de-emphasizing SAT scores discriminates against their children, who do well on these tests. Since for many years Asian American children faced explicit restrictive quotas, their suspicion that the de-emphasis on SAT results aims to keep them from dominating university admissions is reasonable (Izumi 2002).

White racism as culture

The folk-theory insistence that racism is entirely a matter of individual beliefs and prejudices contrasts sharply with critical theories of racism. David Theo Goldberg, one of the most prominent critical theorists, argues that racism is a cultural phenomenon that exists in publicly circulating discourses (Goldberg 1993:92). Goldberg's theory does have a place for beliefs and intentions. However, counter to the folk theory that sees racist beliefs as anachronistic and irrational, Goldberg has argued that they are often quite rational (Goldberg 1999). Goldberg's theory of racist culture (Goldberg

1990, 1993, 1997) does a much better job of explaining the forms and practices of language explored in this book than does the folk theory. The diverse critical theorists who emphasize cultural approaches to racism do not necessarily share all of Goldberg's views. But his theory of racist culture opens up some very useful analytic opportunities.

Goldberg sees racism as a set of "discourses," taking this term from the work of Foucault (see especially Foucault 1972). Foucault uses "discourses" to label sets of fundamental principles that organize the world. Discourses divide rationality from irrationality, truth from error, madness from sanity. They make some things in the world noticeable and discussible, and others invisible, and, in the last analysis, even create "things" themselves. Discourses are not superficial beliefs and practices imposed over a more fundamental way of being. Instead, for Foucault we live in the world only through discourses, and we cannot think or speak outside them. The anthropologist Audrey Smedley captured this dimension of racist culture when she described White racism as a "world view," as "a culturally structured, systematic way of looking at, perceiving, and interpreting various world realities . . . [that] actively, if not consciously, mould . . . the behavior of their bearers" (Smedley 1993 : 17). Feagin (2006) proposes that a systematic and enduring White racial "frame" generates racializing meanings and associated discriminatory actions. The notion of a "frame," from the work of sociologist Erving Goffman (1974), implies a contextualizing perspective, an angle or point of view that endows a racialized world with common-sense properties. Systems of constraint on thought like discourses, world views, and frames exist below the level of consciousness. They are invisible to us, and yet constitute our world. Critical theories of racism aim to make them visible, to parse their terms and logics, and to interrupt their terms with constructive alternative anti-racist discourses.

To understand White racism[21] as culture, as discourse, as world view, or as a generative frame for thought explains why race and racially based practices become common sense. Each time this common sense plays out in talk and behavior, these fundamental ideas become available anew, and people use them to understand what has happened and to negotiate interaction. This constant feedback is dynamic, and White racism at different times and places can be quite diverse. This flexible racism is highly adaptable. Stoler (1997) argues that social formations like capitalism, or colonialism, or liberalism, or modernity, which are sometimes considered preconditions for racism, do not predict it. Instead, she finds that racism can parasitize almost any social formation or political system, and be articulated within almost any economic or political discourse.

Years of grappling with the idea of "culture" (see Brightman 1995 for a summary of recent debates) has led anthropologists to use the term to refer, not to a timeless system that is given to its inheritors as an inflexible package of ideas and practices, but to a set of collective projects that must be continually renewed by the action of human agents. The collective property of cultural projects makes them seem natural, as it is difficult for members to imagine a world other than the one in which so many people move about and speak and act in ways that are intelligible to them. It also makes them effective; since such collective practices create worlds, they make sense and are efficacious within those worlds. But anthropologists have found that such collective projects are never complete, in at least two senses. First, the necessarily diverse kinds of memberships in large collective projects imply that there will always be members who are marginal to them, or who are positively disadvantaged by them and thus resist them. Within a set of cultural projects as enormous as those of White racism, participants will have many different reasons for acting, and these reasons may change even during brief spans of time. Some participants may be in outspoken and active practical opposition even to ideas that seem fundamental. However, such "resistance" does not necessarily lead to interruption of the cultural project. Indeed, it may be entirely constituted within its logics, merely turning their elements on their heads without interrupting their most fundamental presuppositions. Thus resistance runs the risk of power-fully reinscribing a cultural project by both implicitly and explicitly evoking its ideas and making them public once again (Abu-Lughod 1990).

The second reason that cultural projects are never complete is that their logics always contain internal contradictions and lapses. For instance, the *sistema de castas*, the system of racial categories enshrined in law throughout Latin America in the colonial period, broke down due to sheer complexity during the last years of the eighteenth century (Van den Berghe 1978). The *sistema de castas* included almost every imaginable ratio of racial inter-mixtures among people of European, African, and American Indian descent. A few such labels, like "mulatto," "quadroon," and "octoroon," appeared in English as well. When this system broke down, White racism in coun-tries like Brazil (Harris 1964) and Nicaragua (Lancaster 1991) shifted the basis of racial categories from genealogy to color. The baroque proliferation of racial categories recognized in the 2000 United States Census may hint that White racism in the United States is also close to a new phase.

We can understand White racism as constituted loosely by a set of cul-tural projects. Keeping in mind that these are never complete, that they exhibit considerable internal diversity, and that they encounter resistance and exhibit gaps and contradictions, I have found that four projects of White racist culture in the United States in the twenty-first century account for most of the data that I discuss in this book. These are: (1) the produc-tion of a taxonomy of human types; (2) the assignment of individuals and groups within the taxonomy of types through "racialization" or "racial formation" (Omi and Winant 1994); (3) the arrangement of these types in a hierarchy; and (4) the movement of resources, both material and symbolic, from the lower levels of the hierarchy to the upper levels in such a way as to elevate Whiteness and denigrate and pejorate Color.

The first project, toward a taxonomy of human types, reached a local peak in the baroque systems of the United States Census of 2000. But this cultural project dates from the early modern period, when it was entwined in the evolution of biological science itself. The Linnean taxonomy – *Homo afer, Homo americanus, Homo asiaticus, Homo europus* – reflects the same impetus to the identification of human types that is seen in the 2000 Census categories of "White," "Black or African American," "American Indian or Alaska Native," "Asian or Pacific Islander," "Hispanic or Latino," "Non-Hispanic White," and "Two or More Races," nomenclature which reflects the political struggles of our own day. But nearly all combatants share a common underlying logic, that a world of racial types is meaningful, and one without them is disorderly and lacks meaning.

The second project is the assignment of individuals and groups to the categories of the racial taxonomy. This process, often called "racialization," is accomplished in court rulings that determine whether a person or group is a member, or not, of a category of persons eligible for affirmative action. It is accomplished when Americans, often at a glance, assign one another to racial categories (a glance that can have life-and-death consequences, as in the forms of split-second racial inferencing accomplished by gun-toting citizens and police officers described by Armour 2000). Racialization is accomplished when individuals themselves claim or reject memberships. For instance, immigrants to the United States from the Spanish-speaking Caribbean often take up quite different locations in American society based on accidents of appearance and individual life histories, with even members of a single sibling group variously choosing White, Latino/a, or Black categories and walking, talking, eating, singing, dancing, dating, etc., differently depending on which racial choice seems most favorable (Rodríguez 1994). Racialization is dynamic even within the lifetimes of single individuals, as with the 6 million people who changed from being members of single races in the 1990 US Census to being at least bi-racial in the Census of 2000. Racialization can even be dynamic over a few minutes of interaction, as shown by Bailey (2000) for a Dominican American teenager. However, all this real-life dynamism is often erased by an ideology that a person's race is fixed at conception, and that others must be able to determine that race in order to know how to act in reference to that person.

The third goal is the arrangement of racial categories within a hierarchy. This is the project that produces what I will call, throughout this book, "White virtue," the idea that Whites are highest in the hierarchy because their qualities deserve this arrangement. In the history of the United States, federal and state legislation and court decisions that permitted slavery and

Jim Crow segregation enshrined White supremacy for hundreds of years, but many Whites see their ascendancy, not as a historical product, but as a moral imperative. Whiteness is associated with virtue, thought to reside in White "culture." Color is associated with vice, rooted in supposed cultural deficits and historical stigma (Loury 2002). One of the most notorious articulations of this idea of a moral hierarchy was made by Professor Lino Graglia of the University of Texas School of Law in 1997, in a comment on *Hopwood v. Texas*, resolved by the 5th US Circuit Court of Appeals in a decision which halted affirmative action measures in the Texas state universities. Graglia, who approved of the Hopwood decision, was quoted widely as having said,

> Blacks and Mexican-Americans are not academically competitive with whites in selective institutions. It is the result primarily of cultural effects. It seems to be the case that, various studies seem to show blacks and Mexican-Americans spend much less time in school. They have a culture that seems not to encourage achievement. Failure is not looked upon with disgrace.[22]

Any scholar familiar with the relevant literature – and indeed, any person who had ever spent much time among African Americans and Mexican Americans – would know that many members of these groups value educational achievement at least as highly as do Whites, and abandon it as a goal for themselves and their children only in the face of the direst economic constraints, after failing in battles against discrimination, or after assessing the battle as a hopeless one. Much of the differential achievement of children of color in secondary education is explicable by the fact that the schools that serve them – which remain largely segregated even 50 years after *Brown v. Board of Education* – are simply not providing a very good education. In addition, social-psychological factors involving anxiety and distrust, so-called "stereotype threats," that are shaped by years of the experience of discrimination have been found to account for differential achievements on standardized tests by Black and White students in universities (Steele 1997). Since the quantitative effects are found among Latinos and African Americans regardless of social class, it is highly unlikely that they result from some sort of universally shared "culture" of US minorities. There is no concept of "culture" in anthropology, or indeed in any branch of the social sciences, that would encompass everyone from working-class Mexican immigrants to well-to-do African American professionals. What Professor Graglia meant by "culture" was nothing more than a euphemism, a socially acceptable relabeling of the folk-theoretic category of "race." However, his statement was greeted very widely by commentators in the mass media as expressing and explaining an "uncomfortable truth" that the forces of political correctness had attempted to suppress (e.g. Horowitz 1997).

The moral dimension of racial hierarchy is continually reasserted in the United States today by attention in the mass media, often couched in deceptively sympathetic language, to social problems confronted by communities of color – high rates of incarceration, health problems, school failure, and unemployment – that are treated as the results of cultural and personal inadequacies rather than as products of White racism. This media attention often includes the publication of authoritative-seeming statistics showing members of minority populations lagging behind Whites. This reassertion of hierarchy by quantitative method is exacerbated by stereotypical visual representations in all forms of media, as when photographs of African American women illustrate newspaper articles on work-for-welfare programs, or when the role of drug kingpin in action movies is filled routinely by a Latino actor.

The denial of racism, and the performance of what are taken to be antiracist gestures, is one way of constituting White virtue. Whites like the student journalist who wrote the *Arizona Daily Wildcat* op-ed essay that I used to illustrate the folk theory of racism find it easy to think about people of color as racists, but very difficult to think about White racists. White virtue is protected by projecting racism onto an imagined category of "skinheads" and "Ku Kluxers" that Whites seldom encounter in real life. White virtue is also constructed through creating "honorary Whites," whose presence in worlds shaped entirely by White power serves as a sign that Whites who associate with them and give them recognition are not racist. Significant examples today include public figures whose careers are often cited by Whites to demonstrate that race is no longer a problem for Americans. However, Whites are not comfortable when such people exhibit styles and expressions that are distant from White norms. The most famous example of the requirement of this kind of cultural conformity is the case of Bill Cosby and his immensely popular 1980s television show. Williams (1995:195) has pointed out how visible signs of everyday Black ways of life were gradually erased from the show, shaping it, in the view of many African Americans, into a show about White people who happened to look Black.

White racist culture works to shift both material and symbolic resources from the bottom of the racial hierarchy, Color, to the top, Whiteness. This project, the movement of resources, yields what I will call, following McIntosh (1989), "White privilege." Lipsitz (1998) assembles data showing that much of the economic history of the United States can be understood as a vast capture by Whites of resources from people of color, from the labor of Black slaves, to the lands and wealth of American Indians, to the land and water rights of Mexican Americans, continuing today in the super-exploitation and under-compensation of the working poor – a group that includes a high percentage of people of color. I will illustrate the construction of White privilege with the example of residential segregation, which creates White wealth at the same time that it creates poverty in communities of color. Residential segregation will also show us how White privilege and White virtue are intertwined, each feeding the other.

## White privilege, White virtue, and residential segregation: A case study in White racist culture

Residential segregation is a conspicuous feature of contemporary American life. It illustrates how racial disparities result from very complex intersections of individual and institutional choices that share only the presupposition that "race" is a meaningful human category. Residential segregation is simply too complex, too far-reaching, and too historically specific to be satisfactorily explained by the folk theory idea that "people prefer to be with their own kind" (which, of course, presupposes that by "own kind" we mean "own race"). But residential segregation also illustrates how White racist culture can be perpetuated in a sort of closed loop of feedback as Whites gain credit and people of color are discredited through this practice.

Race-based discrimination against people of color in access to housing (both householder-owned and rental) and financing for housing (including mortgages and related housing-based financial instruments) has been illegal in the United States for over 30 years. However, residential segregation has persisted. New forms of discrimination constantly develop, making racial discrimination in housing a "moving target" (Massey 2005). Residential segregation can be expressed quantitatively through the "dissimilarity index," which measures the evenness of distribution of populations across metropolitan areas. The index represents the percentage of people in a particular group who would have to change their place of residence to achieve a racially even distribution. A dissimilarity index of 0 represents complete integration, a dissimilarity index of 1 represents complete segregation. Table 2 gives the dissimilarity indices for African Americans, Hispanics, and Asian Americans (combined with Pacific Islanders), as against Whites, for the last three US Censuses. Table 2 shows that in the year 2000, 64 percent of African Americans would have had to move into new neighborhoods in order to reach complete integration with Whites. The figures in Table 2, for the entire nation, miss some appalling extremes: In New York, Chicago, and Detroit, Black/White dissimilarity indexes run higher than 80 percent, and Latino/White indexes exceed 60 percent in many metropolitan areas (Friedman and Squires 2005).

These statistics are highly visible on the ground in American cities in the twenty-first century, in inner-city ghettoes and even entire cities and

**Table 2** Residential segregation of major non-White populations for all US metropolitan areas[23]

|  | *African Americans* | *Hispanics* | *Asian Americans* |
|---|---|---|---|
| 1980 | 0.727 | 0.502 | 0.405 |
| 1990 | 0.678 | 0.500 | 0.412 |
| 2000 | 0.640 | 0.509 | 0.411 |

inner suburbs inhabited largely by people of color, surrounded by sprawling outer suburbs inhabited largely by Whites. This pattern is not a primordial result of the desire of people to be with their own kind. Instead, it developed largely within the last 75 years (Lipsitz 1998). In 1934 the Federal Housing Administration began to underwrite private mortgage loans. This keystone program of President Roosevelt's New Deal aimed to stimulate the economy, devastated by the Great Depression, by promoting the construction of housing and home ownership. In the early 1950s a massive program of highway construction, justified as necessary to national defense and security, permitted the spread of suburbs at a hitherto unimagined pace as developers sought cheap land outside of cities. Global domination by the United States after World War II guaranteed the low prices for gasoline that permitted even working-class Whites to commute long distances from the sprawl of the suburbs to jobs in cities.

While today's suburbs arose during a period when overtly White supremacist attitudes were still widely accepted in the United States, segregation was not an explicit goal of suburbanization. Instead, suburbanization was thought of as the pursuit of a better, healthier life for families. However, people of color were excluded from this pursuit, because even people who did not dislike or fear African Americans shared the view that their presence in neighborhoods "lowered property values." For this reason, until the 1964 Civil Rights Act, mortgages backed by the Federal Housing Administration (FHA) were not available to African Americans.[24] By encouraging residential "covenants" that prohibited resale to people of color, the FHA policed the suburbs against African American residents even beyond the reach of the jurisdiction it had over the holders of its primary mortgages. In the western United States, these restrictive covenants often also prohibited homeowners from reselling to "Mexicans," "Japanese," or other excluded racial categories. The same concern for "property values" led to mortgage redlining[25] in cities, where people of color remained because they were blocked from moving to suburbs. Redlining made it impossible for city dwellers to acquire mortgages for new purchases of housing, or to finance improvements in housing already owned, and resulted in the deterioration of urban housing stock.

Many of the decisions and practices that produce residential segregation are not racist in the perspective of the folk theory, which requires that racists hold an explicit belief in the biological inferiority of people of color. Nor were they irrational. Instead, within a regime of private property and an understanding that the national economy results from the workings of markets, the idea of "protecting property values" against people stereotyped as deficient in the role of homeowners and householders made eminent good sense. Note, though, that in this case the property values that were protected were those of White citizens and taxpayers. The property values of people of color were eroded by these very same policies.

All White Americans will be familiar with the many kinds of rationalizations that are available as one chooses a place to live. Even a White person with impeccably anti-racist credentials might guiltily decide to live in a predominantly White suburb simply because of its many amenities: a fine system of parks and libraries, good schools, a low crime rate, etc. A second White homeowner might believe that a home is an investment, choosing the suburbs over the city in order to get a better return on her money. A third might fear and detest people of color, and want to live as far away from them as possible, regardless of expense. Only the last decision would be considered racist within the folk theory. The first two types of decisions do prioritize a comfortable lifestyle or a good return on investment over life among diverse neighbors. Most White Americans would probably find the opposite priority to be praiseworthy – but eccentric – anti-racist heroism. But all of these decisions except the eccentric one result in residential segregation when the same latitude for decision is not available to people of color. People of color may rightly fear ostracism or even violence from suburban neighbors. They may be too poor to move to the suburbs. Today, actual denial of home financing on racial grounds is rare, but recent studies have shown that people of color are much more likely than Whites to be steered into the "sub-prime" mortgage market, and even into its criminal sectors where mortgage money is available only under predatory and fraudulent terms.[26]

The material facts of the world that residential segregation creates prop up White stereotypes about people of color. The high crime, poor schools, declining housing stock, poverty, noise, and dirt of cities and inner suburbs become associated with the idea of color. Since White Americans do not know about the history of suburbanization and the role of explicitly exclusionary policies by their government and their financial institutions in this history – and often resist confronting these facts when they are pointed out – the amenities of the suburbs become, not the sign of the accretion of White privilege throughout a racist history, but a sign of suburban virtue, that is to say, of White virtue. And urban decay becomes a material sign of the vices of Color, or even of essential properties of people of color. Thus a non–White applicant for a mortgage may be profiled by a prime-market bank officer as likely to take poor care of property, or to default on the mortgage, because of supposed essential inclination. And a family of color living in an immaculate home in an expensive suburban neighborhood may be seen as "exceptional," their very success and accomplishment indexing the stereotype, calling it up in the thoughts of their neighbors: "We have a Mexican family next door, and they do a beautiful job with their yard. Their children are quiet and well behaved and we've never had to worry about a thing." Who would say: "We have a White family next door, and . . ."? And so the circle of the cultural project of White racism tends to close. Not completely, because cultural projects are never closed, but residential segregation is an exceptionally tangled and dense fact of White racism.

There is resistance, of course. A long series of legal battles made the classic forms of mortgage redlining illegal, and anti-redlining legislation and judicial precedent are among the very few areas of American anti-discrimination law where the courts have held that discriminatory *effects* can justify a finding of illegal discrimination, even when belief and intention cannot be demonstrated.[27] Substantial changes in the culture of the real estate industry mean that people of color are today less likely to experience discriminatory treatment from real estate and rental agents (Ross and Turner 2005). But fair housing projects by a variety of non-governmental organizations continually battle against such discrimination, which remains significant. Residential segregation is difficult to fight in a period of gross economic inequality, where rising unemployment and falling wages among precisely the sectors of the labor market where many people of color have historically found employment exist alongside skyrocketing housing prices and gentrification. In spite of court decisions ruling that such practices are illegally discriminatory (see note 27), it is common for residential developments to make no provision for housing for working-class (or even middle-class) people, with a consequent differential impact on people of color. In many American cities today, less than one-third of households are qualified to purchase a median-priced home. This crisis of affordability inflicts long-term damage on family wealth, and exacerbates racially based economic inequality. People of color trapped in rented residences in inner cities experience a loss of wealth, while suburban property owners, who are largely White, build wealth as property values rise, and because they benefit from tax policies that permit deductions from income taxes of even enormous mortgages, that are very permissive about gains from loans against home equity, and that allow generous roll-overs and exclusions of capital gains from sale of a primary residence. Primary homeowner-occupied residences, unlike rented residences, also receive very favorable treatment in the bankruptcy codes of many states, an important protection against the loss of wealth.

Thus economic advantages that can be found in real estate markets accrue largely to Whites. These advantages feed back into increasing disparities between cities and suburbs. In the United States infrastructures such as schools, libraries, museums, parks, roads, policing, sanitation, and communications depend very heavily on the tax base of local municipalities and counties, and much less on state and federal-level investment. As wealth drains from cities, the tax base collapses there as well, and the capacity of a city to maintain a decent quality of life collapses with it. Even White property owners in cities lose wealth, teaching a stern lesson to those who might want to make the anti-racist choice of inner-city residence. A dire example of what this vicious circle can yield is the collapse of the great city of Philadelphia, graphically described in Buzz Bissinger's heartbreaking *A Prayer for the City* (1997). In summary, residential segregation is a classic vicious circle, and one which very few American cities have been able to avoid or redress.

Most Whites find it easy to ignore residential segregation. I experienced a good example of this inattention when I told a lunch-table's worth of White colleagues at the Center for Advanced Studies in the Behavioral Sciences about the linguist John Baugh's project on "linguistic profiling" (Baugh 2003). Baugh has developed a matched-guise test in which a single speaker uses a "White professional," a "Latino," or a "Black" voice in making telephone inquiries about the availability of advertised rentals in the San Francisco Bay area. The "White professional" voice is much more likely to yield an invitation to make an appointment to look at the property, while the other accents are more likely to result in a response that the rental is no longer available. My colleagues, all sophisticated scholars, were genuinely surprised at this result; several mentioned that they had thought that this sort of discrimination had long since disappeared.

Life at the Center also provided a very good example of discourse silence about residential segregation. The Center, located in the hills above the campus of Stanford University and the city of Palo Alto, California, is very concerned that its fellows be members of a residential community, and insists that they live within an easy commuting distance. Here is the statement on residence from the 2003–04 Fellows' Manual:

> As you know, residence must be in proximity to the Center (i.e., Atherton, Los Altos, Menlo Park, Mountain View, Palo Alto, Portola Valley, Redwood City, Stanford). This requirement specifically excludes San Francisco, Berkeley, other communities in the East Bay, and Santa Cruz.

What is interesting here is a town that is not mentioned in the list of "i.e.'s": East Palo Alto. East Palo Alto borders Palo Alto on the east, and is no further from the Center than Mountain View or Redwood City. I doubt that the Center intended to rule out residence in East Palo Alto. Instead, it is probably not mentioned because it would simply almost never occur to anyone who moves in the Bay Area academic world to want to live there, even though the savings in rent might be considerable. East Palo Alto is the only town in the golden chain of expensive bedroom suburbs strung between San Francisco and San Jose with a substantial concentration of African American residents, and it is notorious for its high crime rate. The failure to mention the town constitutes the Center as a space of privilege, which is to say as a White space. And, since naming East Palo Alto might require a cautionary note, this erasure also constitutes the Center as a site of virtue, of people who would not make any invidious distinctions among local communities. The town simply vanishes from the mental map shared by those who designed the Center's literature.[28]

The case of residential segregation shows that we cannot understand White racism as residing exclusively in individual beliefs about the inferiority of people of color and the superiority of Whites. Instead, it shows how a wide range of motives and behaviors, many of them perfectly rational, and many kinds of silences and inattentions that are at first glance entirely inoffensive, work together to create racist institutions and outcomes. Residential segregation remains stable, decreasing slightly nationwide during the last two decades among African Americans (yet remaining at very high levels in many cities), and even slightly increasing among Asians and Pacific Islanders and Hispanics, as shown in Table 2.[29] Residential segregation cannot be due to the actions of a vicious minority of White supremacists. Ezekiel (1995:xxi) reports statistics gathered by the Center for Democratic Renewal and the Southern Poverty Law Center showing that the militant White racist movement had only about 25,000 "hard-core members," perhaps another 150,000 "sympathizers" who might actually pay for literature or attend rallies, and approximately another 450,000 people who read movement literature. This last number is probably higher now that Internet accessibility means that pamphlets and newsletters do not have to be passed around from hand to hand. However, this is a still a very small number of people, who are stigmatized by their fellow citizens and harassed by law enforcement agencies. The importance of their occasional acts of violence should not be underemphasized – they are rightly feared, and such fear does play a role in decisions by people of color about where to live. But it is surely obvious that in order to create a pattern at the national scale of American residential segregation, the vast majority of Whites, including White elites and Whites who do not consider themselves to be racist within the terms of the folk theory, must somehow be participating. Their participation simultaneously stems from and reproduces White racism as a set of cultural projects and generative principles that are fundamental to the production of White culture and identity in the United States. These cultural projects are not marginal or archaic. They are an active, productive, and dynamic contemporary reality that shapes the beliefs and behaviors of Whites in every sphere of life, and that produces the racial reality in which they, and the populations of color subordinated within this reality, must live.

# Chapter 2

# Language in White Racism: An Overview

## Introduction: Discourse

The central problem for this book is how White Americans, while claiming to be anti-racist, are somehow able to acquire and to share with one another negative stereotypes that they use, consciously or unconsciously, to justify the subordination and oppression of people of color. These stereotypes must circulate among them in discourse, in everyday language, made public in talk and text. In this chapter, we will take a first look at how linguistic ideologies – ideas about language itself that are shaped by political and economic interests – may work to promote the reproduction and circulation of stereotypes.

Negative stereotypes can, of course, be acquired without discourse, by mere gaze. Where brown and black faces dominate the American street scene, the White gaze can often observe a background of unpainted and sagging buildings, abandoned vehicles, graffitied walls, trash-filled gutters, weedy vacant lots, and poorly stocked shops where the price of the purchase is passed to the clerk, not across a friendly counter with displays of small items for impulse purchase, but in a revolving tray through bullet-proof plastic. Not understanding the history of residential segregation, or how it drains wealth from communities of color, or how this erodes a community's capacity for maintaining decent neighborhoods and controlling crime, White Americans conclude that the disorder before their eyes reveals that people of color are deficient as citizens.

But the uninformed White gaze, forming stereotypes through first-hand observation of how people of color often live in the United States, cannot be the most important source of racist ideas. I know about those revolving compartments where your money goes in one side and your bag of groceries comes out the other because I used to work at Wayne State University in downtown Detroit, Michigan, and if I wanted to buy a can of soda or a magazine on a break between classes, the only store in easy walking distance from my office had that system. But most White Americans live and work far from such neighborhoods, and have little social contact with people of color (Bonilla-Silva 2003). So indirect sources of information are probably much more important for them. These include casual conversation with other Whites, information circulated officially and unofficially in institutions like schools and workplaces, and, especially, representations of all types in mass media.

Among these media representations, visual images are immensely important, and the biases that these convey have been carefully studied by specialists (e.g., Entman and Rojecki 2000; Rodríguez, ed. 1997; Weston 1996). But since my training is in the analysis of talk and text, I have chosen to look at the ways racism is reproduced through these channels. This chapter introduces the foundational concepts that we will need for this project.

I use the term "discourse" as shorthand for "all the varieties of talk and text." In doing so, I depart from a meaning of the term introduced in Chapter 1. There the word came up in the sense developed by the philosopher Michel Foucault (1972). In Foucault's theory, a "discourse" is the set of fundamental preconditions not only for talk, but for thought and understanding itself. But when I write "discourse" I include the actual material presence, in structure and content, of language-in-use in history and at particular moments of human interaction. It is in these material presences that ideas actually live, and it is through these that people acquire and share knowledge. In using the term "discourse" in this way, I join a long tradition in linguistic anthropology and discourse analysis.[1] But another reason that my usage is not exactly like Foucault's is that I prefer the more politically loaded term "ideology" for some of the preconditions on language that Foucault labels as "discourse."

Knowledge and ideas are made available in discourse not simply through material presence. They are also made available in absences. We can think of the material surface of discourse, of our talk, as partly a set of explicit articulations, but also as a set of suggestive gaps that trigger inferences and connections among the stretches of explicit utterance. So the analysis of discourse requires us to examine not only what is said, but what is not said. Let me give an example. Last summer I visited my local Social Security office, fortunately located only four blocks from my house, to resolve a problem with my Medicare coverage. While I was waiting, a White woman sat down next to me and volunteered, "I had to drive two hours to get here!" When I was finally admitted to the inner office for an interview, I mentioned to the interviewer that someone in the waiting room had told me that she had driven two hours, and asked what the service area of the office was. The interviewer, a brown-skinned woman whose ethnicity wasn't obvious to me (her last name implied no obvious affiliation), said something very close to this, "Oh, we get that all the time. People come up here all the way from Green Valley because they don't want to go to our South Tucson office. We can't make them go to the office closest to their homes." I said, "Oh. I think I know what you're saying." This is what she did not say: Green Valley is a set of retirement communities inhabited almost entirely by relatively conservative White people. South Tucson is an almost all-Latino community, and, in fact, the whole south side of the Tucson metropolitan area is heavily Latino and Native American. A White person in the waiting room in the Social Security office in South Tucson would probably be very much in the minority. There were quite a few people of color in the waiting room on North Campbell Avenue, but Whites were the majority there. The interviewer's utterance did not make any of this explicit. By the time of my question, she knew I had lived at my present address for over 20 years, so her utterance invited me to apply my local knowledge, of the racial makeup of the communities, and of the kind of attitude that would make someone drive for two hours to get to North Campbell Avenue, instead of perhaps 30 minutes to reach South Tucson. Having made these inferences, I realized that my interviewer had really said a mouthful, in addition to her actual words.

In summary, when I write "discourse" I do not mean just the material surface of the language, although this publicly available surface, the linguistic sign itself, is absolutely crucial because it triggers all the meaning-creating activity accomplished in communication. I include as well the invitations and clues, the silences, the inferences that the literal content of a text or an utterance invites. Following Foucault, I assume that deep principles determine what components of the message are explicit, and what components are recovered through inference. Among the most important of these principles are "linguistic ideologies."

## Linguistic Ideologies

This book argues that "linguistic ideologies" (often called "language ideologies") that are not in themselves racist provide, in interaction with the folk theory of racism introduced in the first chapter, an essential scaffolding for White racist discourse, including both its characteristic forms and the ways that these are visible and invisible. In so arguing, I adapt to the study of White racism a crucial insight of linguistic anthropology: that linguistic ideologies shape and constrain discourse, and thus shape and constrain the reproduction of other kinds of ideologies, such as ideologies of gender, race, and class. Linguistic ideologies are sets of interested positions about

language that represent themselves as forms of common sense, that rationalize and justify the forms and functions of text and talk.

The functions of linguistic ideologies are diverse. They rationalize and
justify what people understand to be the structures of their language (or
languages) and the ways that language should be used (Silverstein 1979).
They sort out language structures and ways of using language as good or
bad, correct or incorrect, and link these with persons who are thought to
be good or bad, moral or immoral (Irvine 1989; Woolard 1998). People
acquire ideologies of language because these make their world more coherent and comprehensible, but also because these beliefs promote their access
to important resources, both economic and symbolic, within that world,
and promote their sense of privilege and well-being. The term "linguistic
ideologies" emphasizes how such interests are crucial to the formation of
ideas about language. Linguistic ideologies persist not only because they
have a certain internal coherence, and because they resonate with other
cultural ideas, but because they support and reassert the interests of many
(but not all) of those who share them.

The label "ideology," then, suggests a way of thinking or a perspective
saturated with political and economic interest. Sometimes, this interest is
glaringly obvious. For instance, when a White speaker condemns African
American usage as ignorant slang, anyone might suspect that this condemnation advances the speaker's interest in the racial status quo, in White
privilege. But other expressions of linguistic ideology are less obviously
interested. Rumsey (1990) pointed out that ideologies of language often
appear to us as forms of common sense. They may even be quite invisible
until they are carefully pointed out. But as we explore the possibility of
political and economic interest in ideology, we find that "common sense"
has that status because it defines a group of people whose interests are
advanced by believing in it, and not because it is necessarily true or even
likely. This does not mean, of course, that the ideas that are part of
"ideologies" about language are always wrong. We will see examples where
ideas that are closely related to vernacular linguistic ideologies show up in
scholarly theorizing about language that has been useful and productive.
But their correctness or logical coherence is not what makes ideologies
attractive to, or persistent among, people who hold them. After all, only a
minute percentage of the people who have ideas about language are
linguists.

## An explicit linguistic ideology: Monoglot Standard

Let me begin an explanation of linguistic ideologies with a fairly simple
and accessible example. This example, which to most people seems

commonsensical and benign at worst, and highly positive at best, turns out to be deeply implicated in the culture of White racism in the United States. Silverstein (1996) called this ideology "Monoglot Standard." The emergence of "standard" languages and the ideologies that have preserved them, and in some cases made them even the objects of legislation and intense government involvement around the world during the last several hundred years, is a large and complex topic that goes beyond the scope of this book. However, we can summarize the major elements of ideologies of Standard, drawing on Silverstein (1996) and Milroy and Milroy (1999).

The first part of the ideology of Standard is the belief that, if there are two or more variants of a form, only one is "correct." This contrasts with the view of linguists, that all varieties of human languages are systematic and rule-governed. For linguistics, correctness is a social and political, not a grammatical, fact. The second part is the belief that ways of speaking can be ranked according to their prestige. Prestige and correctness go together in the ideology of Standard, because it is believed that prestigious people speak the prestigious form, which deserves its prestige because it is correct. Again, the ranking of ways of speaking according to prestige is of interest to linguists as a social phenomenon, but it is considered to be a strictly arbitrary result of politics and history. Linguists have not been able to identify any scientific grounds for such judgments, and they are very fond of sharing a huge repertoire of examples of how a single linguistic feature will have high prestige in one circumstance, and low in another.[2] Third, a "standard" language will be endowed with a respectable history and a set of arguments that explain why it is prestigious and correct. Such popular histories are nearly always rather different from what careful historical scholarship reveals. Finally, believers in the ideology of Standard hold that to speak the correct and prestigious form will bring social and economic benefits, so it is important, as well as possible and desirable, for people to learn to speak this way. Not to acquire the "standard" is a sign of moral failing, or of an absence of proper ambition. Sociolinguistic study, however, shows that even absolute control over a "standard" variety often does not bring economic or social benefits if a speaker is otherwise stigmatized (the study of race and gender discrimination is crowded with examples).

We can look at how the ideology of "Standard" works and how it is entwined with White racism by starting with a belief about correctness that is shared very widely by White speakers of American English: that "double negatives" are incorrect. People who hold this view usually rationalize it by explaining that since "two negatives make a positive" (as in multiplication in arithmetic), sentences with double negatives make no sense, and are ruled out by universal logic. Thus, speakers who use double negatives are not only incorrect, they are illogical. Thus they will be unable to coherently represent and communicate their ideas, and will be held back from success in their endeavors. Because they cannot see this illogic, they are probably unintelligent. While believing that double negatives are incorrect may seem harmless enough, as soon as this belief is used to sort people according to communicative and intellectual – and, as we shall see, moral – potential, it is revealed as less benign. We can make this example clearer by looking more closely at the grammars of negatives and the ways that these are distributed across the English-speaking world.

A nice example of "double negative" usage, uttered by a young African American man who kept homing pigeons in coops on the roof of his apartment building in New York City and was proud of his provisions for their security, was quoted by the sociolinguist William Labov: "It ain't no cat can't get in no coop" (Labov 1972:130). Linguists call the grammatical principle that organizes this sentence "negative concord." In strict "negative concord," if a negative appears anywhere in a sentence, all other negatable elements must also be negative. The variety of American English that Labov labeled "African American Vernacular English" (AAVE) follows this principle. Most White working-class speakers in the United States also use negative concord. Negative concord is a staple of the grammar of some important popular genres of musical lyrics (such as rap music and country music) and appears in representations of working-class speech in film, television, and theater. In contrast, most middle-class speakers of all colors throughout the English-speaking world use varieties of English that exhibit "negative polarity": Only one negative can appear in a sentence. So, if I kept pigeons on my roof, I would say, "There is**n't** *any* cat that *can* get into *any* coop," or "**No** cat *can* get into *any* coop." Every element that follows the first negative (bolded in these examples) must be positive or "polar" to the negative. These polar items are italicized.

Most English speakers know that to utter sentences with negative concord exposes speakers to stigma, to being labeled as crude or uneducated. The association between negative concord and social subordination is so strong that my students are often surprised when they are reminded that Spanish, which they acknowledge to be an important world language, uses negative concord even in its highest registers. On the other hand, Cupeño, a Uto-Aztecan language that was spoken by a small group of hunters and gatherers in aboriginal California, exhibits rigid negative polarity, rather like the classiest forms of English (Hill 2005a). So both types of negative grammar (and several mixed types) are possible, and neither type has any inherent connection with logic, or education, or class. However, English speakers all feel strongly that there is such an association. Middle-class speakers think that African American or White working-class speakers who use negative concord are not just doing something "non-standard," they are speaking illogically, revealing the poverty and disorder of their thought. Thus, this piece of linguistic ideology permits its adherents to hear anew, in sentence after sentence, evidence of the inferiority of those who use "double negatives," and evidence as well of their own superior intelligence and cultivation, which justifies their access to the resources that a middle-class life brings them. It's important to understand that the double-negative shibboleth in English doesn't work because people carefully reason through the "two negatives make a positive" argument – this is an *ex post facto* rationalization. It works at a gut level, and to use a double negative without wrapping it in vivid and unmistakable oral and even gestural quotation marks (as when a middle-class person quotes country music or a hip-hop lyric) would bring instant discredit, rather like blowing one's nose on one's sleeve.

The ideology of Standard and the sub-part of it that stigmatizes double negatives meet resistance. One of the reasons that double negatives are so common in song lyrics is that for working-class people the kind of grammar in which they are embedded can be a proud emblem of personal authenticity, of being an unpretentious and egalitarian person, and, even more specifically, of being authentically masculine. Using this kind of language in hip-hop culture, centered in the African American community, is part of "keeping it real," speaking the truth about life and its circumstances (Morgan 2001, 2007). Double negatives appear in the representation of African American and working-class characters in film, television, theater, and literature because such characters would not seem real to viewers and readers if they did not exhibit this usage. In domains where authentic masculinity is especially at stake, double negatives may be crucial in identity work. Male athletes, even White men known to have tertiary degrees from prestigious institutions, may feel constrained to speak in this working-class style even in the relatively formal context of interviews on radio and television, lest their masculinity be doubted. But the potential for stigma is always present when such usages are advanced, and the stigma is especially acute when the speaker is African American. The cartoonist Jeff Danziger issued a cartoon in 2004 showing Condoleezza Rice (an African American who was then National Security Advisor to President George W. Bush, who has never been overheard using African American Vernacular English), barefoot, in a rocking chair, bottle-feeding a baby aluminum tube and saying, "'I knows all about aluminum tubes' (correction) 'I don't know nuthin' about aluminum tubes'." Defenders of Rice focused on the language attributed to her in the cartoon as an inexcusable display of racism by Danziger (Google returned over 16,000 hits on "Danziger Rice cartoon" as late as July 2007).[3]

Of course the ideology of "Standard" does more work than simply provide a site where stereotypes about African Americans can be repeated. The ideology of Standard and its link to what Irvine (1989) called "moral interest" showed up when the political blogger Joshua Micah Marshall linked to a graphic image of a letter handwritten from a federal prison by former California Republican congressman Randy "Duke" Cunningham, convicted of accepting bribes from defense contractors. The letter, in which Cunningham attacked the journalist who had first exposed his crimes, was filled with misspelled words and grammatical infelicities (no double negatives, though). Marshall commented, "Give it a read and ponder how this fool ever made it into Congress" (Marshall 2006). For Marshall, Cunningham's failure to match a schooled standard for written American English signaled low intelligence, that he was a "fool." The illiterate letter became a natural "icon" (Gal and Irvine 1995) of Cunningham's political corruption. Precisely the naturalness, the ease with which Marshall, a political writer whom I admire, deployed the ideology of Standard against a corrupt right-wing militarist congressman whose fall from grace I was delighted to follow, shows how Standard is such a good, ordinary, commonsensical tool for attacking the intelligence of a working-class White, or questioning the competence of an African American National Security Advisor – or, more broadly, for questioning the intelligence of all African Americans. And Marshall's attack on Cunningham shows that more is at stake than mere intelligence. Once a person lacks the bulwark of logic and capacity for "clear communication" provided by Standard, moral standing as well is at risk, and criminality is not a surprise. As a linguist, I know that the ideology of Standard has no scientific basis, and as a reasonably observant human being, I know that many intelligent and highly moral people produce sentence fragments and spelling errors when they write. But this didn't stop me from enjoying Marshall's jab at Cunningham. My pleasure shows us how deeply linguistic ideologies go in making our world meaningful.

## Some implicit linguistic ideologies: Personalism, referentialism, and their corollaries

Many of the linguistic ideologies that will be important in this book are far less obvious than the ideology of Standard. The ideology of "personalism" (Rosaldo 1981), which holds that the most important part of linguistic meaning comes from the beliefs and intentions of the speaker, is very widespread. The baptismal ideology of meaning, which holds that there is a single correct meaning of a word that can be found by tracing its history to an authoritative original source, is of narrower scope (it is one element of referentialist linguistic ideology [Silverstein 1976]), but just as widely shared. Both of these are interesting in that, unlike the ideology of Standard from which the double-negative shibboleth comes, they overlap with views held by eminent linguists and philosophers of language. I will try to show, however, that as these are deployed in popular rationalizations and justifications, and, specifically, when they are used along with the folk theory of racism in everyday decisions about whether discourse is "racist" or "not racist," they are emphatically ideological, serving the interests of dominant groups just as much as the ideology of Standard. Personalist ideology and baptismal ideology are seldom explicitly articulated. Instead, they function most of the time as unspoken presuppositions about "not only linguistic form and use, but also the very notion of the person and the social group, as well as such notions as religious ritual, child socialization, gender relations, the nation-state, schooling, and law" (Woolard 1998:3).

A central function of language ideologies in the reproduction of White racism is that they make some kinds of talk and text visible as racist, and others invisible. We can illustrate this with referentialist ideology, which is shared by most middle-class White Americans. Reference is the function of language whereby its forms come to stand for things in the world – the understanding that permits us to say that the English word "dog" refers to an example of *Canis familiaris*. Silverstein (1976) critiqued the way that even scientific linguistics focuses almost exclusively on reference, to the neglect of other functions. The idea of the stability of reference, that elements of talk can be linked by referential indexes to elements in the world, is crucial to grammatical analysis. For instance, a grammarian draws on the theory of reference when she points out that in the sentence "Jane knows that Mary loves her children," the word *her* is ambiguous, potentially referring to children of either *Jane* or *Mary*, but not both. But everyday referentialist ideology insists that language exists in order to communicate information, and that it uses words to do this job.

Referentialist ideology insists that words must be used properly. When the logician C. L. Dodgson, writing as Lewis Carroll in *Alice in Wonderland*, wanted to create a topsy-turvy, chaotic world, he invented Humpty Dumpty, who said, "When I use a word, it means just what I choose it to mean – neither more nor less." Dodgson joined other philosophers in equating the stability of reference, the proper use of words in accordance with an authoritative baptismal moment, with the stability of the social world itself. The ideology of Standard incorporates referentialist ideology when it links correct usage to correct beliefs and in turn to moral virtue.

Referentialist ideology makes the question of whether or not statements are "true" into a very salient issue, so that within its terms the utterance or publication of what are called "stereotypes" is highly visible as racist. Referentialist ideology permits stereotypes to be attacked as racist because they are not true, so they reflect false beliefs and moral dubiousness. A recent exchange of letters to the *Tucson Weekly*, a local free weekly newspaper that I pick up every Thursday when I buy my morning coffee, provides an example. On July 5, 2007, the *Tucson Weekly* published an infuriating letter to the editor from Joseph R. Damron under the headline "Education is not a cultural value for Latinos." Mr. Damron argued that while there might seem to be short-term advantages in inviting unskilled immigrants from Latin America into US labor markets, in the long run, this would be very costly, because "although the unskilled laborer's taxpayer-supported children do eventually learn English, they remain educationally resistant for generations" (Damron 2007). I was confident that this stereotype-laden letter would receive an angry reply, and I was not disappointed. On July 26, the *Tucson Weekly* published a letter from Martin Bernal, headlined "Letter writer needs to open his eyes to Latinos in our society." Bernal enumerated the educational accomplishments of his own immigrant family (college for all, and careers as "a nurse, a judge, a public-school teacher and a director of a government department") and mentioned many other counterexamples to Damron's claim. Bernal didn't call Damron a racist, but he did say "Mr. Damron should quit listening to conservative talk radio and open his eyes" (Bernal 2007). That is, Mr. Bernal linked Mr. Damron's publication of false beliefs to an imagined property of Mr. Damron as someone who "listens to conservative talk radio," which in the United States today would entail holding beliefs and attitudes that many people, and certainly many Latinos, would see as discreditable. He also implied that Mr. Damron keeps his eyes closed so that he cannot see the truth.

While referentialist language ideology makes stereotypes visible as "wrong," it leads us to the misleading conclusion that if we merely "educate," revealing the racist errors in stereotypes, they will be discredited. But, although a publication of a stereotype today is guaranteed to attract angry replies that advance better information, the same stereotypes are repeated again and again. Mere education does not seem to interrupt the circulation of racist ideas.

## Performative ideology

Another linguistic ideology that is shared by most Americans holds that words have an active force, that they can soothe or wound. This so-called performative ideology permits the recognition of so-called "hate speech." Rather than being about truth and correctness, this ideology is about how language makes people feel. Silverstein (1979) called such ideologies, that rationalize and justify the usages and functions of language, "metapragmatic." Performative ideology makes it possible to understand some words as assaultive, rather than true or false. The idea that words and utterances are actions appears in the philosophy of language. J. L. Austin's (1962) theory of the performative holds that certain utterances, such as "I sentence you to thirty years in the state penitentiary," or "I baptize you Mary Christine," or "I now pronounce you man and wife," function mainly to perform actions rather than to represent the truth.

Performative ideology makes racial epithets and slurs visible as racist. Ordinary people often use the language of physical assault, of being "cut" and "wounded," in discussing them. The legal scholars known as Critical Race theorists (Matsuda et al., eds. 1993) have developed this idea to argue that, if hate speech is simply assault and has no truth value, then hate speech can be made illegal without violating the constitutional protection of freedom of speech. This point will be discussed in Chapter 3.

## Indexicality and Covert Racist Discourse: Invisible to Linguistic Ideologies?

Stereotypes and slurs are visible as "racist" to most people because they are made salient by referentialist and performative linguistic ideologies respectively. But other kinds of talk and text that are not visible, so called covert racist discourse, may be just as important in reproducing the culturally shared ideas that underpin racism. Indeed, they may be even more important, because they do their work while passing unnoticed. These forms of discourse do not reproduce racist stereotypes by conventional reference, like explicit stereotypes. Instead, they communicate by absence and silence that invite inferences, as in the example that I introduced above, of my Social Security interviewer's oblique utterance. To use a technical term that will be explained in Chapter 5, they work by indexicality, and specifically by presupposition and entailment. These presuppositions and entailments are retrieved by listeners and readers, who make contextually based inferences that may be quite automatic. The presuppositions or entailments invited by covert racist discourse include very negative stereotypes that might be sharply censured if they were made explicit. But, since they are not overtly uttered, they are invisible to referentialist ideology with its focus on the meaning of words. Not only are they not explicitly uttered, these presuppositions and entailments are not easily identified as the products of individual intentions, as required by personalist ideology. Instead, they are co-constructed in the communicative space shared by interlocutors, in the collaborative project that is required to "get" jokes, to share moods, to enjoy sociality itself. Personalist linguistic ideology really has no way to handle the co-construction of meaning among speakers, since for personalism meaning is founded in the intentions and beliefs of individuals acting alone.

An introductory example comes from the lexicon of "Mock Spanish." This is the use of "cerveza" by middle-class White Americans when they talk about drinking beer. Planning a casual hour or two, made more agreeable by inexpensive alcohol, they might say something like "Let's go have a beer." Or "Let's get together for a few cold ones." Or they could say (and as far as I know this could be said anywhere in the United States, and perhaps anywhere in the core English-speaking world[4]) "Let's get together and crack a few cervezas." The last utterance is in the same register or level of usage as the locution "a few cold ones." It is vaguely euphemistic and slightly humorous. It probably means something like this (I will argue for this analysis in detail in Chapter 5): "On this occasion, we will be relaxed about alcohol, the way we believe that Mexicans are relaxed about alcohol, rather than careful and responsible and sober like White people." That is, our imagined party planners recruit a small piece of a stereotyped "Mexican" identity to excuse their own relaxation, and in doing so they briefly make available a very ugly stereotype of the "drunken Mexican." Access to the stereotype is probably required in order to participate in the feeling of relaxed sociability that the utterance should produce. The mood would surely be interrupted if we inquired, "Why did you say 'cerveza' instead of 'beer'? This is America, we speak English here!" Many people who would say "Let's crack a few cervezas" would be shocked to be accused of sharing the "drunken Mexican" stereotype. Yet the constant use of "cerveza" as part of a register of relaxed sociability can do the same work as the explicit utterance of the slur.[5]

None of the linguistic ideologies that are widely shared among White Americans provide any purchase on the phenomenon of indexicality. This is probably an important reason why the racist entailment of this use of "cerveza" and other Mock Spanish usages is not visible to them. As I will show in Chapter 5, they are likely to indignantly reject the idea that there could be anything even remotely racist about using the word "cerveza" in the way that I have mentioned above. On the contrary, they are likely to understand it as charmingly cosmopolitan, or as reflecting their authenticity as westerners or southwesterners. They will even argue that they use it to show their respect for, and appreciation of, Mexican culture and language. I have never found any evidence that they are not completely sincere in these objections, and I believe that the racializing functions of Mock Spanish are genuinely invisible to them. It is even difficult for Latinos to figure out exactly what is going on, although Mock Spanish often makes them uncomfortable (and some Latino/as are intensely aware of Mock Spanish as racist).

## The Metacultural Function of Linguistic Ideologies

Along with their capacity to make some kinds of discourse functions and meanings highly salient, and others invisible, linguistic ideologies have what Urban (2001) has called a "metacultural" function: In Urban's words, they "move culture through the world," putting certain kinds of talk and text into general circulation. A very good example is the role of personalist linguistic ideologies in the circulation of racist slurs and epithets. Slurs are highly visible as racist. However, even though they are stigmatized and discredit the people who utter them, they are astonishingly common. Everybody somehow learns them. So-called "moral panics" (Cohen 1972) are a very important context for the circulation and reproduction of visibly racist discourse. Moral panics often occur when a prominent public figure is accused of making a racist remark. Personalist ideology inspires intense concern about the inner selves of such persons, and the attribution to a celebrity of a racist remark provokes obsessive examination of his or her beliefs and intentions. These obsessions play out in mass media firestorms, during which the offensive remark is repeated again and again, over days and even weeks, both by those who wish to defend the speaker and by those who are on the attack. I strongly suspect that an important effect of the hyper-repetition of overtly racist language that takes place during these affairs is the one noted by the linguist George Lakoff in his title *Don't Think of an Elephant!* (2004) – having been so instructed, one cannot avoid thinking, precisely, of elephants. Thus, when we read or hear, perhaps dozens of times in a week, about how some important public figure was overheard using a racist epithet, that epithet is irrevocably reinscribed in our understanding. Here is an example. During the 2006 congressional elections, Senator George Allen, a Virginia Republican, was videotaped using a racist slur, "macaca," about a dark-skinned young American man of South Asian ancestry. At first, nobody understood the word, and his campaign put out that he had been referring to the young victim's rather edgy haircut, so "macaca" meant something like "Mohawk." However, investigators soon discovered that Allen's mother had been brought up in French Algeria, where "macaca" was a racist epithet for "Black African." This discovery focused intense attention on Allen's racial views. When reporters learned that he had used the N-word often when he was in college (and collected Confederate memorabilia), this was headline news in major newspapers, on talk shows on television and radio, and endlessly on blogs and Internet discussion sites. Weeks after the allegation first surfaced, I was preparing a talk on the "macaca" incident for the annual meeting of the American Anthropological Association. When I typed into the Google search window the words "George Allen nigger" I brought up 237,000 hits. These dated from mid-August to my access date of November 2, 2006 and represented every type of media. That is, a person browsing the web, flipping through the newspaper, picking up a magazine, or channel-surfing for a bit of news or talk, would almost certainly have encountered references to Senator Allen's use of the N-word, thereby seeing the word and reflecting on what it means. Concern about what kind of *person* Senator

Allen might be, given the kind of *language* he used, put the single most stigmatized and ugly racist epithet in the American language into intense circulation (and, of course, added a new one, "macaca," to the American vocabulary). Personalist ideology, which locates the meaning of talk in the mental states of speakers, promoted the circulation of Allen's chosen epithets. This is what I mean by the "metacultural" function of linguistic ideologies. When prominent public figures like Allen are suspected of holding false or racist beliefs, a scandal occurs: In a sense, everyone is implicated, since such people are influential, admired, perhaps elected by popular vote, and otherwise stand in for ordinary people and are important to them in many complex ways. Thus it becomes acutely important to understand their beliefs and to determine whether they are truly racist. The density of reportage and analysis that these concerns produce work metaculturally, promoting the public circulation, in respected and authoritative media contexts, of the most explicitly racist forms of discourse associated with the culture of White racism. Scholars who have proposed that we are now in a phase of "New Racism," where racism is reproduced only with great subtlety, neglect these affairs. Even though the utterance of stereotypes and epithets is stigmatized, linguistic ideologies provide people with occasions where they can be repeated.

## An Overview of Chapters to Come

In Chapters 3 and 4, I consider two major types of discourse which most White Americans can call "racist." Chapter 3 treats "slurs": insults and epithets that convey racial insults. These are highly salient to both Whites and people of color, and when made public they often elicit censure and condemnation. To label an utterance as a "slur" is to insist that it is an intentional violation of a code of conduct that condemns racist speech. I will explore both the nature of racial slurs and the ideological underpinnings of reactions against them, and the ways that discourse about slurs reveal the major themes of the folk theory of racism. Chapter 4 is about "gaffes." Gaffes often contain exactly the same language as do slurs. However, to label an utterance as a gaffe (or a "slip") is to treat its racist meaning as unintentional. Debate then centers around whether the utterance might be an inadvertent revelation of underlying and hitherto-hidden racism, or simply an unfortunate misspeaking or misunderstanding. Gaffes, like slurs, are highly visible, and precipitate elaborate public rituals of conflicting rationalization and condemnation. However, in contrast to a claim that an utterance is a slur, to label an utterance as a gaffe is to insist that its moral significance is open to debate. People accused of gaffes, unlike speakers accused of uttering slurs and epithets, are often defended by others as having "not really meant" what is implied in the gaffe. I will look at what makes an utterance understandable as a gaffe, and how reactions to gaffes reveal ideologies about language, especially ideologies of personalism that maintain that the principal source of meaning must be the beliefs and intentions of a speaker.

The discourse events – the circulation of talk and text over a bounded period of time – that are precipitated by the noticing of slurs and gaffes are important moments in the reproduction of racism, but also in the reproduction of Whiteness itself. These discourse events have at least two major functions that advance the projects of White racism outlined in Chapter 1, especially the project of constructing racial hierarchies. First, they permit Whites to reproduce their folk-theory understandings of racists and racism. This reproduction advances White virtue, in that in recognizing a "racist" or in identifying "racism," a White person shows herself to be a good person. Second, they permit Whites to stigmatize color by reproducing racist stereotypes, since in these discourse events slurs and stereotypes are endlessly repeated. These stereotypes justify White privilege and the oppression of color. Even when people do not believe the stereotypes in the usual sense of "belief," the stereotypes become easily accessible, become an element of automatic, unreflective action and reaction that is very difficult to notice and contest.

In Chapters 5 and 6, I discuss forms of talk and text that I believe to be part of the production and reproduction of White racism, but which are not salient among Whites as "racist," and have no popular labels. These include racist metaphors that pass unnoticed, and linguistic appropriations by Whites of language materials that originate in communities of color. Some such appropriations are highly visible and are identified as racist even by many Whites. These include mimicry: the broad imitation of African American language found in minstrelsy and its descendants, and parodic imitations of Spanish accents such as the old "José Jiménez" or "Speedy Gonzales" routines that today make many Whites uncomfortable. However, many such usages escape White censure as racist, including fairly broad imitations of "Arabs," "Indians," or of African American or Latino "accents." These are very common in popular culture in advertising and popular films; Lippi-Green (1997), Chun (2004), and Meek (2006) treat this sort of mimicry in detail. At least one kind of appropriation, "Mock Spanish" (Hill 1998), the source of the "cerveza" example reviewed above, seems to be quite invisible to Whites as racist. These covert forms do not precipitate the exchange of accusations and rationalizations and denials that we see in the cases of slurs and gaffes. In fact, one cannot use the usual everyday-language denials of racism identified long ago by van Dijk (1987, 1993) with such locutions. One cannot say, "I'm not a racist, but adios, sucker," or "I'm not a racist, but what up, dog?" or "I'm not a racist, but no tick-ee, no wash-ee." Such an utterance doesn't make sense, because even though I think I can show that "Adios, sucker," "What up, dog?" and "No tick-ee, no wash-ee" require the intersubjective recovery of racist stereotypes, such utterances are not racist in the way that something like "Mexicans are treacherous and insincere" or "African American men are exceptionally tough and masculine" or "Chinese people all own laundries and don't speak English correctly" might be taken to be racist. If we hear someone say, "I'm not a racist, but I really think that African American men are exceptionally tough and masculine," the qualification makes perfect sense, because the truth of the claim is debatable, and if the claim is not true, then the speaker might be guilty of believing in a racist stereotype. For this reason, in my analysis of these linguistic appropriations I depart from the case study method of Chapters 3 and 4, which focus on socially occurring discourse events that I could retrieve from the published record. Instead, I use a form of critical analysis that looks at a broad sample of examples from many different events, in order to show that these appropriated forms of language can and do work to reproduce racism.

Since the linguistic appropriations discussed in Chapter 6 are not salient for Whites, they do not precipitate moral panics. So, instead of looking at specific discourse events around instances of appropriation, I have followed a few themes and usages over many years, drawing on a wide variety of media. Major media sources include television, radio (these less so, since I have been unable to make myself acquire a TV-radio habit), newspapers and magazines, and the Internet. I have used also minor media such as slogans on t-shirts and coffee cups, verses on greeting cards, and text on such artifacts as menus, public-service pamphlets, and advertising fliers.[6]

While I analyze mainly materials that were produced without my intervention (so-called "socially occurring" talk and text), I depart from customary "ethnographic" practice in my heavy use of materials from mass media, especially from the moral panics that produce "media firestorms," where a particular incident of talk and text becomes the intense focus of many media outlets at the same time over several days or weeks. While the language of media is socially occurring, rather than elicited by interview or experiment, it is not everyday language. Everyday talk is probably the most important site of social production and reproduction. However, it is extremely difficult to observe everyday talk about race and racism among Whites. Myers (2005) trained college students who were able to record rich examples of shocking "race talk" among their peers. Picca and Feagin (2007) collected thousands of accounts of racist talk reported by college students as occurring among their friends and families. Ezekiel (1995) conducted fieldwork among neo-Nazis and Ku Klux Klansmen, who talk obsessively about race. However, this book deals mainly with White people who do not see themselves as racist and who would not be thought to be so by their fellow Whites. In this world, while "race talk" is by no means unknown, and, indeed, is almost certainly an important element of back-stage solidarity on many occasions, racism is located as well, and very importantly, in an undercurrent of presuppositions that provide no moments of awkwardness or embarrassment for participants, and that permit White privilege to be taken for granted. The theme of race is both everywhere and nowhere, consisting largely of silences, of the failure to be specifically anti-racist, of careful failure to notice racially shaped phenomena. Among such people, as Memmi (2000) pointed out, racism "lurks in the shadows of discourse."

This quality of absence and silence in White discourse exists alongside a very active "presence" of racist discourse that continues in slurs and gaffes. However, the locations where saliently racist talk can be heard have shifted. As I pointed out in the preface to this book, I grew up among unabashed racists for whom race was, as Memmi (2000:5) noted, "a preoccupation, . . . even to the point of obsession." But for the kinds of Whites who figure in this book, race talk has largely retreated to occasions where speakers are among trusted intimates (as recorded by Myers 2005 and Picca and Feagin 2007), or to contexts like talk radio or Internet chat rooms where they can remain anonymous. When such Whites speak "on the record," whether in public or private, if racial issues are explicitly addressed at all (and they hardly ever are), the tone is earnestly liberal. In my own small social world, only the occasional sly jokes – including some from fellow academics – by friends and colleagues who know that I am studying racism and try to tease me, interrupt this bland surface. Living as I do within this White world, engaging in my own turn in these forms of talk, it is difficult for me to notice the silences and deep presuppositions in which our racism is encoded. But when White talk is inscribed as a text in a newspaper or on a website, it is – at least for me –more accessible to reflection and analysis, to the "Aha! Just look at what is happening there!" that interrupts the taken-for-granted world. This is why most of the materials that I analyze in this book come from media sources and not from participant observation in conversation. This is a fault in the work. I do try to watch and listen within the world that I inhabit, and anecdotes from such attention will turn up from time to time, but they are not the center of this study.

This book, then, is about my claim that everyday middle-class White discourse, published in widely distributed and respected media, and circulating as well in ordinary talk, continues to produce and reproduce White racism. Far from being part of America's past, White racism is a vital and formative presence in American lives, resulting in hurt and pain to individuals, in glaring injustice, in the grossly unequal distribution of resources along racially stratified lines, and in strange and damaging errors and omissions in public policy both domestic and foreign. White racism persists because Whites enjoy enormous benefits from being the dominant group in a racially stratified social order, and White racist culture is part of who Whites are. To genuinely confront racism, recognize it, and give it up would require them to undertake both painful and difficult personal reflection and constant attention to thought and action, of the type usually associated with rigorous spiritual disciplines. But I believe that White racism persists as well because beliefs and understandings that count as common sense among Whites, such as the folk theory of racism introduced in Chapter 1 and the linguistic ideologies introduced in this chapter, encourage them to continue to think, speak, and act in ways that make the foundational ideas of White racism enduringly available to new generations. White racism lives in discourse in a wide range of genres and routines, many of them right at the core of "the American language." They range from national rituals like media firestorms over racist gaffes by public figures, down to silly Mock Spanish slogans on coffee cups. These genres and routines are a very satisfying part of everyday social life, and White racism is not a cultural system that mere scholarship and reflection will change. But a first step is surely to try to understand how it works.

# Chapter 3

# The Social Life of Slurs

## Introduction

Among the kinds of talk and text that are visible as racist to White Americans, words labeled as slurs and epithets are the most salient. Slurs are made visible by performative linguistic ideology, the idea that words can perform actions. Slurs are understood to "cut," to "wound." To call a speaker's words a slur is in itself a charge of racism. Within the folk theory, this charge implies that the speaker is backward, ignorant, and filled with irrational hatred, so to label an utterance as a "slur" is to use very strong language.

The folk theory, which holds that racism persists only among marginal and uneducated people, predicts that slurs should be less common today than they were a few decades ago. Yet somehow everyone knows these words. They appear in assault, in moments of interpersonal anger and violence, or in gratuitous verbal muggings of people of color. They show up in jokes, and in the backstage "race talk" documented by Myers (2005). Slurs are important as well for a tough, hyper-masculine register of American English, where they are emblematic of straight talk and the right to unconstrained and "irreverent" expression, even among people who would deny a charge of racism (Eliasoph 1999). Slurs circulate in discourses that attempt to recapture and reshape the meanings of these words, as in the use of "nigga" as a term of affection and solidarity among some African Americans. They are frequently repeated in metalinguistic debates, about whether certain words are slurs, about who can use them and when they can be used, and in debates over whether those who use them are racists or not. Such debates are familiar and even ritualized routines that keep these words in active circulation even among speakers who would hesitate to deploy them in any other kind of discourse. In fact, these routines are among the few sites where White Americans seem to think that they can talk relatively freely, in public, about race and racism, so such talk offers an important opportunity for analysis. The central case study of this chapter examines a battle over the word "squaw," condemned as a racist slur by the middle of the nineteenth century. This debate, over whether a local mountain called "Squaw Peak" should be renamed, took place on an Internet message board hosted by the Phoenix daily newspaper, the *Arizona Republic*. Many participants in this debate insisted that the word "squaw" is not a slur, and so they should be able to use it without being labeled as racists.

While the folk theory insists that slurs appear only in the vocabularies of skinheads and Ku Kluxers, critical theorists of racism have found that the most educated and cosmopolitan Whites frequently deploy these expressions. Thus, while the folk theory predicts that discourse at colleges and universities should be dominated by enlightened anti-racism, in reality a strong current of vulgar racist talk continues on campuses and may even be especially common there (Delgado and Stefancic 2000:227; Myers 2005). The Internet is a symbol of technological progress and enlightenment, so the folk theory predicts that racist discourse should not appear there. Yet the Internet has become perhaps the single most important medium available to racists, an internationally accessible bulletin board where the most scurrilous racist invective is posted with impunity. One project of the National Association for the Advancement of Colored People, a leading American civil rights organization, has been to register all possible Internet domain names containing the epithet "nigger" in order to block White supremacist groups from using it (Kennedy 2002). So, instead of fading into marginality as predicted by the folk theory, slurs and epithets have colonized new environments among the most highly educated and technically competent members of American society.

Slurs and epithets are an object of fascination and even pleasure for White Americans. Scholarly attention to them by dialectologists and lexicographers has continued for over a century. Allen's *Unkind Words* (1990) is typical of this genre, inscribing an exceptionally rich collection of slurs and epithets at the same time that the author expresses the hope that people will stop using them. Contradicting this pious plea is his assertion that "American slang is among the most elaborate, fanciful, and colorful in the world" (Allen 1990:vii). No comparative evidence from other languages is advanced to support this point, but the claim makes clear that Allen, at the same time that he condemns slurs and epithets, takes pleasure in them as a sign of the richness of "American" imagination. This pleasure in slurs is one of their most important characteristics: at the same time that they are censured, they are indispensable in certain kinds of joking and humorous talk and text, and many people enjoy the poetics of a skillful string of slurs.

The deep history of slurs in White American discourse is especially well documented for the word "nigger," which exhibits a very typical social life cycle. First attested in 1574, the word is clearly pejorative by early in the seventeenth century, and was explicitly recognized as a slur at least by the end of the first third of the nineteenth century (Kennedy 2002:4). Even by the mid-nineteenth century the word was stigmatized; polite Whites used "colored people" or "Negro." Today the word is labeled as pejorative in dictionaries in every part of the English-speaking world, and is considered so offensive that it is often no longer spelled out in print. In 1967 the US Board on Geographic Names ruled that all place names in the United States that contained the word "Nigger" – more than 1,000 names – must be changed (Bright 2000).[1] Yet while "nigger" is often said to be the most offensive word in American English, the word is in constant use in many kinds of discourse. Kennedy (2002) summarizes many of the discourse events that have kept the word in active circulation even as it is strongly condemned. An evergreen debate disputes whether Mark Twain's *Huckleberry Finn*, arguably the greatest novel in the history of American letters, should ever be assigned for study or even held in school libraries below the tertiary-education level, because the word "nigger" appears in the novel "about 215 times" (Kennedy 2002:109). Writing in his own voice, Mark Twain used "negro," as in the 1884 "Explanatory" which opens *Huckleberry Finn*, where Twain claims that the book will use "the Missouri negro dialect."

Even "mention" of the word, as opposed to "use," can precipitate a crisis – and consequent repeated use of the word. In my own department of anthropology at the University of Arizona, a graduate teaching assistant, leading a discussion section in an introductory course in cultural anthropology in the late 1990s, cited the word to illustrate a point about racism. An African American student in the section complained to the highest levels of the university administration that this mention constituted a racist attack on her. Students and faculty debated the issue for weeks. In these arguments, they repeatedly recycled the word and obvious circumlocutions for it. A nationwide moral panic which generated immense amounts of press coverage was precipitated in late January of 1999 over the use of the word "niggardly" (which refers to pinch-penny thrift) in a staff meeting by a White assistant to the African American mayor of Washington, DC. The mayor accepted the assistant's resignation, but later rehired him (Kennedy 2002). Linguists like me, who may live for decades without ever encountering discussions of philological issues outside their own classrooms, were astounded to read in the national media technical discussions of the Germanic etymology of "niggardly," from Old Norse, as opposed to the Romance etymology of "nigger," a sixteenth-century loan from Portuguese. More recently, a national moral panic was precipitated when on

November 18, 2006, the actor Michael Richards (famous for portraying the character "Kramer" on the long-running television show *Seinfeld*) shouted "Nigger!" several times at African American members of his audience at the comedy club The Laugh Factory in Los Angeles. Richards's tirade was filmed by an audience member with a video cell phone, posted on the Internet, and endlessly quoted in every kind of media. Thus, the very attempts to condemn Richards's use of the word had the effect of massively increasing its circulation in the center of the American mainstream.[2]

Astonishingly, after 150 years of such discourse events, the stigmatization of "nigger" is not secure. Some commentators argue that it is simply a regional pronunciation or a ruralism, a mere ethnonym with no racist connotations. Conservatives have defended the word as part of an attack on "political correctness," as in an editorial from the University of New Mexico's student newspaper in 2004:

> exactly who is it that is entitled to determine which words are slurs? Should there be a national committee to determine an index of ethnic and other slurs? . . . This type of thinking can and has already led to a lot of silliness, such as the practice of using the expressions "f-word" and "n-word."
>
> (Berthold 2004)

White supremacists insist on their right to use the word. Ezekiel (1995:15) quotes a Ku Klux Klan leader who opened a speech in the 1980s with the following words: "You know . . . before this rally I talked to that fat little cop, that black police chief, and *he* said, 'Now, David, I don't want to hear the word *nigger*.' Well, Sheriff, hear this: *Nigger, nigger, nigger, nigger!*"

Whites who defend the word often argue that, since African Americans use it in both speech and in literary writing, Whites should be able to use it too. A fine parody of this negotiation was featured in the cartoon strip "Opus" on Sunday, July 22, 2007 (see Figure 1).

Opus the penguin claims that because he is 51 percent black (if you look at him from the right angle), he deserves a black license, which will permit him to "just walk around willy-nilly and call other people the N-word." However, when he learns that he "cannot claim dual membership privileges," Opus refuses to surrender his white license, because he needs it for "singing Celine Dion at the gym" (Breathed 2007).[3]

Whites are obviously fascinated with imagining the African American use of the word, which appears very commonly in film and television representations of African American speech (nearly always written by Whites). A famous and much-discussed example appeared in the 1998 film *Bulworth*, where the African American actress Halle Berry, playing White actor Warren Beatty's love interest, was given the line "You're my nigger"

**Figure 1** Opus negotiates the right to use a slur at the Department of Moral Licences. © 2007, Berkeley Breathed. The Washington Post Writers Group. Reprinted with permission.

to utter to him in an affectionate moment. A media debate raged for weeks about whether the line (and other representations of African American speech in the film's dialogue) was appropriate or authentic. Smitherman (1994:168) notes that the debate over the word also occurs among Blacks:

> [T]he frequent use of *nigga* in Rap Music, on "Def Comedy Jam," and throughout Black Culture generally, where the word takes on meanings other than the historical negative, has created a linguistic dilemma in the crossover world and in the African American community. Widespread controversy rages about the use of *nigga* among Blacks – especially the pervasive public use of the term – and about whether or not whites can have license to use the N-word with the many different meanings that Blacks give to it.

On July 9, 2007, at its annual meeting in Detroit, the National Association for the Advancement of Colored People held a symbolic funeral for "the N-word," with speakers arguing that if African Americans are going to insist that Whites stop using it, then they will have to hold themselves to the same standard. However, it does not seem likely that this ritual succeeded in laying the word to rest, given the venerable history of the debate.

## The Legal Status of Slurs

Linguistic ideologies that rationalize the repetition of slurs can be identified not only in the talk of ordinary people, but also in scholarly discussions of language in philosophy and linguistics, and in the discourses of government and law. In the United States public debates about slurs are shaped by the First Amendment to the United States Constitution:

> Congress shall make no law respecting an establishment of religion, or prohibiting the free exercise there of; or abridging the freedom of speech, or of the press; or the right of the people peaceably to assemble, and to petition the government for a redress of grievances.

Americans usually do not think of "freedom of speech" as "ideological." Instead, we understand this as an unassailable universal value. We imagine that the freedom to write and say anything that we want to say is fundamental to the advancement of human understanding. Thus the offensive publications of stereotypes that are a staple of the "Letters to the Editor" section of American newspapers often appear under an epigraph usually attributed to the French Enlightenment hero Voltaire: "I disagree with what you say, but I will defend to the death your right to say it." However, what is often called "First Amendment absolutism" is in many ways specific to American discourse about language. International law limits the freedom of racist speech. Article 20 of the International Convention on Elimination of all Forms of Racial Discrimination of 1966 states that "all . . . propaganda activities, which promote and incite racial discrimination" shall be declared illegal (Matsuda 1993:27). While the United States is technically a signatory to the convention, its endorsement is qualified by a statement of "reservation, understanding, or declaration" in reference to Article 20 that cites the First Amendment to the US Constitution. For this reason, to the distress of many citizens of other countries, in the United States White supremacist groups can legally post websites with repulsive racist messages that are accessible from anywhere in the world.

The doctrine of freedom of speech, beginning in the European Enlightenment in the eighteenth century, was advanced within the terms of referentialist linguistic ideology. Enlightenment thinkers held that freedom of expression was a crucial foundation of the search for truth. Freedom of expression permitted opinions to be made public, where they could be tested in debate. American courts have tended to support this ideology by admitting a very broad definition of "speech" that notoriously includes forms of expression like burning the American flag in protest and making large monetary contributions to political candidates.

The Critical Race theorists, a group of legal scholars, have explored whether or not the First Amendment protections on freedom of expression can be narrowed to permit the proscription of verbal slurs (e.g. Matsuda et al., eds. 1993).[4] Their reasoning draws on Speech Act theory, the theory of performativity in the philosophy of language developed by J. L. Austin (1962) and John Searle (1969). Austin and Searle show that utterances can be "acts" that produce material changes in the world, rather than mere descriptions of the world that can be evaluated as true or false. Invoking Speech Act theory, we can argue that slurs are the equivalent of a punch in the nose, not forms of expression that might expose some truth. Critical Race theorists argue that this understanding is shown to be correct by the evidence that the targets of racial slurs experience them as physical assaults, feeling genuine bodily pain. Indeed, they argue, slurs incite to literal assault and often accompany it. Thus, slurs should be legally proscribed, like assault, not protected like speech. The Critical Race theorists also argue against the idea that to proscribe racial slurs is the first step down a slippery slope that would end with the loss of freedom of speech. They point out that the courts have consistently judged certain forms of speech to be unprotected by the First Amendment. Examples include commercial speech uttered in a conspiracy to fix prices, obscenity, libelous speech, "fighting words," and other "dignatory affronts." Racial slurs have much in common with this class of expressions, and Lawrence (1993) argues that their pro-scription provides legal precedent for treating slurs as "libelous." Matsuda (1993) makes the additional constitutional argument that to protect racist speech violates the equal protection clause of the Fourteenth Amendment, because the "psychic tax" of racial slurs is borne only by people of color.

Critical Race theory, then, understands slurs within the formal theory of Speech Acts. This theory clearly draws on, and has much in common with, everyday vernacular performative ideology which holds that words can wound or soothe. The Critical Race theorists tap into this vernacular ideology by using expressions like "wounds" and "pain" along with a more technical language of "embodiment." In spite of this dual attention to formal theory in pragmatics and vernacular linguistic ideology, their work has not had much practical impact. In the US Supreme Court case *R.A.V. v. City of St. Paul* (1992), over an incident in which a White teenager burned a cross on the lawn of an African American family, Justice Scalia's majority opinion found cross-burning (historically associated with White supremacist terrorism during the Jim Crow era) to be a protected form of expression. His opinion also severely restricted the "fighting words" option for legal action against slurs and epithets. In a more recent cross-burning case, *Virginia v. Black* (2002), the majority opinion did rule that threat and intimidation were the dominant features of such conduct, over the expres-sive features, and thus it was not protected. However, Justice Scalia dis-sented, and it seems unlikely that this opinion would survive a test in today's Supreme Court, where Scalia votes consistently with the new majority.

The Critical Race theorists were deeply involved in legal battles over the so-called "campus speech codes" promulgated in the 1980s and 1990s, an era which produced an epidemic of what Matsuda (1996:105) called "gutter racism" on American campuses. However, again the Critical Race theorists and their allies have not been very successful. The campus speech codes proscribed slurs and other racist, homophobic, or misogynistic state-ments by members of college and university communities. But opponents of such codes have consistently prevailed in the courts.[5] Campus speech codes have fared poorly in popular opinion as well, victims of a right-wing campaign against "political correctness." Even major academic organizations such as the American Association of University Professors argued that slurs should be handled on campuses within the normal processes of education and the exchange of ideas, and not by the development of regulations. In August 2003 the Office of Civil Rights of the US Department of Educa-tion indicated in a letter to officials of all American universities that it did not support campus speech codes (Limbaugh 2003). On campuses, so-called "First Amendment absolutism" currently prevails.

In summary, the "eradicationist" (Kennedy 2002) position on slurs advanced by the Critical Race theorists has not fared well. Instead, some scholars have argued that slurs are best controlled by recapturing them from racists and endowing them with positive, identity-enhancing connotations. Thus Kennedy (2002:139) argued that "there is much to be gained by allowing people of all backgrounds to yank *nigger* away from white suprem-acists, to subvert its ugliest denotation, and to convert the N-word from a negative into a positive appellation." Butler (1997) has developed a techni-cal argument against eradicationism, drawing on Speech Act theory. The essential points of Butler's argument are these: First, slurs are unquestionably acts, but their power is not just assaultive. It is productive, constituting subjectivity itself. "Subjectivity" is a term in culture theory that refers to the cultural human being composed, classically, of two dimensions. The first is the person, the individual as a social being vis-à-vis other social beings. For instance, in J. L. Austin's (1962) famous example of a perfor-mative sentence, "I now pronounce you man and wife," the two people who become a married couple are changed as persons, because the utter-ance assigns them rights and obligations to one another that can only be dissolved by annulment, divorce, or death. By extension, any label can constitute the individual as a person. The second dimension of subjectivity is the self, the domain of interior experience, intention, belief, and emotion. Labels for these properties can also be shown to have constitutive functions. For instance, in American English in the twenty-first century we can speak of experiencing "stress," of being "stressed out." The *Oxford English Dic-tionary* dates the noun "stress" in this psychological sense from the 1950s, and the verb only from the 1970s. To speak of being "stressed" actually creates a certain kind of modern self, subject to very specific culturally produced tensions. Butler extends examples like this to the most general case: subjectivity is produced in the act of naming and being named, as with a slur. But, crucial to her argument, not naming, and not being named, is also performative and constitutive. Thus, once the label is avail-able, and can be "not uttered," there is no escaping it.

The second point in Butler's argument is that speech acts are "iterable":[6] they require predecessors and predict futures. So she argues that speaking subjects never act as sole controllers of words. Instead, they are linked by a historical chain of discourse to those from whom they hear and those to whom they speak. Butler argues that there is no logic by which such a chain can be broken, by which a speaker can be singled out and punished, or a word singled out and proscribed. Instead, she holds that punishments and proscriptions mainly accomplish "unintended proliferation" of what they censor (a point with which I agree). But hope, for Butler, lies in this very quality of slurs, that they are fundamentally repeatable. Slurs are available not only to racists, but to anti-racists. Butler admits that slurs carry an immense burden of history. But she argues that, since they cannot be proscribed, the best political strategy is to try to reshape them to new ends, to use them to create new kinds of subjectivity. She clearly has in mind cases like the use of "Black" in the Civil Rights movement, "Queer" by gays and lesbians, and "Nigga" by hip-hop activists, which function as badges of pride and solidarity. The dilemma, of course, is that this circulation makes them continually available for malign re-reappropriation as well. Mark Twain intended *Huckleberry Finn* to make the racist use of "nigger" absurd by using it to label the single most sympathetic character in the book, the Christ-like "Nigger Jim." But more than 100 years after the publication of his text, many readers still cannot hear his irony. The same fate may await current efforts to reappropriate the word, unless the foundations of White racism can somehow be shaken by some effort even more profound than Mark Twain's magnificent epic of our common humanity.

## Naming the Peak: Attacking and Defending a Racial Slur in Arizona

Now that we have reviewed debates about slurs among scholars, we are ready to undertake a case study of how referentiality, performativity, and other linguistic ideologies, linked with the folk theory of racism, play out in the discourse of ordinary people, who live among slurs, respond to them, label them, and link talk about slurs to talk about race and racism more broadly. In 2003 and early 2004, the citizens of Arizona debated whether the name of a mountain near the city of Phoenix, "Squaw Peak," was a slur. Those who believed that it was argued that the landmark should be renamed "Piestewa Peak" after Pfc. Lori Piestewa, a Hopi woman who died in combat in the American invasion of Iraq in March 2003. Before turning to the debate itself, I review the debates about the word "squaw," which, as in the case of "nigger," have a long history.

### Massachusett "skwa" and American English "squaw": The history of a slur

The word "squaw" is attested in English-language documents from 1624. It was borrowed from Massachusett, an American Indian language belonging to the great Algonquian family.[7] In that language the word *skwa* means "young woman." Cognates of the word appear throughout the Algonquian language family in similar meanings and are never pejorative or offensive (Bright 2000). There is no dispute among linguists who specialize in Native American languages over the Algonquian etymology of the word. The claim that the word comes from Mohawk *otískwa* "female genitalia" is wrong.[8]

When "squaw" was borrowed into English in the seventeenth century, so-called "scientific racism" was in its earliest stages. Most Europeans believed that American Indians, Africans, and the peoples of Asia were distinctive "natural kinds," almost different species, who were located below Whites on a Great Chain of Being that was established at the time of Creation. To express that belief, they invented technical language to talk about the males, females, and children of these lesser human kinds, comparable to terms like "bull, cow, calf" or "stallion, mare, colt" or "buck, doe, fawn" for the various species of animals. For Africans these were "buck, wench (among other terms), pickaninny," and for American Indians "buck, squaw, papoose." The unmarked English words "man, woman, child" were used for Whites. Thus "squaw" in English from the very outset presupposed the biological inferiority of American Indians.

"Squaw" early picked up unmistakably pejorative connotations. By the first years of the nineteenth century it was especially likely to be used of Indian women thought to be undistinguished or ugly. Bright (2000) cites "the crafty 'squaw' . . . the squalid and withered person of this hag" from James Fenimore Cooper's *The Last of the Mohicans* of 1826. These extreme pejorative meanings were available in part because in English (although not in Algonquian languages) the word has an unfortunate sound. The sound-symbolic sequence /skw/ (written as "squ") is associated in English with flatness of shape and/or an unpleasant sort of liquidity, as in words like "squint, squelch, squat, squish." The "rhyme" of the word, the "aw" sequence, evokes a kind of gap or hole, especially associated with the mouth, as in "maw, craw, yawn" (Rhodes and Lawler 1981). These English-language sound-symbolic associations are surely an important reason for the persistence of the erroneous belief that the word comes from an Indian source meaning "vagina."

The argument that "squaw" is a destructive slur dates back at least 150 years. McWilliams (1943:52) quotes John Beeson's "Plea for the Indians," published in 1859. Beeson writes of his fellow Oregon settlers:

[I]t was customary to speak of the Indian man as a buck; of the woman as a squaw; until, at length, in the general acceptance of the terms, they ceased to recognize the rights of humanity in those to whom they were so applied. By a very natural and easy transition, from being spoken of as brutes, they came to be thought of as game to be shot, or as vermin to be destroyed.

### Changing "Squaw Peak" to "Piestewa Peak"

The most recent campaign against the word "squaw," led by Native American activists, began in the late 1960s. Native American websites often do not write out the word, but use instead the expression "the S-word," parallel to "the N-word." The spelling "s★★★w" is also common. In testimony before the Arizona legislature in January 2004, the chairwoman of the Fort Mojave Reservation refused to say the word out loud because, she said, it is "offensive to us as Native American women" (*Indian Country Today*, 2004). The campaign has focused especially on place names, and by the 1990s several states had considered, and a few had passed, legislation to change all place names containing the word. In January 1993, Native American members of the Arizona legislature introduced a bill to change the name of "Squaw Peak," a small mountain in the Phoenix metropolitan area. They faced strong opposition from the White community. The *Arizona Republic*, the major daily newspaper for Phoenix, polled 339 respondents and found that 86 percent "said the word [squaw] did not have a negative meaning." Seventy-two percent of respondents "opposed any name change for Squaw Peak . . . or the freeway that carries the name." Only 10 percent felt the name "had a negative reference," and only 11 percent "favored change" of the name (Maricopa Residents 1993). In 1997 two young women from an American Indian Movement youth group formally proposed to the Arizona Board of Historic and Geographic Names that the peak be renamed "Iron Mountain," a translation of *Vainom Do'ag*, which their research had suggested was the Akimel O'odham (Pima) name of the mountain. However, ethnohistorians at Arizona State University determined that the Vainom Do'ag was a different mountain. No historic O'odham name for Squaw Peak could be found, and the Board voted in July 1998 not to accept the change (Bright 2000).

The final campaign to change the name "Squaw Peak" began in a tragedy. On March 23, 2003, Pfc. Lori Piestewa, a Hopi tribal member from Tuba City, Arizona, serving with the 507th Maintenance Company of the US Army's Vth Corps, was mortally injured in combat and died while a prisoner of the Iraqis. Pfc. Piestewa was the first American Indian woman in history to die in combat while serving with the United States military. She was only 23 years old, and she left two small children. News of her death touched Arizonans deeply. On April 3, 2003, an editorial in the *Arizona Republic* proposed that Squaw Peak be renamed Piestewa Peak in her memory. On April 12, 2003, Governor Janet Napolitano announced that she would officially petition the Arizona Board of Geographic and Historic Names to rename the peak "Piestewa Peak." The Board's chairperson refused to consider the petition, observing that the board's rules required a five-year waiting period after a death. Napolitano insisted that by law he had to consider her petition, and requested his resignation from the Board if he would not agree to receive it. The governor's "high-handed" and "bullying" tactics became a major issue in the controversy that followed.

The Board met to consider the name change on April 17, 2003, with its chairperson and the other "public member" (a member appointed by the governor from the general public instead of from among state officers and employees) both absent in protest. After consultation with its attorneys, the Board agreed that it could waive both the "five-year rule" and the rule that at least one public member had to be present for a vote. The members present voted 5–1 in favor of the new name, Piestewa Peak. The name of the Squaw Peak freeway was later changed by the Arizona Department of Transportation. The Phoenix Parks and Recreation Board met in early March 2004 to rename the Squaw Peak Recreational Area. In spite of heavy lobbying for "Piestewa Park," this Board selected "Phoenix Mountains Park and Recreation Area," with the chairman of the Board stating that "It's too significant a park to be named for anyone" (Anchors 2004). The Pointe Hilton Squaw Peak Resort continues to bear that name as of this writing (Hilton Hotels 2007), and many other businesses in Phoenix also retain it. None of the names was changed on national maps, since the Executive Secretary of the US Board of Geographic Names insisted that "There's never been an exception" to the five-year cooling-off period after a death (Baker 2003a).

Intense local resistance greeted the name change. As soon as the Arizona legislature convened in January 2004, Assemblyman Phil Hanson, Republican of Peoria, introduced a bill which would remove from the governor the power to name members of the Arizona Board of Historic and Geographic Names. Representative Hanson claimed that he was "just trying to reinstate the board's integrity" (Diaz 2004). Native American representatives countered by introducing a bill that would change all "squaw" place names in Arizona by 2007.

The *Arizona Republic* ran an on-line message board for public discussions on the name change during April, 2003 and January 2004.[9] During the periods of most heated debate (April 4, 2003–April 29, 2003 and January 10, 2004–March 3, 2004) I monitored the message board, but also regular reportage, unsigned editorials and signed opinion pieces, and letters to the editor in the newspaper. From the April message board I collected 278 messages, beginning on April 9, when the "online editor" posted the question: "Should we rename Squaw Peak in honor of fallen soldier Lori Piestewa?" The last message was posted April 18, 2003. From the January 2004 message board I collected 123 messages responding to the online editor's query, "Should Squaw Peak Park be renamed in honor of fallen soldier Lori Piestewa? Should the name 'Piestewa' go away entirely?"

posted on January 9. After January 24, 2004 the on-line edition no longer showed any message board entries.

While signed letters to the editor of the *Arizona Republic* were heavily in favor of the name change (56 letters in favor, 36 against by April 12, 2003), on the message board, with its anonymous postings, the opposition led by a ratio of almost three to one, with 154 against and 54 in favor in April, and 64 against, 28 in favor in January. Anonymity on the message board not only encouraged citizens opposed to the name change (and therefore vulnerable to charges of racism) to freely express their views, it also left them free to use explicitly offensive language. While an automatic on-line editorial program substituted "(expletive)" for words barred by editorial policy, contributors could easily defeat the online editor by not spelling out epithets completely.[10] In signed letters to the editor, reportage, and opinion pieces that appeared in the newspaper, authors writing under their real names all used careful and moderate language.

The messages on the board contain many deviations from school-book American English in spelling, grammar, and punctuation, but these contributors cannot be dismissed as marginal or uneducated people. Most of them are probably posting from their home computers, since workplace computers are usually carefully monitored by employers and can be used only for work-related projects. The 2000 US Census reported that about one-third of adults in the US used e-mail from home (a number that had probably increased by April 2003 and January 2004 when the message boards were active), so these contributors belong to that minority (9-in-10 School-Age Children . . . 2001). Many contributors were clearly very familiar with the issues involved, including legal technicalities such as the five-year delay rule.

## Is "squaw" a slur? The *Arizona Republic* debate and the folk theory of racism

While "squaw" was labeled as a slur by the 1850s, many Whites still, astonishingly, consider it to be a technically correct expression.[11] It appears not only in place names, but in many other contexts such as Internet advertising for "squaw and papoose" dolls and in expressions like "squaw dance" (a dance where women choose their partners) and "squaw dress" (a dress for women in a supposedly southwestern style, with a full ruffled skirt). And of course almost every non-Indian in Arizona had for many years uttered without a second thought the name of "Squaw Peak" and the roads, parks, and businesses in the Phoenix area that bore the name. If the word is a slur, this entails that its users are racists. In the folk theory of racism, to call a person a racist is a dire insult, since racists are uneducated, marginal, and backward individuals. Thus the stakes in the debate were very high. To call "squaw" a slur attacked not only White virtue in general, but the good opinion most participants in the debate had about themselves. Since many contributors to the message board had obviously used the word all their lives, they sharply rejected both the label and the entailment.

Contributors to the message board who identified themselves as Native Americans, like those seen in (1), all made clear that they believed that the word is a slur, and the people who use it are "ignorant and low-life."

(1)    a. "I grew up on the Navajo reservation for 18 years until it was time for me to leave for college. I grew up in a very traditional home. I was never allowed to say the word 'squaw' in our house just like many of the other four letter words that are around today. I was told that the word was another way of calling a Native American woman a B★★★★. And to see that word plastered all over Arizona signs? Its upsetting and at the same time hilarious because it makes the Arizona State Board of Geographic and Historic Names look like idiots. Aren't they supposed to research this kind of stuff before they go naming things? So how can anyone say that this is not offensive?" (April 12 2003 5:24 PM)

b. "My familly comes from the Chicarilla, Picuris and Navajo Nations. The word 'squaw' to me means a female B. only ignorant or low life people speak in derogatory terms." (January 12 2004 1:14 PM)

This universally held Native American perspective was, at best, ignored, and at worst attacked. Only 25 of 401 postings joined Indians to argue that the word "squaw" is offensive. These supportive postings, however, showed clearly that their authors wrote from within the folk theory of racism, assigning those who wanted to use the word to the folk-theory category of the backward and ignorant racist. They also make clear the role of performative ideology in making slurs visible. In (2) we see appeals to the "words that wound" ideology, as interlocutors are invited to put themselves in the shoes of Indians and think about how they would feel if slurs on their own ethnic group appeared in place names.

(2)    a. "Some say that s@#!aw does not mean anything, but to some it is as racist a word as whop, kike, (expletive), cracker etc. . . . I use these words to try and make you think!!!! If you were Italian would you want a place in your state officially named whop ridge? Or if you were Jew would you want the gov. to officially name a hill Kike peak? I do not think so. So why name a hill something that we find a racial slur????" (January 24 2004 4:58 PM)

b. "If a term is demeaning to a group it should not be used, end of story! I'd like to see how far we'd get trying to refer to a landmark as Gook,

Jap, Kike, (expletive), Taco, Lesbo, (expetive), etc. If someone tells you a term offends them, who are you to say they're wrong ???" (January 10 2004 11:08 PM)

A number of contributors supported their arguments that "squaw" is a slur by offering versions of the false etymology of the word as a reference to female genitalia in the original Indian language, as shown in (3):

(3)    a. "Hey Idiots ... don't you know that squaw means ((w_hore)) in Indian??????? It's offensive and should be changed." (April 12 2003 8:21 AM)
b. "Most people who live in AZ know that the word 'squaw' is a very derogatory term, similar to a 'white' term for a woman that most decent people wouldn't use. The continued use of this word shows that AZ is still rooted in its ignorant, wild west past." (January 10 2004 3:25 PM)
c. "Squaw means c_nt ... meant that 50 years ago and it hasn't changed ..." (January 10 2004 5:03 PM)

The contributions in (2) and (3) show how these debates put slurs into circulation. During these debates, very vulgar language is used by both sides to score points in argument. This repetition simultaneously makes the words available for those who find them meaningful and pleasurable.

## Slurs and racists

The real danger sensed by debaters on the message board, that to use a slur is to be a racist, is facilitated by the linguistic ideology of "personalism," which holds that the meanings of utterances are determined by the intentions of speakers. In personalism, speakers believe something, and intend to communicate about it. In order to do so, they choose words that match their beliefs and that will therefore best fulfill their intentions. Personalism is usually linked to a dimension of referentialist ideology that holds that the meanings of words are stable, determined in a baptismal moment by an authoritative source (this point will be discussed further below). That is, under this baptismal ideology of word meaning, speakers do not reshape the meanings of words, they choose them in order to correctly represent the world. Thus a word reveals the speaker's state of beliefs about the world, and also reveals the speaker's communicative intentions to assert some truth.

Linguistic anthropologists reject a simplistic personalist account of meaning in favor of one that understands meaning as the complex product of long chains of historical negotiation, where each exchange of utterances is a moment of renewed intersubjective creation of meaning (Agha 2007).

But personalist linguistic ideology is part of the common sense of most Whites, and it has important consequences for the debate we are analyzing. Within personalist ideology, if the word "squaw" can be shown to be a slur that has ugly and pejorative meanings, then a person who uses it must be a racist who believes that the targets of the slur are ugly and deserving of the label and intends to communicate this fact. The examples of postings in (4, 5) show that this is what participants in the message-board discussions believed. They also show that participants subscribed firmly to the folk-theory definition of "racists" as marginal and backward people.

Message board contributors who opposed the name change often opened their postings (as in (4)) with well-documented hedging language like "With no disrespect" or "I am not a racist, but" (van Dijk 1993), signaling that they knew that their views would be understood as controversial.

(4)  "I am sure that I will be labeled a racist because I do not agree about renaming Squaw Peak." (April 11 2003 2:01 PM)

Opponents of the name change were indeed labeled as racists. For instance, a posting by "Albert" in (5a), using what this contributor surely thought was an all-American language of democratic majority rule, drew the response in (5b).

(5)  a. "The heavy-handed tactics used by the governor to change the name of a landmark is inexcusable. This is not a way to honor a fallen soldier. And I can't believe that just because a few people were offended by the name 'squaw,' the government felt like it had to spend our time and money to change the name. ('Squaw' comes from the Algonquin language, and means simply 'woman,' so being offended by it is stupid). It's amazing that when only a few people are offended by something in this country, huge changes are made to please them. I thought that the majority ruled and that we voted for people in office because they'll represent us and do what the majority thinks is right! I guarantee that the majority of the people who voted wouldn't have changed the name. Even if the name is official, I and I'm sure many others will always call it 'Squaw Peak'." (January 10 2004 1:56 AM)

b. "Spoken like a true white supremacist there, Albert! Is there a KKK after your name, or is it 'Grand Klukker,' or 'Grand Draggin,' or whatever you call your leaders these days?/Let's break out the Georgie flags with tha Stars 'n Bars on 'em an' go git some Blue Ribbon or Schitz, an' thin we kin bild sum krosses 'n burn 'em in sum yards 'a' them we hate!/The name might have originally been Algonquin, but it has become a racial slur – and you know it as well as we do./Take note of my name and e-mail address so you can have your gutless sheet-wearin' budz from Happy Holler, Alabama, burn a cross on my lawn./Kuk Klux Kluk!" (January 10 2004 7:56 AM)

This attack illustrates the folk-theory stereotype of a racist. "Albert" is accused of being a "Ku Kluxer." Even though there are no southernisms in his posting, his opponent imagines Albert as hailing from "Georgie" (Georgia, in a stigmatizing eye-dialect) or "Happy Holler, Alabama." That is, while "Albert" is a reasonably literate inhabitant of Phoenix, Arizona, who is posting on the Internet, to call him "racist" requires that he be marginalized as a southern redneck. This displacement precludes any constructive analysis either of the specific local context or of White racism more broadly.

Just in case the reader has concluded that Albert's moderate language in (5a) was the strongest assertion of a potentially racist position on the message board, it must be pointed out that examples of extremely offensive language did appear there, as in (6), a posting by "PhxResident."

(6)    "If Indians feel that they need politicians to kiss their ass, then they should find another country to live in. Renaming Squaw Peak 'Piestewa Peak' is a slap at all the non-Indian men and women who served./And the Indians should take the Hispanics with them. They should all go to Mexico and stay there." (April 16 2003 9:33 PM)

Two from at least half a dozen angry replies to (6) are seen in (7), both from Native Americans.

(7)    a. "I being a Native AMERICAN was very offend by your comment. The Native AMERICANS do not need to have politicians kiss our asses!! And why would we need to find somewhere else to live? We were here first!! Obviously you are not very smart or you would know that. So go back to school and read your history book." (April 17 2003 11:19 AM)
    b. "PhxResident, I'll mention to you what I said about another entity on the board, Rokk./Some of the comments that have been made could very easily fall under the Federal Hate Crimes Act. If the Sysop's [System Operators, responsible for editing contributions] can't police the manner in which people express themselves, perhaps someone else should./I will volunteer to make the call and can be in Arizona before lunch." (April 17 2003 9:34 AM)

While PhxResident's contributions infuriated Native Americans, White contributors defended him or made excuses for him. The debaters in (8) tried to soothe tempers, using a "First Amendment" argument; (8a) even uses a version of the famous "Voltaire" quotation.

(8)    a. "A suggestion to all, ignore PhxRes, it'll only get worse./Joseph Red-Cloud [the author of (7b)], as all of this falls under the catagory of free speech doubt the feds will bother, unless it blatantly breaks BBS rules the

sysop won't either./I may not like what some have to say, but I'll die for their right to say it." (April 17 2003 9:39 AM)

b. "Mr. RedCloud [the contributor of (7b)], I'm afraid you'll find vitriol and invective an ocassional commenplace in this venue./While most posters typically conduct themselves within the decorum expected of conversations in public discourse, there are some who use the anonymnity of the medium to exercise a license they would would not were attribution possible./I think we can all agree this speech is in poor taste, insulting to the reader and generally abhorent. The greatest insult it does is to perceptions of the character of those authors themselves./But exept for those abuses that either interfere with the function of the venue (such as uncontrolled SPAMing or Conterfeiting handles), I think it much better to allow them their say, however distasteful." (April 17 2003 10:05 AM)

Other contributors, like those in (9), suggested the Indians who posted the contributions in (7) were overly sensitive, because PhxResident was "misguided" or a "troublemaker." This illustrates a corollary of the folk theory of racism: since racists are few and marginal, no one should be "thin-skinned" about what they say.

(9)   a. "Actually . . ./There is a dearth of 'racist' comments toward Indians on this thread or any other. Those few posters who wish to focus on the one troublemaker – knock yerselves out./By the way, he does that to everyone so get a thicker skin or don't pay any attention – your choice./'Ow 'bout 'PCP'??/Politically Correct Peak." (April 17 2003 12:59 PM)

b. "Look folks, this is not about racism. It really bothers me that anytime someone disagrees with a suggestion from a minority group, they are labeled a racist. I am not including the obvious racially driven remarks from a few misguided people that have already posted." (April 17 2003 2:04 PM)

Charges of "racism" were made as well by opponents of the name change against supporters, as in (10), illustrating the folk-theory idea that the prejudices of people of color are morally equivalent to those of Whites. As pointed out in Chapter 1, within the folk theory racism consists simply of having a negative belief about another group, and does not take into account differences in power and the ability to have one's bad opinion make a difference.

(10)   a. "I don't know what 'squaw' means, but I don't think it's any of those things the overly sensitive and racist Indians say it is." (April 12 2003 12:10 PM)

b. "Hey B.J., you're an overly sensitive white-hating racist. Go back to your tribe and stay there. People like you are a threat to a civilized society's well-being. I am sick and tired of the politically correct nonsense of appeasing minority groups." (April 12 2003 12:27 PM)

While the charge of racism was repeatedly made on the message board, many participants considered it to be an unfair argumentative gambit. Especially, it was said to be "divisive." This is illustrated in some of the longest threads of exchange on the message board. Two of the most important proponents of the name change were "RedCloud" and "Betty Ann." Both stayed active on the board over hours and days and conducted extensive give-and-take with opponents.

Joseph RedCloud, Agency and Political Liaison Officer for the Presidents' Office of the Oglala Sioux Tribe of the Pine Ridge Indian Reservation in South Dakota (the author of (7b) above), posted a long message in support of the name change at 11:40 AM on Monday, April 14, 2003. There is no reason to doubt that Mr. RedCloud is who he says he is. His postings were in formal and elevated language; the selection in (11) is typical:

(11)    "To my White Brothers and Sisters, some of you have managed to learn and expand your horizons and yet there are great numbers who seem to be concerned only for themselves and the present. There is much more to life than collecting money, imposing your beliefs upon others, punishing those who worship differently than you and living just for the moment. Why can't you understand that some people are not 'honored' by your efforts to absorb our names and symbols in your quest for the almighty dollar? Why can't you do something that is 'just' and 'correct' simply because it's the right thing to do? You are surrounded by Indians. If you don't understand how a word or phrase affects us, why don't you simply ask us? Haven't we done as much for you? [. . .] You have all been blessed with an opportunity to right an old wrong. The situation before you is that and nothing more. You can remove a shameful name from a public place and rename it with a name that holds honor. This issue is not about male or female. It is not about veteran or civilian. It is not about Indian or White. It is not about dollars or votes. It's simply about right or wrong. Do the right thing. Don't listen to the polls. Don't listen to your wallet. Instead, listen to your heart." (April 14 2003 11:40 AM)

RedCloud's posting elicited sharp replies from opponents who attacked him not only as "oversensitive," "divisive," and "playing the race card," but also as "arrogant."

(12)    a. "Your remarks are disturbing and only creates a wider division between Native Americans and non-Indians." (April 14 2003 12:56 PM)
        b. "Isn't it a little arrogant of you to be calling this Indian Country? Aren't you and your people complaining that we don't recognize you as Native Americans?/Isn't it also arrogant that you want to put down

people that came here from elsewhere, when it was your ancestors that came from Asia across the Bering Sea? People didn't just pop up in the Dakotas. Isn't anyone born here a Native American?" (April 14 2003 7:38 PM)

Another long series of exchanges was precipitated by a posting to the message board from "Betty Ann Gross." Betty Ann writes as a person of color, labeling her opponents as "you white folks . . . you white Americans." Like RedCloud, she hung in and debated her opponents over many exchanges. Her first posting appears in (13):[12]

(13)   "Jessica Lynch (white) can make millions of dollars of her ordeal and become white American's hero./Shosona Johnson (mixed cultures) received very little media attention and has become a faceless US soldier./ Lori Piestewa (American Indian) died, she left behind two small children and a family./And yet America still complains and carries that white supremacy arrogance and superiority when a state want to honor a fallen US Soldier . . . get it a fallen US Soldier by renaming geographical site in her memory./America fell all over the white girl Jessica Lynch and America discriminated agains Shosona. You want America to stand up for what she says she does, One Nation Under God, United We Stand, Justice and Equality for all her children . . . and yet, you posters have not shown that you are ready to reach out your hands to other nations other than white./I believe that if you white folks want that damn peak so bad to remain Squaw Peak then go change it bak and let Lori rest in peace. After all for all you white Americans for you I say, Your deep ignorance is bliss, for you move within the confinements of racism, prejudice and hatred for a fallen US Soldier." (January 10 2004 2:55 PM)

Within minutes replies appeared:

(14)   a. "People trying to play the race card with this whole ordeal are hilariously out of their minds. This has absolutely nothing to do with race. This has to do with the naming of a geographical area and people having two points of view as to what it should be./Betty Ann Gross − Your post was undoubtedly the most ignorant thing said yet in regards to the Peak. Your anti-white attitude makes you exactly what you hate. A racist. Get a dose of reality and occupy your mind with something useful instead of hate-mongering. 'You white people.' How would you react if I said 'you black people' or you this or that. You'd say I was a racist./I saw we name it BetttyAnn Gross Peak so we can make this maniac happy." (January 10 2004 3:32 PM)

One obvious symptom of the delicacy of the issue of whether "squaw" was a slur is the striking difference, pointed out above, in the distribution of opinion between signed letters to the editor, which heavily favored the name change, and postings on the largely anonymous message board, where the name change was overwhelmingly opposed. This suggests that opponents of the name change feared being accused of racism, and thus preferred the anonymous forum. But even the journalists and editorialists for the *Arizona Republic* who favored the name change avoided labeling the word "squaw" as a slur. They preferred expressions like "some Native Americans find it offensive," "some activists find it offensive," or "many find it offensive." This kind of hedging occurred even in most signed letters to the editor, as in (15a). These formulas unfortunately encouraged the widespread opinion that "squaw" was not offensive to most people and that the name change was an example of political pandering to a minority. In (15) the hedges are italicized.

(15)  a. ". . . something that *may be perceived* to be a cultural slap in the face *to many Native Americans*" (Sands 2003).
b. "[The state] can end the long-running concern *by some Native American activists* that the word 'squaw' is demeaning and insulting to the first Americans" (Piestewa Peak!. . . 2003 [unsigned editorial]).

The word "squaw" was explicitly condemned in the main newspaper only in quoted speech, a strategy that appeared not only in reportage (as in (16a, b)), but even in editorials (as in (16c)), where the expression of unhedged opinion is customary. The *Arizona Republic* journalists were apparently very concerned to be seen as "balanced".

(16)  a. "A derogatory term" [quoting Rep. Sylvia Laughter, I-Kayenta] (Baker 2003a).
b. "A derogatory word for Native Americans" [quoting Wayne Taylor, Hopi Tribe Chairman] (Baker 2003b).
c. "The governor's counsel cited a half-dozen dictionaries. 'Squaw' is considered 'an insult,' 'offensive,' and 'derogatory' in dictionaries published by Webster's, Random House, Cambridge, and American Heritage, he said. Observed Maricopa County Supervisor Mary Rose Wilcox: 'We don't use "squaw" in our deliberations at the County Board of Supervisors. We don't hear "squaw" on the floor of the Senate or House. We don't use the word "squaw" in our churches, and we certainly don't use "squaw" to teach our children in school'" (Piestewa Peak: Our Stand: Board rights a wrong . . . 2003 [unsigned editorial]).

Only a few op-ed pieces and letters to the editor in the on-line edition of the *Arizona Republic* used a full authorial voice, rather than a quoted voice, to condemn the word as a slur. The *Republic*'s columnist E. J.

Montini, writing in (17), was very active in supporting the renaming of the peak for Pfc. Piestewa, and had devoted an entire essay to this point under the title "Who would call warrior 'squaw'?" as early as the April 8, 2003, edition of the newspaper.

(17)  "[Squaw is an insult, because] if it were not, we would use it in conversation. If it were not, someone by now would have used it in reference to Piestewa or to other Native American women. That will never happen" (Montini 2003).

On both the message board and in the newspaper itself, debate in the *Arizona Republic* was carried out entirely within the terms of the folk theory of racism. Both sides understood racism as a matter of individual prejudice, not as an immensely productive form of power that is distributed across a wide range of institutions and practices. In these terms, Indian opposition to White opinion could be called "racist" as easily as White opposition to Indian opinion. The folk theory provided no way for those accused of this kind of "reverse racism" to answer this charge. Both sides thought of "racists" as backward and ignorant, as Ku Kluxers, rural southerners from "Happy Hollow, Alabama," or as overly sensitive Indian hatemongers. Ironically, postings that used the kind of very offensive scatological and obscene language that might justify such an accusation were dismissed as the views of an "ignorant minority," untypical of communications on the board and therefore not worthy of attention, or even defended as exercising the right to free speech. This understanding that "racism" is something undertaken only by marginal people contradicted the evidence of the message board itself, that White racism in a raw form was alive and well in 2004 among residents of Phoenix, Arizona, with on-line access to their daily newspaper.

Only one of over 100 contributors to the message board ever wrote from the perspective of a critical theory of racism. A number of his messages were at least partly in an Algonquian language that he eventually identified as Anishnaabe (Ojibwa). Participating in both the April and January message boards (although he changed his handle, appearing in April as Assinamaagun A. [Adj_ibik] and in January as Mister Ibik [Nimah_win-nomin]), he played a sort of trickster role, posting an obscene limerick, short notes attacking irresponsible Indian leaders and do-gooder White liberals, and support for RedCloud in untranslated Anishnaabe. He observed (correctly) that this was largely a White person's debate, since it was not Indian custom to name landmarks after themselves. His contributions in (18) on the proper understanding of racism went unanswered; other participants on the message board did not seem to know exactly what to do with him.

(18)   a. "Racism isn't just an anomoly in this society, it's fundamental." (April 17 2003 2:52 PM) [Replying to a poster who asked why the peak hadn't been renamed years ago if "Squaw" was offensive]
b. "And still largely oppressed . . . it's built into the fabric of the US baby" (April 17 2003 9:35 PM) [Replying to a poster who referred to Native Americans as a "once oppressed people"]


### Defending "squaw," defending White virtue

Given the terms of the debate illustrated in the previous section, it is not surprising that the overwhelming majority of postings on the message boards defended the word squaw as "not a slur," and therefore those who wished to use it as "not racist." Statements in defense of the word depended on a very short list of rhetorical elements, often chained together in single contributions. These are listed in (19):

(19)   a. The word is not offensive in its original language so it is not offensive
b. The name is historical and traditional and should not be changed
c. The writer insists on his or her right to use it.
d. The name is not offensive except to people whose judgement has been ruined by political correctness and bias, to "a few activist Indians," or to politicians who are "pandering to Indians"
e. Alleged Indian friends and acquaintances of the writer were said to find "squaw" unobjectionable.

Another way of defending the right to use "squaw" was to argue that "Piestewa Peak" was not a good name. Again, the argumentative themes were very restricted. They are listed in (20):

(20)   a. The name change singles out one person and one ethnic group over others who had also sacrificed (this "colorblind" theme often included a charge of "reverse racism")
b. The name "Piestewa" is difficult and unpronounceable
c. Pfc. Piestewa was "not a heroine" and does not deserve to be honored; she died because she "made a wrong turn" and not in some glorious moment of combat.[13]

The rhetorical gambits listed in (19) and (20) are all grounded in widely shared linguistic ideologies. Let's look first at the kinds of ideas people must share in order to believe in (19a) "The word is not offensive in its original language so it is not offensive" and (19b) "The name is historical and traditional and should not be changed." These claims reflect the "baptismal ideology" of word meaning, a position that is in conflict with the views of linguists, who recognize that words constantly change their meanings. The match between sound and meaning that constitutes a word as a linguistic sign is, in technical terms, "arbitrary," the result of human choice, not universal law. The range of meanings of a word is a social fact peculiar to a particular speech community at a particular historical moment. Thus for linguists the meaning of *skwa* in the Massachusett language nearly 400 years ago has no bearing on the question of whether "squaw" is a slur today in English. The message-board debates showed that very few members of the public share this view. Indeed, the commitment of Native Americans to the baptismal ideology of meaning leads to serious misunderstandings between activists working to eradicate "squaw" and linguists who support their cause. As is evident from the examples in (3) above, the idea that "squaw" was somehow originally a sexual insult was an important resource for people who wanted to label it as a slur. This erroneous view is widely shared by Native Americans. Ives Goddard of the Smithsonian Institution, perhaps the foremost living authority on Algonquian languages, has tried to correct the false etymology associating "squaw" with the Mohawk word for female genitals (Goddard 1997). Many Indians took this to mean that Goddard believed that "squaw" was not a slur in English today, and was trying to undercut their campaign. More than one contributor on the message board referred to a rumor that "linguists" or "a linguist" had said that the word was not a slur (as in (23b) below). This misunderstanding, along with a great deal of other evidence from the message board, showed that most participants neither shared nor understood linguistic understandings about the mutability of meaning.

The baptismal ideology of meaning is loosely connected to scholarship in the philosophy of language. I have adapted this term from Kripke (1972), who argued that the meanings of words can be traced historically to "baptismal events" that exhibit social-institutional legitimacy (see also Putnam 1975). However, Kripke's theory does not preclude changes in meaning. Nor does it include a crucial idea in vernacular ideology, that change is always a falling away from truth. This "degenerative" component of baptismal ideologies dates back to the idea that the true names of things, given by Adam following God's directions, were lost at the fall of the Tower of Babel. Baptismal ideology does not admit inference from everyday usage as a method of determining the changing meanings of words, but understands change only as evidence for degeneration and corruption.

Baptismal ideology is evident in the postings in (21):

(21)   a.   "And Squaw is not what they say it means, it really does mean Young Woman. Janet [the governor], you are just plain wrong this time!!!" (April 18 2003 10:01 AM)

b. "What was wrong with 'Squaw Peak' anyway? A squaw means 'a little girl' in an overwhelming majority of Native American Languages. When did a little girl become so repulsive?" (April 18 2003 5:52 AM)

A corollary of baptismal ideology held that the word "squaw" was probably very old, correct simply because it was historically established (in fact the name "Squaw Peak" dated from 1910). This idea is seen in (22):

(22)    "Geographic names like Squaw Peak have a history that date back hundreds of years. Changing those name for political correctness or political gain is wrong. Very wrong!" (April 18 2003 5:59 AM)

A very important theme in the message-board debates was a language of "rights," which I have characterized in (19c) above as "The writer insists on his or her right to use it." These assertions made very clear that White privilege, the right to decide what words will mean and to control those meanings, was at stake. This is consistent with an important goal of White racist culture pointed out in Chapter 1, to control both material and symbolic resources, to recruit these for White privilege, and to deny them to people of color. Sometimes the idea that Whites, and not Indians, had the right to decide what words mean was made explicit, as in the postings in (23):

(23)    a. "I wish the Native Americans would stop being so sensitive over the word 'squaw' and stop distorting what 'squaw' means. I don't know what 'squaw' means, but I don't think it's any of those things the overly sensitive and racist Indians say it is." (April 12 2003 12:10 PM)
b. "The peak should revert to the historic name of Squaw Peak. Most Linguists agree that the word 'squaw' is not offensive. The controversy over this word was invented in the 1960's by Indian activists. The Anglos don't feel the word is derogatory, why do Indians accuse us of insulting them by its use?" (January 10 2004 11:31 AM)

Some contributors who claimed their "rights" to call the peak "Squaw Peak" did so with the full-throated libertarian excess in which many White Arizonans take considerable pride:

(24)    a. "Long live SQUAW PEAK.
Long live SQUAW PEAK PARK.
Long live SQUAW PEAK PARKWAY
Long live SQUAW PEAK FREEWAY" (April 17 2003 11:41 PM)
b. "They can name it Tutti Frutti Peak for all I care. I am still going to call it Squaw Peak. Squaw Peak [repeated 36 more times]. f|_|ckin' bite me." (April 18 2003 3:01 AM)

Invocations of the "rights" theme often recruited the language of democracy. We have already seen the invocation of the freedom of speech (as in (8)). This "democratic" rhetoric included the idea of "majority rule," with the implication that a minority, "activist Indians," have no right to tell the majority – Whites, of course – what to do. This discourse showed up in "Albert's" posting in (5a), and is illustrated again in (25):

(25)    "This is so infuriating. When did the word squaw change meaning in the english language. Oh, thats right it hasn't. No, it supposedly sounds like an 'offensive term' in a Native American dialect spoken by a small tribe who lives some thousand miles plus from this state. The fact is (oops, better watch it with that concept, p.c.er's find it more offensive than the word squaw) that the word squaw never carried a negitive connotation to 99.999% of us UNTIL activists in the Native American community started this campaign. The irony of this is lost on such people. By the way, What if Piestewa means some vile, evil word in a language spoken by the 6 members of a tribe of people in the deepest darkest forests of Borneo? Can we risk offending them? They might sue!!!" (April 18 2003 8:08 AM)

We also see the language of "democracy" and "the rule of law" in the postings in (26). The "law" being referred to here is not an article of the Arizona constitution or an act of the legislature, but the 1981 bylaws of the Arizona Board of Geographic and Historic Names, which its attorneys agreed could be waived to consider the proposal for "Piestewa Peak." (26c) is a response to an attack on opponents of the name change that called them "Ku Kluxers."

(26)    a. "If we got to vote, it would still be Squaw peak" (April 18 2003 8:32 AM)
        b. "Squaw Peak will always be Squaw Peak and no so called unlawful ruling will change that." (April 18 2003 9:53 AM)
        c. "I see. So anyone who wishes to follow the law of this state is now a member of the KKK./Anyone who wishes to see justice for two criminal acts comitted by an elected official is a racist./Wow, I had no idea that the eight hundred thousand plus of us that have been born here are all white supremists! Pretty amazing, considering more than half of us born here are not white. I am so glad you associate fascism with respect for ethnic diversity and democracy with totalarianism and white supremacy./I need say no more." (April 18 2003 6:09 AM)

Exemplary participation as a citizen was also cited as source of rights:

(27)    "I am a veteran and also live in the Squaw peak area. I Live here because I liked the name, and will always call it Squaw Peak, with no disrespect.

The people who feel offended will always find something to complain about, so we would be better off if they moved out, than they would not have to deal with their imaginary problems, and allow me to enjoy my life." (January 10 2004 8:00 AM)

Some contributors seemed to feel that their right to use the word derived from the intensity of their family connections with the peak, their emotional commitment to the name, and the psychic pain they would feel if it was changed:

(28)   "But to change the name of significant landmarks smacks our psyches with unnecessary change. If Sky Harbor, South Mountain, Thunderbird Mountain, the Salt River, or countless other entities were changed, almost everyone would continue to refer to them as the previous name." (January 10 2004 1:56 AM)

The next set of themes, in (19d), shows up in a discourse that finds that any ideas that are "biased" or "political" are illegitimate. "Biased" people include "a few activist Indians" or politicians who are "pandering to Indians" just to get re-elected. The idea that participants in public debate should be "unbiased" dates to the dawn of modern forms of civil society in Europe in the seventeenth and eighteenth centuries. Warner (1990) has shown how contributors to political debates in the early years of the American republic insisted that they spoke "from nowhere," with no position of bias or interest. Contributions to the message board share this idea: as soon as an opinion can be identified as "political" or "biased" it is immediately dismissed. On only one occasion, however, in (29), was an accusation of bias leveled at a contributor who had posted a list of very negative stereotypes of Indians.

(29)   "You said you are not Native American yourself, so who are you really to claim that 'you' give and give and give, while 'we' take and take and take? And how is anybody supposed to take your post seriously when you obviously hold some ill will against Native Americans? One can't obviously judge this situation fairly with bias like the one you demonstrate." (April 12 2003 11:43 PM)

The more common opinion was that Indians were biased just because they were "Indians," and thus unqualified to speak for themselves. A good example of this type is seen in (30):

(30)   "Our lame brain governor . . . and all the idiotic politicians in both political parties are just trying to appease the Indians & the overly sensitive P.C. crowd who take offense to the word 'squaw.' They just want a quick resolution to the age old controversy over this 'squaw' term. We

have more important issues to be concerned about, instead of worrying about how offended a few dorks are over an old Indian term. Lighten up & get over it!" (April 17 2003 11:22 PM)

The posting in (31) attacks Joseph RedCloud, arguing that his "political agenda" disqualifies him as a contributor to debate:

(31)  "Is the post of tribal political liaison officer the same as that of a Propaganda Minister? It's attitudes like yours Mr. Redcloud, that cause divisions in this country. Then again you are willing to use the name of a dead soldier to promote your political agenda. How sad and unfortunate for the Piestewa family." (April 15 2003 12:12 AM)

Governor Janet Napolitano's role in the debate was repeatedly attacked as merely "political," as in the example in (32):

(32)  Janet KneeJerk Napolitano. Big Squaw kneeJERK say we change name now./A mountian for some one who got lost. what next?/Looks like we have a new Fife or Even [references to disgraced former Arizona governors Fife Symington and Evan Mecham, both Republicans] in the Gov. office. It's just time before Big Squaw KneeJerk screws up Arizona just like the rest. All he is doing is looking for the indain votes. I wish I could change laws just like BIG Squaw KneeJERK./But the Dumb O Craps can not see it. If He was a Replican doing the same thing you all would be running around spouting your normal Dumb O Crap dribble." (April 17 2003 7:04 PM)

Several contributors who objected to the name change as an absurd example of political correctness used parody, as in the grossly offensive posting in (33a) (which drew only the reply in (33b)):

(33)  a. "Why not name a rock in the Navajo Nation a.k.a. Tuba City or the Hopi Nation. That is were she is from not here. Why not Goldwater Peak after some one who did something for this state./I don't see how getting lost (took a wrong turn P.C.) makes you a hero. Fact is she was lost and it cost them. Sad yes. People get lost in Arizona all the time and die but are not heros./But we are now all a bunch of P.C. people here in the US so if you do something dumb and die you are now a hero./Next we need a road named after the first Afrian American woman killed in the war. Black Canyon Hwy bothers me (What you find in the Bottom of an African American womans swim suit) lets change that. Now the first Irish American Woman is killed needs a place too. The White Tanks need to go. (It is what you find in the top half of an Irish American womans swim suit)/What is next Tonto Forest, Grand Canyon etc.etc." (April 12 2003 7:35 AM)

b. "ROFL [rolling on floor laughing] . . . omy goodness . . . all i can say is . . . YOU GO TIGER koodoz to AzBaja . . . that was gr8!!!!" (April 12 2003 7:53 AM)

While the claims of "activist Indians" were stridently rejected, many contributors invoked the theme in (19e), submitting anecdotes about alleged Indian friends and acquaintances who had no problem with the name "Squaw Peak" or the word "squaw." Every Arizona tribe through its official spokesperson and all Indian public officials in the state supported the name change. This unanimous official opinion, however, was dismissed as "politics" or "activism" and trumped by anecdotes, often framed in elaborate claims for the contributor's authentic access to Indian opinion.

(34)   a. "When this whole thing started around the word Squaw I had the pleasure of visiting the Navajo Nation and found not one Native American woman that thought 'squaw' was a slanderous term. So what's the big problem? Who are all these 'do gooders' trying to clean up the names of area landmarks and useing Lori as an excuse to do so?" (April 12 2003 7:10 AM)

b. "As a second generation native Arizonan whose grandparents worked on the reservation in Sacaton and the San Carlos Apache Reservation and whose father was raised speaking fluent Apache and Navajo, I have always had the highest respect for Native Americans. While I am primarily of Italian descent, my grandfather was listed as an Indian (Sioux) teacher at the school where he taught in sacaton. While I am considered an Anglo, I was the only 'non Native American' to serve on the Indian Health Advisory Board representing Arizona's Indian tribes in the late 1970's. To me squaw was not derogatory. I still do not think it is." (April 12 2003 3:54 PM)

c. "As far as the term squaw goes, I feel sorry for you if you feel it is offensive. My parents grew up in Phoenix and as a young married couple spent a lot of time with various tribes on the reservations. The term squaw was never implied as a negative, and I have always felt it to be endearing when I used it towards all my Navajo 'aunts' & 'grannies'." (January 10 2004 1:56 AM)

d. "If the indians are complaining now, well then it's the new generation. The older ones don't have a problem w/ it. I also work w/ an Indian and he is also upset of the name change. He has also told me that he has heard of no other Indian complaining of the name 'Squaw Peak'." (January 10 2004 3:54 PM)

## Colorblindness, reverse racism, and "fairness"

In proposing the name "Piestewa Peak," Governor Napolitano followed a precedent established by the Minnesota State Board of Geographic Names, which had voted in 1995 to substitute the names of Indian women for the state's "squaw" place names (Bright 2000). But contributors to the message board often argued that honoring an Indian woman was unfair. This shows up in the "colorblind" theme in (20a) "The name change singles out one person and one ethnic group over others who had also sacrificed." This theme often included a charge of "reverse racism." "Colorblindness" is an extremely popular point of view. Many Americans, especially Whites, oppose any racial preferences, especially so-called "affirmative action." The idea that affirmative action makes Whites victims of "reverse racism" erases any notion of White power or privilege, and casts White males especially as victims. Contributors to the message board proposed in all seriousness that "a white male will never get honored." These ideas are entirely coherent within the folk theory, which holds both that all discrimination is morally equivalent, and that White racism is no longer a factor in the distribution of resources in the United States. Both these ideas, of course, assert White virtue. Contributors to the message board often developed an absurdly counterfactual extension of these claims, arguing that Indians have been given immense political clout and economic resources that threaten White well-being.

Contributors urging "colorblindness" insisted that honors like the assignment of a geographic name should not single out a person of a particular race. They often mentioned other Arizona warriors who had died in the invasion of Iraq or in the Gulf War ten years earlier as equally or more deserving than Pfc. Piestewa. Contributors often veered into questioning whether Pfc. Piestewa herself was deserving of honor. Many objected that her actions in the Iraq invasion had not been particularly heroic: instead of dying while "taking out a machine gun nest," she was "lost" because of having "made a wrong turn." Others argued that all military personnel were equally worthy of honor, so that the peak should be called "Veterans' Peak," "Patriots' Peak," "Freedom Peak," "Memorial Peak," or "Heroes' Peak." Several proposed "Code-talkers' Peak" or "Windtalker Peak," after the Navajo soldiers who specialized in coded Navajo communications in World War II (these heroes are very well known and much honored in Arizona). Others suggested looking for a name in the local Indian language, O'odham (these contributors were apparently unaware that ethnohistorical research had been unable to identify the peak's O'odham name). Several posters suggested naming the peak after Ira Hayes, an Akimel O'odham man who participated in the iconic raising of the American flag at Mt. Suribachi on the island of Iwo Jima in World War II. But many contributors to the message board objected specifically to singling out an Indian woman. A selection of these postings is shown in (35).

(35)   a. "What about all the other folks who died in the war in Iraq? Sounds
          like more reverse discrimination to me./Who cares whether Piestewa was

Native American, White, Black, or Hispanic? That shouldn't matter. It's crap like this that breeds racism. She'll get her memorial with all the other lost soldiers on the memorial in Washington. Why does she need this?" (April 18 2003 9:34 AM)

b. "It's not fair to PFC Piestewa, her family, or all 3000+ Arionans who've made the ultimate sacrifice for their country. You are singling her out for her race and ethnicity. In war, there are only three colors we fight for . . . Red, White, and Blue." (April 18 2003 6:26 AM)

c. "Piestewa was the first NATIVE AMERICAN women killed in combat, not the 'first female killed in combat.' Many, many other females have died in combat, just not with the 'appropriate' ethnic background./ Meaning, simply, that if you are a soldier killed in combat who is not a Native American female, your death is less worthy and deserving of less honor./We know that a white male will never get honored, but how about a white female soldier? Black female? Sorry, you're both out of luck. Black male soldier? Nope. How about a Native American male soldier? No, you're not on the list either." (April 15 2003 10:44 AM)

The postings included parodic versions of the idea that renaming the peak for Piestewa constituted some sort of special pandering to Native Americans in violation of a code of colorblindness, similar to the parodies of politically correct name changing in (33a) above. Examples are seen in (36).

(36)    a. "I think it also offensive that we have a war machine named the Apache attack helicopter. That is so sterotypical of the white man. Maybe we should rename it the Hopi wrong turn helicopter?" (April 17 2003 10:55 PM)

b. "I could go with 'Cracker Peak'[quoting an earlier posting]./ Go ahead and offend me. I don't care. Maybe that would make everyone feel better – to just get it off of their chest. You know, take this opportunity to right every social injustice perpetrated against all people of color by us insensitive white folk./Maybe even 'All Conservative Heterosexual War-mongering Whitey Males are Scum Sucking Pigs Peak'." (January 13 2004 6:55 AM)

Some posters attacked the name "Piestewa" itself, as difficult and unpronounceable.

(37)    a. [Argues that Piestewa did not do anything heroic] "Besides, people would have no idea how to spell Piestewa." (April 17 2003 8:05 PM)

b. "Please do not rename the Peak or the Parkway. Piestewa is such a long name." (April 17 2003 10:42 PM)

c. "Imagine tellin some out of towner to get on how every you say it parkway. Don't ask me to even spell it." (April 18 2003 12:22 AM)

A subgenre of the objection that the name was long and difficult was expressed in (often offensive) parody:

(38)   a. "it will always be Squaw Peak. For a few simple reasons; we all know it as that name; it's easier to pronounce than Pieintheskya or whatever and because Piestewa is difficult to spit out; soon it will be called Pizza Peak." (April 18 2003 9:11 AM)

b. [In a message that opens with a note that the late diet guru, Dr. Atkins, who recommended a diet containing no carbohydrates, had probably had more influence in Arizona than Piestewa] "How 'bout 'Skip-the-pie-estewa Peak'." (April 17 2003 10:55 PM)

This argument, that the name should not be used because it is long and difficult, is an old one in the United States. Generations of immigrants have been encouraged to "Americanize" their names. Even perfectly straightforward short names may be changed; I once met a "Carmen" whose first-grade teacher had insisted that she be entered on the class roll sheet as the more American "Carol."[14] Resistance to generic American names developed in the African American community after the end of slavery, but names that are identifiable as African American, such as DeShawn and Tamika, subject their bearers to racist discrimination (Bertrand and Mullainathan 2003). English translations of Plains Indian names (RedCloud's name is an example) are often the objects of parody by Whites. Hopi names are less familiar to Whites, but they are easily assimilated into the category of "long, difficult" names that are considered marginal to the White American norm.[15] Thus contributors to the message board can assert without embarrassment that the name *Piestewa* is too difficult to spell or pronounce. Indeed, such an assertion is a proud claim of all-American White normalcy.

Some correspondents objected that if some site was to be named after Piestewa, it should be one with special significance to Native Americans. Many of these postings suggested that Indians could use casino money to honor Piestewa. Many Whites (like the contributor in (38b)) consider casino income to be undeserved, a form of ill-gotten gains.[16]

(38)   a. "If the Native American community feels so strongly about it, then they should rename something in northeastern Arizona in her honor" (April 11 2003 2:01 PM)

b. "Also isn't reservation land considered a sovereign nation? Seems to me they can put something in honor of Piestewa there. Native Americans have quite a lot in this state, including control over casino gambling. They also show their heritage to many of us and it is one to be admired. However, I can't help but feel now with this Piestewa and Squaw Peak issue that they want to totally control the state with Napolitano's help." (April 17 2003 8:05 PM)

c. "Erect a statue in Tuba City for Piestewa. Leave Squaw Peak the hell alone." (April 18 2003 9:34 AM)

The argument that Pfc. Piestewa had nothing to do with the Phoenix area, so any monument to her should be in Tuba City, not in Phoenix, or on Indian land, elides what is well known to Arizonans: Phoenix is the capitol of Arizona, a White-majority metropolitan area located close to the geographical center of the state at the intersection of the major transportation networks that today define the flows of resources and people. Tuba City is a remote, dusty, and impoverished small town on the Navajo Reservation, inhabited primarily by Indians, without political or economic importance for Whites, off the main highways and far from the center of Arizona. Just as "Indians" are marginal to the White center, Tuba City is geographically marginal and thus an appropriate place to honor a person who is made marginal by metonymic association with the place and with the race of people who live there.

Thus far, I have quoted mainly rather short contributions to the message board. Some of the longer ones chained together many of these themes in single contributions, and this deserves an illustration. The repulsive example in (39) develops nearly all of the themes that we have seen so far, using primarily the tool of parody:

(39) "I fell like I need to go to pist-of peak and pee on it. This just burns me up. Not a Vote just another Dictator./Janet is a political (expletive) so I can see how squaw peek is so upsetting to her. But give me a break./Goldwater peak or goldwater highway is better than pist-on-it peak./Imagine tellin some out of towner to get on how every you say it parkway. Don't ask me to even spell it./Point number 2 how come she gets 2 places named after her an the poor white guy who was realy shooting at the bad guys get non?/Well I forget he was shooting and not just being a lost target some were./ Don't we have some dead black guy the was killed?/We need to get the Spook Hill in Mesa changed too./ Black Canyon and the White Tanks the Beaver Creek. I can see naked woman parts here too. But black are no longer PC and whites never were and mexicans are still just a bunch of illegals./So indains with the big vagus [Vegas] casinos are now the new PC mofia./And we just killed? one dictator to get a new dictator here in Arizona. She is just a carpet bagger sucking up to the indain mofia." (April 18 2003 12:22 AM)

This contribution attracted a version of the "Ku Kluxer" attack that was, for once, entirely deserved (at least in my opinion):

(40) "EXCUSE ME BUT THE DRY CLEANERS CALLED AND SAID THAT WHO EVER LEFT THEIR HOOD AND ROBE THERE IS

READY FOR PICK UP, she was the first native american woman to
be killed in combat, as far as she was concern she couldve stayed at home
and raised her 2 kids, but no she choice to serve this self centerd spoiled
rich fat country of ours, so stop your crying and get over it, its done!
remember we where the ones that took over this country and casted
them (native americans) to the middle of nowhere, i guess what they say
about this state is true nothing but a bunch of bigots live here, im truley
ashamed in how my state has been ruined by all these transplants, you
ppl need to go back east where you belong and leave my state the f#@#
alone . . ." (April 18 2003 4:39 AM)

Readers will by now not be surprised to learn that expressions of the
unworthiness of Pfc. Piestewa, the un-Americanness of her name, and the
marginality of Indians as geographically isolated and inherently "biased,"
occasionally led to very explicit attacks on Indians that included the grossest
and most offensive stereotypes, as in (41).

(41)    "You seem to enjoy the benefits of living in a county that was founded
        by individuals that wanted to better themselves. By the way, these are
        the same benefits that the Indians now enjoy as well. I'm not a racist,
        but I am a REALIST. I can see with my own eyes and make logical
        perceptions. I am 1/4 Cherokee and ashamed to admit it. In fact, I don't.
        The poor, por Indians. Lost their land, live in dumps, boo hoo. I don't
        see them moving. Such a proud people, ya right. Have you been to the
        reservation? What a dump. Cars flipped over in the yards, three legged
        dogs running around, kids poking rattlesnakes with a stick. What happens
        to the money we give them every year? FIREWATER. They drink it
        up. The reservation is no better than Iraq was. A few of the 'leaders'
        reap the benefits of a billion dollar casino industry and the rest live like
        peasants. And then put out public service announcements about how
        they can't afford medical treatment and they have kidney failure because
        the white man raped all the nutrients from their water. Take vitamins!
        My kidneys work just fine./Take your casino money and BETTER
        yourselves! Sop crying about the past. That will gain more respect in this
        country than celebrating some 'victory' because you got a road renamed."
        (April 18 2003 8:02 AM)[17]

This posting, astonishingly, received no reply. However, sometimes
threads on the message boards included very sharp exchanges of insults, as
in (42b), a reply to (42a), which shows how easily contributors slipped into
explicit racism.

(42)    a.  "Thank you, governor Napalitano for changing the name . . . it's about
            time . . . this is not about being PC, it's about respect . . . i would also
            like the governor to start changing team mascot names . . . In honor of

the many naysayers on this board, i suggest calling teams the 'CRYING WHITIES' instead of the chiefs, braves, etc . . . if you snivelers don't like the name change, go back to whereever your ancestors are from and whine there . . . this is indian land . . . don't forget it" (April 17 2003 11:51 PM)

b. "Yeah, right. If it wasn't for us 'sniveling white folk,' this nation would probably still be living in mud huts, the chief industry would be farming, we'd be fighting wars with bows & arrows, and the average life expectancy would be about 38./Oh . . . and you'd be sending your message board posts via smoke signals." (April 18 2003 12:00 AM)

## Conclusion: Slurs and White Privilege

Contributors to the message board defended the place name "Squaw Peak" using diverse rhetorical strategies. However, underlying this diversity is a consistent theme, of White privilege, White control of symbolic resources, and the White virtue that licenses these. Many lines of evidence point to this conclusion. First, contributors to the message board who supported the name change believe that this is what is going on, as when "P.J." asked in (43):

(43)  "My god – does everything have to be white with you guys????" (April 12 2003 8:27 AM)

Second, the ideological positions developed on the list exhibited striking inconsistencies and incoherencies. The ideology of performativity holds that slurs are hurtful and wounding. However, when Native Americans expressed their pain at having to constantly encounter "Squaw Peak," this was dismissed as "over-sensitivity." At the same time, White contributors felt that their own mild preferences against change were important reasons to keep the name "Squaw Peak." Third, some of the departures from obvious facts in the message board suggest that something larger than a mere name change of a not-very-grand geographical feature is at stake. In an environment where Indians are few, powerless, and poor, contributors to the message board represent them as numerous, powerful, and rich.[18] In the face of a well-known history where Whites used every device of power including genocide to strip resources from Indians, contributors to the message board insist that Indians "take and take" while Whites "give and give." Such absurd exaggerations and outright falsifications suggest that those who make them are motivated by acute anxiety.

A few contributors to the message board even attempt to rescue White virtue by suggesting that names like "Squaw Peak" were intended to honor Native American tradition:

(44)    "Having lived in AZ for over 50 years, I have always considered the name Squaw Peak as a tribute to the Indian role in developing this great state." (January 10 2004 9:50 AM)

While this discourse of "intention to honor" is very common (we will see it again in Chapter 6), the actual historical facts are that Native American place-naming traditions were almost never honored by White North American settlers in Arizona. This contrasts with Spanish colonial practice, which retained many Native American names, often pairing these with the names of Catholic saints, as in *San Xavier del Bac* and *San Agustín de Tucson*, where *Bac* and *Tucson* are both place names in the O'odham language. Instead, early White American settlers relabeled the entire landscape using their own conventions. Many Native Americans in Arizona are today involved in mapping projects that aim to recover and encourage the use of names in the local languages (Basso 1996). Thus when "tradition" is invoked in favor of "Squaw Peak," it is White tradition, not Native American tradition, that is being honored. This privileging of White traditions above all others is especially obvious when a place name is known to be universally offensive to Native Americans.

That White privilege is at stake is also suggested by the tone of some of the correspondence on the message board. While opponents of the name change directed a good deal of invective against the governor of Arizona (as a woman, she was an inviting target), the most vicious attacks are reserved for Indians, and we see repeated on the message board the most scurrilous stereotypes of "firewater" and filth. Indeed, the intensity of attacks on Indians in the context of this debate over a mere symbolic resource, the meaning of the word "squaw," and the name of the peak, approached the levels encountered by Bobo and Tuan (2006) in their study of the battle over Chippewa fishing rights in Wisconsin in the 1970s and 1980s, where a material resource was at stake. Astonishingly, even Pfc. Piestewa herself is attacked. This occurred during weeks in April 2003 when the universal attitude in Arizona and throughout the United States was one of jingoistic support for the American soldiers in Iraq and reverent mourning for those who had died. Yet this very young woman, a private soldier, was frequently accused of being "unheroic," of making personally the mistakes that led to her death. These departures from the usual norms of civility, rationality, and even American patriotism as it was expressed in the early days of the invasion of Iraq suggest that deep-seated anxieties were raised by the idea that Squaw Peak would be renamed for an Indian woman.

As the extensive attention to race and racism on the message board attests, nearly everyone thought that a discussion of the word "squaw" was at root about these issues, and contributors who argued that "this is not about race" seemed to protest too much. Yet many contributors, fully aware that race and racism were at stake, insisted that they had never thought of "squaw" as a slur. I think that we have to take these contributors at their word. Indeed, they never thought it was a slur, because they grew up in a period when the many tools of White racism were deployed without fear of contradiction. Whites were thoroughly insulated by segregation from people of color, and actively oblivious to their concerns. Even where Whites were in contact with Indians, they could use "squaw" with impunity. A White message-board contributor recalled using the word "endearingly" to her "Navajo aunts and grannies," during the same period when a Navajo contributor points out that she was never allowed to utter the word, associated by her family with a "four-letter" vocabulary. The first contributor was protected by White power; she would never have been corrected by those "aunts and grannies." If her parents were welcomed in Navajo communities, they were probably providing crucial resources, perhaps buying rugs or jewelry, or mediating access to important services.

In spite of the fact that "squaw" was identified as a slur by the middle of the nineteenth century, the word remains in very widespread use. Over 1,000 places in the United States bear the name, including well-known sites like the California ski resort of Squaw Valley, venue of the 1960 Winter Olympics. Thus the message-board postings constitute a moment when one small tool of White racism — the unquestioned right to use a term that presupposes an alignment of Indians with animals rather than fully human Whites — begins to emerge from the taken-for-granted structure of fully hegemonic White power into the light of criticism, and begins to be associated, by at least some Whites and by nearly all Indians, with a well-established metalinguistic category of racial slurs. Unfortunately, within the folk theory of racism, the only voice that is heard if "squaw" is really a slur is that of the Ku Kluxer, the redneck, marginal and ignorant, who in full intentionality assaults a victim with his foolish prejudices. Thus it is no wonder that the advocates for "Squaw Peak," linked to the Internet through their home computers in the booming sunbelt city of Phoenix, are so defensive. They — and their parents and grandparents who used the word — cannot possibly be as bad as someone who would use a racial slur, therefore, "squaw" cannot be such a word.

The emergence of words like "squaw" into full consciousness and contestability probably does not signal the beginning of the end of White racism. It is more probable that this episode is one symptom of a slow shift of White racism into a new stage, where linguistic resources are being reallocated along the continuum of institutions and practices through which race and racism are reproduced. Racial slurs do not disappear. They shift instead into new environments. The change in the forms of circulation takes place over century-long intervals; both "nigger" and "squaw" have been identified as scurrilous since at least the middle of the nineteenth century. "Nigger" was removed from American place names in 1967. Kennedy (2002) points out correctly that no White person wishing to maintain public credibility in the United States today could be heard or overheard saying the word, and it is risky even to mention it in scholarly debate. Yet it continues in very active circulation. Some of the sites where the word is favored have been driven underground and marginalized, but new sites have emerged and flourished,[19] and the very arguments over the word continually reinscribe both the label and the racializing stigma that it imposes. "Squaw" will no doubt go through a similar trajectory, and we can expect that our descendants 40 years on will still be debating its use.

# Chapter 4

# Gaffes: Racist Talk without Racists

## Introduction: Gaffes, Personalism, and Moral Panics

"Gaffes," like slurs, are visible to White Americans as racist language. Like slurs, gaffes attract metalinguistic and metapragmatic discourse. But when an utterance is called a gaffe or a "slip," the discourse that follows is interestingly different from that around slurs. As we saw in Chapter 3, to call a word a slur entails that the speaker is a racist as defined in the folk theory: a Ku Kluxer or a redneck. Those accused of uttering slurs can defend themselves against this charge of racism by insisting that the utterance in question is "not a slur." In the case of gaffes or slips, the defense focuses, not on the words, but on the speaker. The speaker is defended as "not a racist," but as someone who has uttered racist words without having racist beliefs or intentions. The actual linguistic content of slurs and gaffes can be identical; one commentator's slur is another's gaffe. And both types of metalinguistic discourses – defending words in the case of slurs, but speakers in the case of gaffes – reproduce racializing stigma, protect White virtue, and advance White privilege by denying the existence of White racism.

### Personalist linguistic ideology

Because metalinguistic discourse around gaffes focuses on persons and their beliefs and intentions, it permits us to explore an important theoretical question, the relationship between ideologies of language – interested ideas about how language is organized and what it is for – and ideologies of persons (Woolard 1998:3). Many Whites in the United States share a linguistic ideology called "personalism" (Duranti 1993; Rosaldo 1981). Personalism insists that each individual has an invisible interior self which is the site of beliefs and intentions and emotional states such as love and hatred. Personalist ideology permits us to say that when a speaker speaks, he or she "means" something. That is, meaning resides not only in the content of words, as determined by baptismal ideology, but in what speakers intend by uttering them. Because of these intentions, words not only represent the world, they represent the inner states of persons. The task of interlocutors is to retrieve meaning by assessing those states. Personalist ideology invites attention to speaker intentions even in the most mundane interactions. For instance, a passenger giving directions who has just told a driver to "Turn left!" can offer as a legitimate apology, when the maneuver gets them to the wrong place, "Oh, I didn't mean 'left', I meant 'right'." And of course speakers accused of being rude or insulting can excuse themselves by saying, "I didn't mean it that way."

Alongside speaker intentions, speaker beliefs are crucial for personalist linguistic ideologies. Speakers are supposed to choose their words (which, as we learned in Chapter 3, are often understood within the terms of the baptismal ideology of meaning to have an inherent meaning that corresponds to the truth of the world) to correctly represent their beliefs. Personalist and referentialist linguistic ideologies intersect, because referentialist ideology, with its focus on accurate communication, holds that people should believe what is true (Sweetser 1987). So, just as they assess intentions, interlocutors must be able to assess beliefs. For instance, personalist ideology permits a distinction between a "lie," where a speaker uses words that do not match their beliefs in order to mislead, and an error, where a speaker uses words that match their beliefs, but the beliefs are wrong.

Personalist linguistic ideology also permits the recognition of forms of talk such as irony and parody. In order to recognize irony, interlocutors must be able to assess the speaker's state of belief and infer that the speaker could not really believe the meaning of the words as uttered. For instance, if someone mentions President George W. Bush, and I, a life-long lefty, contribute an aside like "America's greatest president," people who know me would understand the remark to be ironic. In order to understand talk or text as parody, an even more complex assessment is required. A fascinating example occurred during a notorious incident that took place on November 18, 2006. The actor Michael Richards, famous for his role as Seinfeld's zany neighbor Kramer on the long-running television sitcom *Seinfeld*, was performing in Los Angeles at a comedy club, the Laugh Factory. A party of African American guests was being seated and ordering drinks during his act, when Richards, apparently annoyed at the disturbance, began to scream "Nigger! Nigger! Nigger!" A cell-phone video of the incident posted on many Internet sites[1] revealed that initially the audience was confused, waiting for the joke that would reveal these cries to be a parody of a racist display, since Richards had no reputation as a bigot. Indeed, several audience members interviewed later confirmed that they had thought at first that the words were leading into a comedy sketch. When the anticipated punchline did not come, audience members began to shout Richards down with cries of "Oh my God" and "That's uncalled for, man." But the pause of a second or two before these shouts began was extremely telling. During this interval, the audience obviously was processing the kinds of inferences that are invited by personalist ideology: Does he really believe that? Did he really mean to say that? Is he the kind of person that would say that seriously, or is this a joke? The incident shows that even this most censurable of all slurs was not reflexively unacceptable. Instead, personalist ideology permitted it to be treated, at least briefly, as a moment in which Richards parodied the voice of a stereotypical racist, a voice that was not "his own."

Rosaldo (1981) pointed out that personalist ideology appears in the core literature of pragmatics and the philosophy of language. The elaboration of Speech Act theory by the philosopher John Searle (1969) postulates that interlocutor's access to speaker's intentions and beliefs (and speaker's access to interlocutor's beliefs and intentions) is required for speech acts to be accomplished. Grice's (1975) analysis of the production of meaning in conversation similarly requires that speakers and hearers be able to make inferences about one another's beliefs and intentions.

Keane (2002) has pointed out that personalist ideology is linked to referentialist ideology, which holds that the most important function of language is "reference," to label a pre-existing world and to convey true statements about it (Silverstein 1976). As noted above, referentialism is linked to personalism by an understanding that beliefs should be true, that they should match the world. Utterances should precisely reflect these true beliefs (Sweetser 1987). Failures to conform to this correspondence are discreditable. If beliefs do not match truth, this is a sign of ignorance. If utterances do not reflect beliefs, they are lies. Both ignorance and lying are moral failures of speakers. Personalism, with its characteristic appeals to intentions, provides escape clauses for both ignorance and lying, but these require the use of the complex apparatus of inference made available precisely by personalist ideology itself.

Personalism and referentialism are invisible to those who share them. They are simply taken for granted, and, when they are pointed out, people find them commonsensical and simply right. However, anthropologists have encountered societies in which personalism and referentialism are not dominant. In a pioneering paper Rosaldo (1981) showed that the Ilongot of the Philippines find the act most prototypical of human talk to be, not the communication of a truth, but a kind of command called *tuydek*. For instance, a husband might say to his wife, "Bring me my betel nut chewing equipment." Interpreting such a command involves not interpretation of the husband's intentions (Does he really mean it? Did he say it to annoy?), but understanding of his position in a hierarchy of humans arranged according to "passion," a potential for action and motion possessed in full measure by men. Men must command women, who would otherwise lack motivation, as a part of their responsibility to order the world. Duranti (1993), examining Samoan understandings of language, found that for them meaning lies in the social results of utterances, and not in speaker intention. Coleman and Kay (1981) and Sweetser (1987) show that middle-class White Americans define a "lie" as an utterance made with the intention to deceive. Duranti found that Samoans hold any utterance that turns out to be consequentially wrong to be a lie, regardless of speaker intention. Thus what in mainstream White American language ideology would count as a perfectly sincere statement, like "I'm bringing guests for dinner tonight, so set two extra places," for Samoans could become a lie if the guests cancelled at the last minute, leaving food to go to waste and the host inconvenienced. Ochs and Schieffelin (1984) pointed out that Samoan adults do not speculate about the meanings of unintelligible utterances by small children. Only when the words are clear are they thought to be meaningful; the idea that the child intends a meaning, and that adults are charged with figuring out what that intention is, so reasonable to American White middle-class parents, is quite irrational for Samoans. For them, meaning is public, not an internal state of some person.

African Americans in some contexts permit departures from personalism. Mitchell-Kernan (1972) points out that African American ideologies of interaction place as much responsibility for the production of meaning on the hearer as on the speaker. For instance, Mitchell-Kernan reports an incident when one woman became angry at a perceived insult from another. The speaker said of the angry woman's reaction, "I wasn't signifying on her, but I always say that if the shoe fits, wear it." In teaching, I have often illustrated this point with a television interview I heard in 1989 or 1990, during an early episode of panic over misogynist language in rap music precipitated by 2 Live Crew's album *As Nasty as they Wanna Be*. The rapper being interviewed defended this kind of language, asserting, "When I say 'bitch', you don't have to turn around." Morgan (2001) calls this "baited indirectness"; the hearer must accept the bait for meaning to be generated. Another dimension of the public, interactional nature of meaning in African American linguistic ideology is that a speaker can be strongly blamed for a slight or insult, even if, from a personalist perspective, it was done "unintentionally" (Morgan 1999).

Philips (2004) has pointed out the problem of "ideological multiplicity," that ideological systems are often neither homogeneous nor very coherent. The distinctive discourses appropriate to different contexts in a single society may express diverse linguistic ideologies. Ideological multiplicity can be observed in metalinguistic discourse around gaffes. For instance, a metalinguistic discourse exists that holds that banter, joking, and flattery permit and even require insincere talk, which departs from the referentialist ideal. Within such contexts, speakers are allowed to separate what they say from what they believe. Indeed, they may insist that it is unfair to suggest that they believe what they say in such contexts. Such "light talk" is a very important site for the explicit use of racist language by White Americans, and Feagin (2006:207) has found that White speakers very often claim that they were "only joking" when interlocutors accuse them of having made a racist utterance. That is, they claim that what they said did not match what they believe, and that this does not discredit them. Note, however, that this excuse remains personalist. While "light talk" permits words to be separated from beliefs, speaker intentions must be evaluated in order to determine that the context is indeed one of light talk and joking.

## Moral panics and their metacultural function

Racist utterances by public figures precipitate episodes that I label here "moral panics" (adapting this term from Cohen 1972), which play out in mass media firestorms where the potentially offensive utterance is repeated again and again over days and even weeks, both by those who intend to discredit the speaker and by those who intend to support and defend him. These debates take the form of intricate personalist discourses in which folk psychology is deployed to explore every dimension of the speaker's self-hood. Furthermore, every detail of the context of the utterance is examined in order to evaluate speaker intentions. In these discourse events, personalist and referentialist language ideologies play a "metacultural" (Urban 2001) role, facilitating the circulation of the words and ideas of White racism. Indeed, such panics precipitate what we might call "hyper-repetition" of slurs and stereotypes. Linguistic ideologies make this circulation natural and commonsensical. The case of truly appalling racist language used by the radio talk-show host Don Imus on his morning show April 5, 2007, is exemplary. Imus referred to the young African American players on the Rutgers University women's basketball team, which had played the night before in the NCAA tournament's final game, as "nappy-headed hos."[2] Imus's remark and the aftermath (he was forced to resign from the show) made headlines every day for weeks. On August 5, 2007, four months later, his epithet still returned 265,000 Google hits.

These episodes of panic probably occur because when utterances of racist words and propositions by public figures, especially by highly placed White men, become public, this is profoundly unsettling for many White Americans. They have invested, at the very least, attention to these figures in their role as celebrities. And many have invested far more: admiration, envy, votes, financial contributions, hero-worship, and the like. George Allen, whose political career probably ended after he called an opponent a "macaca," was not only a United States senator. He was widely admired by White men because of his association with the all-American sport of football. He had himself played varsity football in college at the University of Virginia, and his father, also named George Allen, had been a legendary professional coach of major teams including the Chicago Bears, the Los Angeles Rams, and the Washington Redskins. Since "racism," in the folk theory the practice of rednecks and Ku Kluxers, is held to be incompatible with the exemplary character and courage that many fans associate with football, and certainly incompatible as well with service in one of America's highest elected offices, evidence that Senator Allen used racist slurs was profoundly unsettling to the self-image of his admirers. And it was unsettling to anybody who believed that White Americans are people who believe in racial equality, and who would be able to detect and reject racists as unqualified for public office. Those who had invested enough in Allen to feel attacks on him as a racist as an attack on their own creditable selves and on White virtue more broadly rose to his defense to preserve that credit and virtue.

## Personalist discourse in moral panics

This chapter centers on the two-week media firestorm that followed a remark in support of legal racial segregation made on December 6, 2002, by Trent Lott, the senior US senator from Mississippi. This remark cost Lott what is arguably one of the most powerful political positions in the world, the majority leadership of the United States Senate. However, elite media opinion was almost unanimous in concluding that Lott was not a racist. Reportage and opinion essays consistently called his utterance a "gaffe" or a "slip." Before looking in detail at this case, let's look at a few other panics of this type, to get a general sense of the kinds of discourse that surround them.

My first example is the only one where the public figure involved was a woman. Not surprisingly, this was a woman connected with sports: Marge Schott, once owner of the Cincinnati Reds baseball team. Mrs. Schott's *New York Times* obituary, published March 3, 2004, exemplifies the focus on beliefs and intentions that accompanies the labeling of utterances as "gaffes." In the early 1990s Mrs. Schott had been ordered by the commissioner of baseball to give up her direct involvement in her team after a whole series of embarrassing public incidents in which she uttered anti-Semitic and racist slurs. Richard Goldstein, the *New York Times* obituary writer, used the term "gaffe" to describe these incidents:

(1)   "But a series of gaffes and intolerant remarks caused Mrs. Schott to lose control of the Reds in 1999 . . . Mrs. Schott's image first soured in November 1992 when several former Reds executives said that she had referred to players and business associates using racial and ethnic slurs . . . Mrs. Schott denied she was a racist, but acknowledged she had sometimes used a racial epithet" (Goldstein 2004).

Goldstein is at pains to find extenuating information, quoting the Mayor of Cincinnati as saying: "While there is no excusing some of the indelicate things she said, there was a kindness to Marge that made her a woman of the people." The former commissioner of baseball was quoted as saying: "I think she tried very hard to do the right things for baseball, but she had some enormous limitations and she had some difficulty overcoming them." The obituary characterizes Mrs. Schott as a big-hearted but eccentric person who said racist things.

Another famous "gaffe" again involves a sports celebrity, the golfer Fuzzy Zoeller, who made disparaging racist remarks about the golfer Tiger Woods, whose mother is Thai and whose father is African American. On April 20, 1997, Woods, only 21 years old and the most exciting new star in golf, was playing the final holes of the US Masters golf tournament, and it was clear that he would win. Zoeller, the 1979 champion, had just finished his own final round, and volunteered the following statement to reporters as he left the course:

(2)   "Little boy's driving well and he's putting well. He's doing everything it takes to win. So, you know what you guys do when he gets here? You pat him on the back and say congratulations and enjoy it and tell him not to serve fried chicken next year [it is the responsibility of the Masters winner to host a dinner for past winners in the following year]. Got it?" Zoeller snapped his fingers and began to walk away, but turned back briefly and said, "Or collard greens or whatever the hell it is they serve" (Fuzzy 1997; on the videotape on the CNN website, "they" in the final sentence is de-stressed).

Zoeller's statement was repeated again and again in all media for days, accompanied by extensive analysis of what he might have intended by calling Woods a "boy," by his stereotyping cracks about fried chicken and collard greens, and, of course, the de-stressed, utterly distancing "they" in the last sentence. Zoeller lost his K-Mart sponsorship, withdrew from a tournament in Greensboro, North Carolina, when the local African American community threatened to picket the affair, and was forced to make many public apologies.

Although Zoeller paid a high price for his remarks, most writers labeled them as a "gaffe" or "slip," an inappropriate attempt at a joke, the racist content of which was not consistent with what was thought to be his character. For instance, John Feinstein (1999) in a bestselling golf book wrote of Zoeller:

(3) "He is a gregarious, funny man who loves to tell jokes . . . But with a national TV camera rolling, Zoeller picked the wrong time and the wrong place to try to be funny . . . Many of his friends have pointed to his exemplary record over a period of many years in race relations and said it is unfair to wipe all that out because of a thirty-second slipup" (Feinstein 1999:26).

Note that Feinstein attends closely to motives: Zoeller "loves to tell jokes," he was "trying to be funny." Feinstein continued with a classic note on speaker intention: "What no one has ever been able to explain is what Zoeller was thinking at the moment that he made the comments" (Feinstein 1999:27). Woods himself was quoted as having taken intention into account when determining (after four days) to accept Zoeller's apology:

(4) ". . . having played golf with Fuzzy, I know he is a jokester; and I have concluded that no personal animosity toward me was intended" (Accept 1997).

Not only did many commentators defend Zoeller, they attacked Woods for being slow to accept Zoeller's apology, and for making inappropriate remarks in his own right. Frank Luksa of the *Dallas Morning News* commented:

(5) "Based on their respective backgrounds for bad taste, Woods and Zoeller deserved to play together" (Luksa 1997).

Luksa equates Zoeller's remark with off-color jokes about African Americans made by Woods himself and reported in the men's magazine *GQ* (Pierce 1997).

The Zoeller case, where a racist and stereotyping utterance was framed as a joke, brings out a fundamental tension in White American linguistic ideologies. The excuse that a racist remark was a joke is always available for Whites, and those who reject this excuse are likely to be accused of lacking a sense of humor. Yet this idea that the facial meanings of words are somehow suspended in joking, so that the joking intention of the speaker supersedes that meaning, conflicts with the baptismal ideology of meaning, which holds that meaning inheres in words themselves. If speakers choose particular words, they must believe in them and intend these meanings. If the baptismal theory that we saw speakers drawing on in Chapter 3 were consistently employed, then racism would always lie in the words themselves, and the intention to joke would not make the words acceptable. So we can see that personalist ideology here is licensing the joking (and thus, within this ideological system, forgivable) use of racist language.

Both the idea that speaker intention is primary and the idea that words have inherent meanings leave out a third possibility: that if language is found to be racist by its targets, then it is racist language. A watered-down version of this is the prescription of "civility": that talk "should not give offence to actual and potential addressees" (Cameron 1995:134). However, flagrant violations of civility often accompany the defense of racist language. We saw in Chapter 3 examples of people who argued that it was simply ignorant and stupid for anyone to find racist content in the word "squaw." Those who objected to the slur were labeled as over-sensitive, thin-skinned. Personalist ideology insists that speaker intention, not the feelings of the hearer, is always most important in evaluating meaning. Thus both personalist and baptismal ideologies validate and make commonsensical a nearly total inattention on the part of Whites to the sensitivities of people of color. This is repeatedly attested in materials I have examined. Feagin (2006:27, citing a proposal by Hernán Vera) has called this curious absence of empathy "social alexithymia." Indeed, "social alexithymia" is more than inattention; in my research data, there are many, many examples of outright and explicit rejection of the authenticity of the feelings of people of color who object to racist language.

A good example of this kind of rejection is illustrated in the "Dame Edna" affair from February of 2003. This case shows how tension develops around racist jokes between baptismal ideologies of inherent meaning, personalist ideologies of speaker intention, and the right of the butts of racist language to object to it as wounding. "Dame Edna Everage" is one of the stage personae of the Australian comedian Barry Humphries, a spectacularly politically incorrect lady of a certain age, costumed in rhinestone-studded eyeglasses, a huge bouffant pouf of purple hair, and absurd frilly tea gowns. "Dame Edna" contributed a parodic advice column to the February 2003 issue of *Vanity Fair*, a glossy US monthly magazine that combines investigative journalism with celebrity news. This issue was purchased by many Latinos and Latinas because of its cover picture and feature article on Mexican actress Salma Hayek. In thumbing through the issue looking for the article on Hayek, these readers bumped into Dame Edna's advice column, which included the following exchange with an imaginary correspondent:

(6)  "Dear Dame Edna, I would very much like to learn a foreign language, preferably French or Italian, but every time I mention this, people tell me to learn Spanish instead. They say, 'Everyone is going to be speaking

Spanish in 10 years. George W. Bush speaks Spanish." Could this be true?
Are we all going to have to speak Spanish?

Torn Romantic, Palm Beach

Dear Torn, Forget Spanish. There's nothing in that language worth reading
except *Don Quixote*, and a quick listen to the CD of *Man of La Mancha*
will take care of that. There was a poet named Garcia Lorca, but I'd leave
him on the intellectual back burner if I were you. As for everyone's speaking it, what twaddle! Who speaks it that you are really desperate to talk
to? The help? Your leaf blower? Study French or German, where there
are at least a few books worth reading, or, if you're American, try English"
(Ask Dame Edna 2003).

Dame Edna's remarks were widely noted; the *New York Times* reported
them under the headline "Gaffes on Hispanics, from 2 well-known mouths"
(Carr 2003).[3] They were big news on the Internet and in newspapers in
cities like Miami, San Antonio, and Los Angeles. Major Latino organizations including the League of United Latin American Citizens and the
National Council of La Raza called for an apology by *Vanity Fair* magazine
and its publisher, Condé Nast.

Many respondents focused not on Dame Edna's intentionality as a paro-
dist (some commentators, not being familiar with the character, missed this
entirely), but on the fact that her words were untrue. This focus emanates
from referentialist ideology, which permits stereotypes about people of
color to be condemned as racist because they are not true. Dame Edna's
parodic column could thus be called racist because it was factually wrong
and "ignorant." A catalytic letter to *Vanity Fair* that was widely discussed
and copied was posted to a website by Wendy Maldonado, who described
herself as

(7)  "a 31-year-old Mexican-American woman, with three Ivy League degrees,
     working in New York City at a major firm. I sure as hell am NOT the
     leaf blower or the help. . . . Dame Edna could have chosen any number
     of amusing responses, however, she responded using cheap, two-dimen-
     sional stereotypes of Latinos and Latin Americans, revealing not only her
     racism, but also her profound ignorance of who we are. We are not just
     'the help' and 'the leaf blowers.' We are architects and activists, journalists
     and doctors, governors and athletes, scientists and business people. We are
     Nobel Prize winners and Rhodes Scholars . . . If Dame Edna were even
     remotely cultured or educated, she would have read and lost herself in the
     exquisite writings of Nobel Prize winners Octavio Paz, Gabriel Garcia
     Marquez, and Pablo Neruda. She would know that Sor Juana Inez de la
     Cruz was one of the first feminists and poets of the Americas. She would
     admire Isabel Allende and Sandra Cisneros for their passionate prose and
     vibrant spirits" (Maldonado 2003).

The staff at *Latina* magazine addressed Dame Edna's ignorance by packing up a box of books by Spanish-speaking authors for Dame Edna, the editors of *Vanity Fair*, and the "hardworking researchers in your [*Vanity Fair's*] fact-checking department"; the package included Gabriel Garcia Marquez's *One Hundred Years of Solitude*, Julio Cortazar's *Hopscotch*, Carlos Fuentes's *The Death of Artemio Cruz*, and Jorge Luis Borges's *Labyrinths* (listed on Latina.com; Vanity Fair 2003).

While Maldonado (in 7), the editors at Latina.com, and many other respondents took the view that Dame Edna's language was racist on its face because it was a stereotyping misrepresentation, other discussants argued that since the column was meant as a joke it should not count as racist. *Vanity Fair* published an apology that advanced this position:

(8) "*Vanity Fair* regrets that certain remarks in our February issue by the entertainer and author Barry Humphries, in the guise of his fictional character Dame Edna, have caused offense to our readers and others. In the role of Dame Edna, Humphries practices a long comedic tradition of making statements that are tasteless, wrongheaded, or taboo with an eye toward exposing hypocrisies or prejudices. Anyone who has seen Dame Edna's over-the-top performances on TV or in the theater knows that she is an equal-opportunity distributor of insults, and her patently absurd comments about Spanish literature and Spanish speakers were offered in the spirit of outrageous comedy and were never intended to be taken to heart" (*Vanity Fair* Apology 2003).

Many Latinos and Latinas rejected this argument, observing that they understood that the piece was an attempt at humor, but that it was in poor taste and unfunny. Juan Gonzalez, the President of the National Association of Hispanic Journalists, and Rafael Olmeda, Chair of the Issues Committee of this organization, wrote the following to *Vanity Fair*:

(9) "Humor and satire are not safe hiding places for ignorance and bigotry. Frankly, we're tired of people hiding behind 'it was just a joke' after taking broad and unwarranted swipes at our culture and heritage" (Gonzalez and Olmeda 2003).

Of course those who objected to the column were accused of lacking a sense of humor. Even some Latinos made this argument. For instance, op-ed writer Helen Urbinas argued that:

(10) "'La Dama's' column was not 'thinly veiled bigotry' but an obvious, albeit failed, attempt at humor . . . So, when can we laugh at ourselves? . . . Take a joke without being seen as a sell-out, a traitor?" (Urbinas 2003).

An anonymous contributor to HispanicOnline.com wrote that if Hispanics truly embraced their diversity, including the leaf blowers and the help,

(11) "Maybe then we would not be so sensitive about some cartoon making fun of us" (Readers' Response 2003).

## The Case of Senator Trent Lott: Personalist Discourse in the Media in a National Moral Panic

The cases sketched above show that much is at stake in determining whether a racist utterance by a public figure is labeled as a slur, a gaffe, or a joke. The example I detail here involved exceptionally high stakes, because of the extraordinary prominence of the speaker, Senator Trent Lott, Republican of Mississippi, majority leader of the US Senate. This episode of moral panic engaged the most influential and prominent political writers in the national media, and so gives us a good look at how their linguistic ideologies shape discourse about racism among White elites.

The majority leadership of the Senate, which Lott had held from 1998 to 2002, is the most important office in the legislative branch of the US government and one of the most influential political positions in the world. Lott had long been associated with the most conservative wing of the Republican Party. At a 100th birthday party held in Washington, DC, on December 5, 2002, for Strom Thurmond, Republican of South Carolina, the oldest and longest-serving member of the United States Senate and notorious for his many years of advocacy of racial segregation, Lott was one of the most prominent of the national figures who came to the podium to offer birthday good wishes. His remarks included the following 45 words:

(12) "I want to say this about my state: When Strom Thurmond ran for president, we voted for him. We're proud of it. And if the rest of the country had followed our lead, we wouldn't have had all these problems over all these years, either."

Lott referred to Thurmond's bid for the US presidency in 1948 as the candidate of the States' Rights Democrats, the so-called "Dixecrat" party. The Dixiecrats broke from the national Democratic Party, walking out of its 1948 national convention when the Democrats adopted a platform plank endorsing civil rights legislation. The Dixiecrat platform stated, "We stand for the segregation of the races and the racial integrity of each race," and the party's slogan was "Segregation Forever." Thurmond carried Louisiana,

Alabama, his own home state of South Carolina, and Lott's home state of Mississippi, gaining over a million popular votes and 39 electoral votes in the largest showing by a third party in a US presidential election in the last 100 years.

Although Lott's remarks were delivered in the presence of many journalists and were televised by C–SPAN, major media coverage of the party included no mention of Lott's astonishing statement. On the Internet, though, liberal blogger Joshua Micah Marshall immediately noted the racist content of Lott's remarks in the December 6 entry in his weblog *Talking Points Memo* (Marshall 2002a). Marshall continued to push the issue throughout the next two weeks. On the conservative side of the web, blogger Andrew Sullivan also immediately labeled Lott's statement as racist.

The first mainstream media figure to note Lott's speech was an African American, Gwen Ifill, moderator for the Friday-evening PBS television program, *Washington Week in Review*. At the end of her half-hour program on Friday, December 6, Ifill played the C–SPAN clip of Lott delivering his statement and, with a quizzical expression on her face, invited her audience to "Let me know what you think of that."

On Saturday, December 7, well inside the first section on page A6, the *Washington Post* ran a negative comment on Lott's statement (Edsall 2002a). On Sunday, December 8, Lott's remarks were the topic on two major national television political discussion programs, CNN's *Crossfire* and NBC's *Meet the Press*. On Monday, December 9, Andrew Sullivan labeled Lott a "bigot" and a "racist" and called for his resignation. On Tuesday, December 10, 2002, *New York Times* columnist Paul Krugman advanced the themes that became central to the debate. "Was Mr. Lott . . . ignorant of the aims of the 1948 Thurmond campaign? Or was he just, in the excitement of the moment, blurting out his real views?" (Krugman 2002a). From this point a classic media firestorm built until Lott resigned as Senate Majority Leader on Friday, December 20, 2002. Lott retained his senatorial seat and was not censured. When the Senate allocated leadership positions at the beginning of the 2003 session, Lott was given a prestigious and influential position as chairman of the Rules Committee. In January 2005 he was awarded a significant honorary post as chairman of the inauguration ceremonies for George W. Bush's second presidential term.

Moral panics like the one that followed Lott's remark are significant moments in cultural production and reproduction. I adapt the label "moral panic" (Cohen 1972) for such episodes, not to downplay the importance of the issues, but because I think the label "panic" captures the frenetic energy of such discourse events. Moral panics play out at multiple sites. No ethnographer can listen in on every tavern conversation, workplace joke exchange, Internet chat room, or boardroom backstage where these social dramas develop. However, a moral panic can be tracked through journalistic discourse, when reporters and commentators in all media, from provincial talk radio to the editorial page of the *New York Times*, from web loggers to the news readers on the national television networks, join in developing reportage and commentary. Over a very short period of time, these events generate an immense quantity of discourse on a single narrow subject. Such a discourse event produces multiple refractions of the same rhetorical formulas, permitting the recovery of what is stable and what is variable in a particular rhetorical system at a very fine level of delicacy.

The Trent Lott firestorm produced over slightly more than two weeks many thousands of words of reportage and commentary. In order to contain the volume of material, I consulted only a few major media sources. From the *New York Times* and the *Washington Post* I collected every mention of the Lott crisis between December 7 and December 21, 2002. On many days, each of these newspapers ran up to half-a-dozen pieces of reportage, feature sidebars, editorials, and op-ed pieces on the controversy. The *New York Times*, for which I used the print version of the national edition, for a week and a half devoted to the controversy an entire two-page spread inside the front section, under the title "Divisive Words." In addition, front-page coverage, editorials, and op-ed essays appeared daily in the *Times* throughout the two weeks. During the week of December 15 to December 21, in order to determine whether elite media on the West Coast were handling the story the same way as the big eastern newspapers, I searched the website of the *Los Angeles Times*, the major western US daily newspaper. *Los Angeles Times* coverage was indistinguishable from that in the two eastern papers.

The Trent Lott episode was an early example of the influence of a new media force, the web loggers or "bloggers," independent commentators who publish on websites, often several times a day. I used the archives of two influential web loggers, the conservative blogger Andrew Sullivan, then at www.andrewsullivan.com, and liberal blogger Joshua Micah Marshall at www.talkingpointsmemo.com. Print and broadcast media during the Lott panic frequently quoted both of them.

While restricting the sample of journalistic discourse to only three newspapers neglects some diversity, Jamieson and Campbell (1992:18–19) argue that newspapers like the *New York Times* and the *Washington Post* are more than merely representative of journalistic rhetoric and opinion. They are taken as standards by other media for what is newsworthy and for what range of opinion about the news is appropriate. Thus, while my material comes from only three newspapers, writers for these papers shape the national discourse, and their journalism reveals core values and ideologies that make sense to a sizable sector of the US population. Especially, these writers are the voice of the elites that are crucial in the reproduction of White racism in the United States in its current phase.

News reportage, opinion pieces, and editorials in newspapers, while they often have "authors," should not be taken to represent the views of these writers in any simple way. These texts are produced through a complex journalistic process, during which multiple writers and editors select from a range of preliminary texts and utterances from documents and from people who are judged to be appropriate "sources." They are shaped in a small social sphere, the newsrooms of the three major US newspapers. Importantly, the language of journalistic texts is governed by in-house style sheets that are closely guarded. However, it is known that these guidelines include policies against language thought to be inflammatory. For instance, word leaked to the press in 2004 that the *New York Times* style editors had decided that the word "genocide" could finally be used about the Turkish massacre of Armenians in 1901–02 (Bass 2004). The *Times'* public editor recently addressed the use of the word "liar," arguing that it "is a loaded word that presumes you know someone's intent" (note the invocation of personalist linguistic ideology), that would be problematic even in an editorial and "should never be used in a news story, except when quoting someone" (Hoyt 2007). Thus there is every reason to believe that words like "racist" and "racism," widely understood as offensive to their targets and threatening to the White elites who constitute the social world of the mainstream media, will appear, if they appear at all, only in quotes from sources. Finally, journalists depend heavily on the good will of senators and their staffs and are therefore cautious about giving insult. In summary, we cannot know what individual journalists or sources might have said about Trent Lott had they been recorded chatting privately with their friends or family. What we can see is the journalism that these newspapers produced, which is intended, in the final analysis, not merely to inform and to influence, but also to present a corporate image that will advance their interests as profit-seeking businesses.

Trent Lott's words invited the question: Was the Majority Leader of the United States Senate in 2002 a racist and a segregationist? This question was profoundly threatening to White elites in the United States, who tell themselves a story of racial progress. As a student leader in the early 1960s, Lott had opposed the integration of the University of Mississippi. Senator Thurmond had been one of the most notorious White supremacists and segregationists in the US government through the 1970s. In the narrative of racial progress, such people are said to have changed, to have become colorblind or even anti-racist. Much is made of their good works for impoverished minority communities, their contributions to college scholarships for African Americans, the people of color on their staffs both national and local. Thus, a great deal was at stake.

Within the folk theory of racism, to answer the terrible question, "Is Senator Lott a racist?", in the affirmative would require proof that he believed that people of color were biologically inferior to Whites. Thus media discourse during the Lott firestorm was about beliefs and motives. Superficially, this discourse satisfied the well-known journalistic ethic of balanced coverage, quoting sources with different points of view, and publishing columnists from right, left, and center. However, it was astonishingly homogeneous in its consistent attention to beliefs and motives rather than to the effects and impacts of speech. All sides drew on the presupposition that words reflect speaker beliefs and that meaning is the product of speaker intention. These personalist presuppositions permitted journalists to develop elaborate hypotheses about Lott's inner nature, his thoughts, beliefs, and motives.

## The folk psychology of personalism: Head and heart

Media discourse in the Lott firestorm made explicit the folk psychology that underlies the presuppositions of personalist and referentialist linguistic ideology. The folk psychological concepts of "head" and "heart" emerge in three propositions: (1) the meanings of a person's words are determined by intentions that reside in a stable core of belief and thought, the heart; (2) the meanings of a person's words are inherent in the words themselves and speakers can be assumed to choose words that reflect their beliefs; (3) certain circumstances interrupt this connection between belief and meaning and can produce talk that reflects only an unstable and error-prone animating psychological locus, the head. These include careless inattention to speech, but also "light talk" and joking.

The contradictions and loopholes provided by this folk psychology and by the linguistic-ideological terms of the debate around Lott's words permitted the extraordinary threat to the story of White American progress raised by his remarks to be explained away, and made it almost impossible for the media to label him as a racist. Lott was accused of a multitude of sins, but the word "racist" was attached to him directly only three times in the 150 pieces of journalism that I assembled: once by Andrew Sullivan on his web log of December 9, 2002, and twice by African American sources quoted by journalists. The word "racism" appears only 14 times.

As with many other terms in the language of the debate, the folk-psychological contrast between "head" and "heart" was introduced by Lott himself. In an apology for his remarks telephoned to Sean Hannity's show on the Fox television network on December 11, 2002, Lott said that he had made "a mistake of the head, not of the heart."[4] This language was repeated again and again. In (13a), the *Washington Post* columnist Philip Kennicott uses the language to attack Lott. In (13b) an African American source is quoted using it to support him.

(13)   a. "... On Sean Hannity's radio show, he made a classic distinction between thought and feeling: 'This was a mistake of the head, not of the heart,' he said. ... In a society that has abolished most forms of legal discrimination, that has made the N word more offensive than the F word or the S word, racism persists because people become adept at *not* saying what they really think when it will get them in trouble. In this sense, Lott's statement that this was a mistake of the head, not of the heart, sounds rather ominous: He seems to say that he didn't betray his heart at all – that he is at heart the same politician he was more than 20 years ago when he made very much the same remark about the Dixiecrats" (Kennicott 2002).
b. "I can't say, honestly, that no long-term damage has been done, which is unfortunate because I think this was a mistake of the head, not of the heart" (Hockstader and Dewar, 2002, quoting J. C. Watts, African American Republican Congressman from Oklahoma).

The term "heart" as a metaphor for the site of intention appeared very frequently, as seen in the following examples.

(14)   a. "One should be very hesitant about ascribing bigotry. It is hard to discern what someone feels in his heart of hearts" (Krauthammer 2002).
b. "'It is not like it is just a few things,' said David Bositis, senior political analyst at the Joint Center for Political and Economic Studies. 'What was most damaging about what he said is that Trent Lott came across as saying what was in his heart'" (Hulse 2002).
c. "Senator Mitch McConnell of Kentucky ... credited Mr. Lott with expressing 'heartfelt regret'" (Nagourney and Hulse 2002).

Alongside the "heart," where "heartfelt" beliefs reside, folk psychology also provides a second intentional locus, the "head." The head is a site of superficial views, associated with the moment-to-moment conduct of communication instead of deep and lasting beliefs. The "head" is invoked in proposals that the meaning of words has been disengaged from deep and consistent belief. Lott himself contributed not only the expression "a mistake of the head," but an elaboration in which he tried to capture the exact circumstances of such disengagement. He excused himself by claiming that he had been "winging it," speaking without careful preparation. This language was repeated again and again, as seen in (15).

(15)   a. "I take full responsibility for my remarks. I can't say it was prepared remarks. As a matter of fact, I was winging it" (Excerpts from News Conference Held by Senator Lott in Mississippi 2002).
b. "It was almost endearingly ingenuous of Trent Lott, the serial apologizer, to say in major apology No. 4 – the tone-deaf news conference-

cum-soliloquy in Pascagoula, Miss. – that his remarks at Strom Thurmond's 100th birthday party should be excused because he was 'winging it.' Meaning he was talking without a script when he said how sad it was that Thurmond lost to Harry Truman in the 1948 presidential election, thereby leading to the 'troubles,' aka the civil rights revolution. It is dangerous for Republicans to have a leader who not only cannot be trusted without a script but who is utterly unembarrassed about citing scriptlessness as an exculpation for any embarrassment he causes" (Will 2002).

Attempts to disengage the facial meaning of Lott's words from his beliefs employed a rich lexicon of expressions for superficial error, including "winging it," "mistake," "gaffe," "mis-speak," and the like. Another one of Lott's own characterizations, a "poor choice of words" (a nice expression of the intersection of personalist ideology noted in "choice" and of referentialist ideology presupposed in "poor . . . words"), was also taken up both by his defenders and by his opponents.

(16)  a. "'A poor choice of words conveyed to some that I had embraced the discarded policies of the past,' Mr. Lott said in a statement" (Kurtz 2002a).
b. "Some [members of the Black Caucus of the US House of Representatives] warned that Democrats would anger blacks if they dismissed Lott's remarks as a poor choice of words" (Edsall 2002b; quoting *USA Today*).
c. "And while few Republicans defended what Lott said, many questioned whether quitting his leadership position was too steep a price to pay for poorly chosen words for which he has since apologized" (Morin 2002).

The word "mistake" was used repeatedly by both Lott and others:

(17)  a. Lott speaking: "I accept the fact that I made a terrible mistake, used horrible words, caused hurt" (BET Interview with Sen. Trent Lott 2002).
b. "Sen. James M. Jeffords . . . said he believes Lott made a mistake and said something in a manner that doesn't reflect his true feelings" (Hockstader and Dewar 2002).

In summary, the folk psychology underlying media discourse about Lott's utterance holds that language that comes from the "heart" is the authentic voice of a person's intentional core, but when we hear the "head" we hear only superficial and fleeting expressions that can include "mis-speaking," "blundering," "mistakes," and "poorly chosen words."

Personalist linguistic ideology requires that to determine the true meaning of words, we must somehow have access to a speaker's "heart." An important contradiction emerged from this requirement, between referentialist linguistic ideology – that beliefs are revealed by the "plain meaning" of the words, which give a direct route to the heart – and personalist linguistic ideology with its focus on intention, which suggests that more evidence is required than simply "plain meaning" to assess a speaker's inner states. We have seen that many people assume that words derive an inherent meaning from some baptismal event that occurred in the distant past. Further, we have seen that these words are supposed to match a speaker's beliefs, which should be true. Another important component of referentialist ideology is the "conduit metaphor" (Reddy 1979). This is the idea that words carry information from the speaker to the hearer in an unproblematic way, without interruption, just like water passes through a conduit and emerges from the spout as the same water that entered at the source. The following examples show these elements of referentialist ideology.

> (18)   a. "That's what the guy believes. You can tell that from listening to his words" (Marshall 2002c).
>
> b. "It was not a 'poor choice of words,' as he later pleaded. It was a perfectly clear choice of words articulating a perfectly clear idea" (Krauthammer 2002).
>
> c. "Everyone deserves a break for a 'poor choice of words' but it wasn't the words that really offended. It was the plain meaning of the words. What other words would have sufficed?" (Kurtz 2002b, quoting Andrew Sullivan).

While the journalists quoted in (18) drew on referentialist ideologies to insist that Lott's words had a "plain meaning" that revealed his beliefs, others held that to accuse Lott of being a segregationist or a racist, more evidence than the plain meaning of his words was required. Some of these debaters appealed to Lott's "record" of beliefs and actions. The basic idea was that if Lott was found to have consistently made remarks like the ones at Senator Thurmond's birthday party, then those words might indeed reflect his beliefs. This idea involves an important linguistic ideological category, "word," seen in expressions like "to keep one's word" and "to be a man of his word." "Word" is the continuity of reference from utterance to utterance, and from utterance to deeds. Unchanging "word" is an important index of "character," the nature of a person's moral center (Hill 2000). From a racist character, we expect consistently racist words. For this reason, the discovery that Lott had used language almost identical to that of his birthday-party remark in December 2002 20 years earlier, when he introduced Senator Thurmond at a rally for Ronald Reagan in 1980, became an important weapon for Lott's opponents. However, a record of action, as well as speech, was also brought to bear on the question of Lott's character. Both supporters and opponents often explicitly invoked versions of the slogan "actions speak louder than words." Thus Lott's voting record and other dimensions of his public career were carefully examined. Evidence against him included his membership in groups devoted to uncritical celebration of the southern Confederate heritage and speeches before such groups, and his votes against honors for victims of White terrorism during the years of the Civil Rights movement. Evidence in his favor included his success in getting resources to African American communities in Mississippi and his record of hiring African American staff. Examples of appeals to "the record" are seen in (19):

(19)   a. "After a fiery speech by Mr. Thurmond at a campaign rally in Mississippi for Ronald Reagan in Nov. 1980, Mr. Lott, then a congressman, told a crowd in Jackson, 'You know, if we had elected this man 30 years ago, we wouldn't be in the mess were are in today.' Last week, in remarks he later characterized as spontaneous and a poor choice of words, Mr. Lott repeated his opinion about Mr. Thurmond . . .The fact that Mr. Lott uttered similar comments in 1980 threatened to intensify the controversy" (Hulse 2002).

   b. "This isn't the first piece of evidence that Lott is an unreconstructed racist. He has spoken before gussied–up white supremacist groups before" (Kurtz 2002a, quoting Andrew Sullivan).

   c. "I have looked at Trent Lott's record, and I don't see that vitriolic thing toward the blacks" (Rutenberg and Barringer 2002, quoting Bill O'Reilly, Fox Channel Talk Show host).

   d. " 'We have examined Senator Lott's record, and we are deeply disappointed to find that this is not an isolated incident but a longstanding pattern of behavior that can no longer be ignored.' Mr. Lott's office sought to defuse such criticism by distributing papers showing his support for black colleges, trade with Africa, and a resolution condemning a string of arson attacks on black churches" (Nagourney and Hulse 2002, quoting "Two leaders of the all-Democrat Congressional Black Caucus").

The power of the record as evidence of a stable core of belief and intention residing in the heart put Lott into a double bind. As his apologies grew more elaborate, he was attacked by both sides for not sticking to his principles. When he said in an interview on Black Entertainment Television that he supported affirmative action, a position in diametric opposition to two decades of Republican Party platforms, he was attacked by both sides for having no stable beliefs. The apparent shift in Lott's views was said to call into question whether Lott had a "heart" at all, or whether this folk-psychological zone, the site of consistency and character, was simply empty.

As seen in (20b and c), both Lott and his words shared this quality of being "hollow," an interesting iconic link between word and person.

> (20)   a. "It's hard to think of anyone more hollow than Lott . . . Trent Lott is now the archetypal Washington figure. He runs for office just to stay in office. He is now bailing frantically, throwing belief and principle overboard, just to stay where he is. He is the majority leader of the US Senate. That is who he is. That is the totality of his beliefs . . . What do you want him to say? He'll say it. I have turned from loathing Lott and what he stands for to pitying him for standing for nothing" (Cohen 2002c).
> b. "Mr. Lott made matters only worse by embarking on a last-ditch campaign full of abject apologies that rang hollow to most witnesses" (Mr. Lott Steps Down 2002 [editorial]).
> c. "All the evidence indicates that what Lott truly meant to say was nothing – nothing at all . . . Critics and alarmists have taken Lott's empty and meaningless words at a public event and injected them with substance they never had" (Rogers 2002).

## Light talk, public and private: What light talk reveals about speaker beliefs

A second line of evidence used to explore the link between Lott's words and his beliefs and intentions was the context for his remark. In the review of joking and parody above, we have seen that personalist ideology includes the possibility that some contexts permit disengagement between belief and the plain meaning of words. Journalism about Lott's remark consistently contrasted private "light talk" with public "serious talk." Public talk is thought to require a certain level of "seriousness," while private talk can be "light," of no relevance in the formation of opinion.

Light talk among intimates provides an opportunity for White Americans to indulge in explicit "race talk" (Eliasoph 1999; Myers 2005; Picca and Feagin 2007), including epithets and stereotypes. To the degree that a particular stretch of talk is keyed as "light," it is relatively opaque to criticism and censure as racist. This opacity derives from cultural models that associate style, person, and space in simplistic default configurations. Light talk and joking are prototypically private, associated with the spaces of intimacy, where interpersonal solidarity is more important than strict adherence to truth. Indeed, the assumption of a key of "lightness" actually constitutes intimacy, so to reject the content of such talk is to reject the intimacy itself, and thus to threaten important social ties (Eliasoph 1999). Light talk and joking are prototypically vernacular, so they are associated with private persons. While, as we saw in Chapter 3, evidence of "bias" is grounds for dismissing the views of a public speaker, bias and interest in private space are unproblematic. "In private," among intimates, a speaker need not claim neutrality or innocence, but may express her strongest and most authentic opinions. Thus to censure offensive talk in the light style/ private space/intimate relationship context is to attack, not interest, but character or judgment, a dangerous threat against the speaker (Hill 2001:92). This kind of intimate talk can, in fact, be used "in public." But such a usage constitutes a metaphorical code switch (Blom and Gumperz 1972) that layers a frame of privacy and intimacy into the interstices of a larger public context. This frame insulates the speaker from many kinds of challenges that might be made of public, serious talk.

This contrast between "public" and "private" appeared frequently in the discourse of the Lott debate. Many commentators argued that his remarks were prototypical "light talk" – in Lott's own words, "flattery to an old man on his birthday" – and that it was absurd to take them seriously or to seek in them some deeper meaning. Thurmond's birthday party was said to be a "trivial" event, not a moment in which serious policy talk was being uttered. In a sense, then, Lott's words were "private," in spite of the fact that this particular birthday party was televised live on C-SPAN and attended by the President of the United States. Lott's supporters argued that "light talk" can interrupt the connection between word and intention, so that people need not be "held responsible" for things said on "light-hearted" occasions. Lott himself asserted this point, as seen in the two quotations below:

(21) a. "It was a lighthearted affair . . . I was too much into the moment. . . . I was trying to make happy an incredible legendary human being . . . I was just into the event . . . Really, it was just an effort to help, to encourage an elderly gentleman to feel good on that occasion of his 100th birthday. So there were no venal thoughts in my mind" (Excerpts from News Conference Held by Senator Lott in Mississippi 2002).
b. "This was a lighthearted celebration of the 100th birthday of legendary Senator Strom Thurmond. My comments were not an endorsement of his positions of over 50 years ago, but of the man and his life" (Edsall 2002b).

After his remarks at the birthday party began to attract attention, Lott's office staff argued that the context of his utterance was more important than the apparent meaning of his words:

(22) "Spokesman Ron Bonjean issued a two-sentence statement: 'Senator Lott's remarks were intended to pay tribute to a remarkable man who led a remarkable life. To read anything more into these comments is wrong'" (Edsall 2002a).

Journalists who had initially failed to report Lott's remarks excused themselves by appealing to the context. Note the use of the first name "Strom" in the quote from *Washington Post* reporter Mark Leibovich in (23), which, if it is accurate, suggests that he felt that he had attended the birthday party as a friend of the ancient senator, rather than as a journalist.

(23)  "Baltimore Sun reporter Julie Hirschfeld Davis says there was so much 'tongue-in-cheek' talk at Thurmond's birthday party that a lot of us probably tuned out remarks that we might have been more careful listening to if it hadn't been such a jubilant atmosphere. Most people were writing this as a featury 100th-birthday bash. 'I wanted to use it but it seemed too parenthetical, given that the story was about Strom,' says Washington Post reporter Mark Leibovich. 'I feel badly about it in retrospect. I kick myself' " (Kurtz 2002c).

Lott's remarks were categorized as "light" by using trivializing verbs – "blurted," "burbled," "brayed" – to describe them. Such labels were insulting, but given the linguistic-ideological complex in which they were embedded, their result was to give Lott a free pass on the racist meaning of his words. And Lott's supporters explicitly used the idea of "light" speech to dismiss the significance of his remarks.

(24)  a. "I think it was a mistake. I don't think he was at all serious, and I don't even think we should dwell on it . . . I mean, this is the kind of thing that makes people infuriated with the media, is they pick up something that's said at a birthday party and turn it into a case of whether he should be impeached" (Kurtz 2002a, quoting Robert Novak).
b. "Some [Whites in Mississippi] seemed to resent Democrats, blacks and liberals for making a fuss over what many whites here regard as a trivial event – praising the 100-year-old Thurmond (R–S.C.) at his birthday" (Hockstader 2002).

The categorization of Lott's words as "light talk" did permit a contrary interpretation, derived from a folk psychology influenced – as noted by the commentator in (25c) – by the Freudian analysis of jokes and slips of the tongue. This interpretation holds that it is precisely in "slips" and "gaffes," moments of being "out of control," that the inner core of meaning, meaning "in the heart," "true belief," is most likely to be revealed. From this perspective, Lott's "cheerleader ebullience" was a quality that was likely to trip him up, and being "into the moment" loosened his tongue.

(25)  a. "Today, undone by the same sort of ebullience he once showed as a cheerleader at Ole Miss but unfortunately displayed again at a 100th-birthday party for Senator Strom Thurmond 15 days ago, he quit" (Clymer 2002).

    b. "Or was he just, in the excitement of the moment, blurting out his real views?" (Krugman 2002a).

    c. "It was a heady moment, he was overcome, there was a birthday cake and punch and he 'went too far' [quoting an apology by Lott]. The question, however, is what it means to go too far. Lott's efforts to explain and excuse the remarks implicitly acknowledge the thing that makes public gaffes so disturbing: the belief (see Freud) that we tell more of the truth when our tongue slips than when we say exactly what we intend to say" (Kennicott 2002).

In summary, some commentators thought that the "lighthearted" context excused Lott's remarks, and others held that the context had loosened Lott's tongue and revealed him as a racist. While these are very different positions, they agree in being personalist, in insisting on the central importance of intention, emanating from some inner site of motivation, as a shaper of meaning.

Yet another invocation of the public–private dichotomy occasionally appeared. Several texts, like Joshua Micah Marshall's cited in (26), suggested that "public figures" like Lott should be held to higher standards of responsibility.

(26)    "Trent Lott may not believe in civil rights for blacks. It's a disaster for the country if he doesn't. But if he doesn't, it's still important – given who he is – that he *say* he does, that he genuflect publicly to the idea. It's important for him to say something like this if for no other reason than to underscore the fact that anyone who doesn't support racial equality – even in this most general sense – is politically beyond the pale" (Marshall, 2002b).

## Does Personalist Linguistic Ideology Insulate Speakers from Accusations of Racism?

The discourse published during the Trent Lott firestorm reveals that elite journalists, regardless of whether they are part of the "mainstream media" or the "blogosphere," all adhere to the premises of referentialism, baptismal ideology, and the conduit metaphor: Meaning inheres in the "plain meaning" of words. But this position about plain meaning is complicated by personalism, by the folk psychology that holds that talk can emanate from either of two possible sites of intentionality: the "heart," the site of true feelings and continuity of authentic belief, and the "head," where mistakes and poor choices of words are produced. Talk can be further divided into light, private talk and serious, public talk. Light talk and private talk are, on the one hand, thought to release speakers from the constraints of truth and sincerity in order to permit flattery and the joys of intimacy that Lott called "getting carried away." On the other hand, some commentators endorsed folk Freudianism: light talk, since it is not carefully considered, may be especially revealing, providing a context where discreditable beliefs can slip out.

This intention-saturated personalist ideology of language made it difficult for commentators to make an accusation of racism, even in a case as plain as the shocking remarks by Senator Lott. In the folk theory, racism is a form of belief. Beliefs reside in the stable core of the self, in the "heart" of folk psychology, and it is broadly agreed that it is hard to know what is in another person's heart. Furthermore, if words are so tightly linked to their intentional sources, in criticizing words the critic is criticizing a person, indeed, the moral core of that person. Such a criticism threatens not only Lott, but all those who have voted for him, praised him, excused him, kow-towed to him, and permitted him to occupy one of the nation's highest offices for many years, and who will share Lott's stigma if he is found to be a racist. Thus to advance such a criticism requires the strongest kind of evidence for his intentions. This, in addition to the policy of avoiding inflammatory language apparently specified in the style guides of newspapers like the *New York Times*, may be the reason for the astonishing fact that these thousands of words of text, quoting many people, contained only three instances where Lott was directly labeled a "racist." In every other case the word "racist" was only indirectly linked to Lott in expressions like "I doubt that Senator Lott is a racist."

Personalist ideology helps speakers avoid the label "racist" or "bigot" by providing a rich and diverse lexicon for motives. Instead of being accused of being a "racist," Lott was accused of "blindness," "tone-deafness," "cluelessness," "insensitivity," "not getting it," "stupidity." While these were taken seriously, they were consistently distinguished from "racism." In order to give a sense of how strongly Lott's attackers preferred these labels, I give in (27) a large number of examples, including passages from many of the best-known op-ed writers and reporters in the national press, as well as quotes from ordinary citizens that reporters chose to use to illustrate popular reactions to Lott's remarks.

(27)  a. "Was he also ignorant of the aims of the 1948 Thurmond campaign? . . . Mr. Lott declared himself ignorant of the group's aims" (Krugman 2002a).

b. "The majority leader of the senate may not be a racist, but he is remarkably incapable of appreciating what it was like to walk in those shoes" [referring to an anecdote about an African American man who wasn't allowed to try shoes on] (Cohen 2002a).

c. "This is about getting wrong the most important political phenomenon in the past half-century of American history: the civil rights movement. Getting wrong its importance is not an issue of political correctness. It is evidence of a historical blindness that is utterly disqualifying for national office. . . . What is so appalling about Lott's remarks is not the bigotry but the blindness. One should be very hesitant about ascribing bigotry. It is hard to discern what someone feels in his heart of hearts. It is less hard to discern what someone sees, particularly if he tells you. Lott sees the civil rights movement and 'all these problems over all these years.' He missed the whole story" (Krauthammer 2002).

d. "This doesn't mean the senator from Mississippi harbors secret segregationist desires. But it does suggest that he doesn't quite get the self-inflicted damage here" (Kurtz 2002b).

e. "The trouble with Lott is that he combines the worst part of some Democrats . . . with the worst part of some Republicans – racial obtuseness in this case, to the brink of outright bigotry" (Kurtz 2002b, quoting Andrew Sullivan).

f. "The birthday party controversy is only the latest evidence that Mr. Lott . . . has never figured any of this out, or come to grips with the bad old days in his state" (Fire Trent Lott 2002 [editorial]).

g. "When you read that Lott said the same thing about Thurmond in 1980, it's like he's thinking that what worked well in Mississippi in 1980 will work for a national audience. It's like he's got a complete blind spot" (Applebome 2002, quoting Merle Black, Emory University professor).

h. "Obviously, I had a blind spot" (Excerpts from News Conference Held by Senator Lott in Mississippi 2002).

i. "the clueless majority leader himself" (Rich 2002).

j. "Senator Chuck Hagel, a Nebraska Republican, called Mr. Lott's remarks a 'dumb statement' . . . 'It raises questions about his judgment'" (Nagourney and Hulse 2002).

k. "Trent Lott doesn't deserve the death penalty for what he said . . . It was foolish to the extreme, but it's an occupational hazard we have" (Bumiller and Hulse 2002, quoting Senator Arlen Spector, R-Pennsylvania).

l. "Lott apologized for saying something stupid and putting people in a box like this" (Milbank and VandeHei 2002).

m. "How can Trent count the votes in the Senate if he can't count the C-Span cameras in a room? The man's dumber than concrete" (Dowd 2002).

n. "What he said was stupid, and it was racist" (Hockstader 2002, quoting an unnamed African American man, Pascagoula, Mississippi. This is one of the three direct uses of "racist" in the data).

Some commentators chose to condemn Lott for misplaced "nostalgia," as evidenced by his admiration of Confederate President Jefferson Davis (who spent much of his life in Mississippi), his enthusiasm for the Confederate battle flag, and the like. They distinguished "nostalgia" from "racism," as can be seen in (28):

(28)    a. "And it's clear from the man's long history of hobnobbing with neo-conservative wing-nuts and general nostalgia for the pre-civil-rights era South. . . . You don't have to believe that the guy's an out and out racist, but it's very hard not to conclude that he sees the old Jim Crow days as the good ol' days" (Marshall 2002c).
    b. "But if it's impossible to believe that Lott is a racist . . . Lott is intellectually stunted by a pernicious and – if the Senate had any sense – politically lethal case of Margaret Mitchell Syndrome" [Margaret Mitchell is the author of *Gone With the Wind*, a novel that celebrates the pre-Civil War South] (Cohen 2002a).
    c. "'He waxes nostalgic from time to time without meaning anything racist,' Wiseman said of Lott" (Edsall and Fears 2002, quoting Marty Wiseman, Director of Mississippi State University's Stennis Institute).

Even where commentators recognized that such "nostalgia" is racist, they resisted an explicit label. The lines in (30a) are a very good example of using the word "racist" without directly labeling Lott:

(30)    a. "Right now we're debating whether the Republican Senate majority leader is a racist who yearns for the days of segregation or just a good ole boy who *says* a lot of things that make it *seem* like he's a racist who yearns for the days of segregation" (Krugman 2002b, quoting Josh Marshall).
    b. "He cannot apologize for being who he is, for seeing in the cratered face of the ancient Thurmond the vaunted Lost Cause instead of a racist, which is the same thing. He heard 'Dixie.' He should have heard Billie Holiday's 'Strange Fruit'" (Cohen 2002b).

## Performative ideology: Did Lott's words wound?

The linguistic ideology of performativity played a very small role in the Lott debate. While Lott himself had apologized for "wounding . . . hurting many Americans who feel so deeply in this area," this received almost no uptake. Journalism in the elite newspapers in my sample gave very little attention to the intensely hurtful impact that Lott's words must have had on African Americans. Thus the elite media discourse around Lott's remark is a good example of Feagin's (2006) "social alexithymia," inattention to the feelings of people of color. Not surprisingly, it was mainly African American journalists and sources who reported deeply visceral reactions to

Lott's statement. A rare piece of reportage that sought out Black Republicans reported them using language like "slapped in the face," "like a rifle going off," or "jolted." One source said that the experience of hearing Lott's language "was like being cut with a chainsaw" (Clemetson 2002). Civil rights veteran John Lewis told *Washington Post* reporter Thomas Edsall that he had been "stunned" on hearing of the remarks (Edsall 2002a). Donna Britt, an African American columnist for the *Washington Post*, wrote a thoughtful account of her own pain:

(31)    "Despite the 'shock' certain black folks profess to feel when racism arises, the fact is we are seldom deeply surprised. Yes, we feel the jolt – that initial, head-jerking, 'huh?' that hits every human being when what we see as divine order slides out of whack . . . our reaction is . . . utter disbelief. Then, black folks get over it. Because we expect racism. Most of us are ready, waiting and, on some level, prepared for its appearance – which doesn't make it hurt less" (Britt 2002).

White hearers of Lott's remarks wanted to believe that they, too, had been viscerally shocked. Thomas B. Edsall (2002a) of the *Washington Post* reported that Lott's remark at Thurmond's birthday party had been greeted by "an audible gasp and general silence." I have listened to the C-SPAN broadcast, and I heard no such reaction from the almost entirely White audience. Another *Washington Post* reporter, Amy Argetsinger (2002), reported the reaction to Lott's remark to have been a "stony silence" that caused Lott to "lose his groove." Again, I did not hear this silence, or see any break in Lott's performance.

Most of the attention within the general framework of the ideology of performativity preferred to avoid any mention of who might have been hurt by Lott's remarks. They were very frequently called "insensitive" or "divisive," without specifying who might have been divided from whom, or whose sensitivities had been assaulted. The *New York Times* special feature coverage ran for two weeks under the heading "DIVISIVE WORDS."

(32)    a. "racially divisive comments at a birthday celebration" (Allen and VandeHei 2002).
        b. "These findings underscore the divisiveness of Lott's remarks" (Morin 2002).
        c. "After making what were construed as racially divisive remarks" (Hulse with Bumiller 2002).

Lott himself repeatedly called his language "insensitive" without saying exactly how this was the case, and this term was taken up by others:

(33)   a. "You can, you know, say it was innocent, but it was insensitive at the very least and repugnant, frankly" (BET Interview with Sen. Trent Lott 2002, quoting Trent Lott).
b. "the [Republican] party has shown its clear resolve to have zero-tolerance for insensitivity to these racial isses" (Purdom 2002, quoting Florida Republican Party Chairman Al Cardenas).

## Conclusion: The Function of the Label "Gaffe" in White Racism

The Trent Lott firestorm illustrates the usefulness of the "gaffe" label for the project of White racism. Once the label is applied, the intricate personalist discourse of motives illustrated here takes over as a form of common sense, and makes serious critical discussion of White racism extremely difficult. Since racism is located "in the heart," it is difficult to detect. Furthermore, this location makes racism exclusively a property of individual persons, their beliefs and their motives. A vague "insensitivity" or "divisiveness" is distinguished from "racism." These texts make clear that Whites can be stupid, insensitive, clueless, divisive, hurtful, and nostalgic for Jim Crow and a society based on African American slave labor, and still not be "racist." This situation is slowly changing. However, the discourse we can observe in the Trent Lott panic shows one reason change is so slow. Everyday commonsense understandings of the relationship between language, persons, and actions make it very easy to avoid seeing racists even when they have been transparently exposed.

Ironically, at the very same time that the excesses of personalist discourse documented here deny the continuity, forms, and functions of White racism, they vividly reinscribe and reinforce its terms. The ideas of segregation, of the stigma of color, of the forms and contours of race were repeated again and again in the debate over Lott's words, in a discourse of great detail and intensity that occupied every level of the US media and, if my own experience is any guide, many private conversations, for weeks.

As I finish this chapter, the great Trent Lott firestorm is five years behind us. And it appears to have been almost completely forgotten. The revelation that a public figure as highly placed as Lott was patently a racist and a segregationist did not fit into the White American narrative of racial progress. It lay outside what Foucault called the "regime of truth." During the weeks of moral panic, many commentators suggested that Lott's words provided a golden opportunity for Democratic politicians to attack the Republican Party with one of the most insulting labels that White Americans have for one another: racist. But leaders of the Democratic Party have not exploited his words. Lott himself remains a powerful figure in Washington. Even today, with a Democratic legislative majority, Lott is often quoted as a significant source by journalists on a wide range of issues. The *New York Times* continues to use the most oblique possible language about Lott; in a recent article reporter Carl Hulse recalled the remark as "what some saw as a racially charged comment" (Hulse 2007). There are many reasons why Lott's "gaffe" has been buried. But, I would argue, linguistic ideologies shaped the rhetorical trajectories that made this interment possible. Even well-meaning people who were horrified by Lott's remarks wrote within the broad framework of personalist/referentialist linguistic ideologies, locating Trent Lott as a respectable person who had merely "slipped."

The Lott firestorm also worked metaculturally to reinscribe personalist discourse as normal and natural. Indeed, the metacultural functions, the reinscription of personalism and the reproduction of crucial ideas about race and racism, may be vital functions of these moral panics. They surely have made little impact on beliefs or behavior. Their structure and language are highly ritualized and repetitive, and do not seem to evolve from one incident to the next. The discourse around Fuzzy Zoeller's racist insult against Tiger Woods in 1997, the discourse around Trent Lott's endorsement of segregation in 2002, that around George Allen's use of racist epithets in August 2006, around Michael Richard's cry of "Nigger! Nigger! Nigger!" in November 2006, and around Don Imus's repulsive racist and sexist epithets in the Spring of 2007 are all very similar. And they have passed by, headlines and all, without making any impact on the nearly universal belief among White Americans that their racism is a part of history, irrelevant to our present. After all, these are "gaffes," "slips," "mistakes." Personalist discourse provides no critical purchase on where they might be coming from.

It might be useful to think of incidents of racism as providing an opportunity to defend personalism, rather than thinking of personalism as an ideological framework within which to evade charges of racism. Personalism may be linked in its own right to some of the most important interests of our era. Anthropologist Webb Keane (2002), who was able to observe changes in linguistic ideologies during the late phases of the monetization of a traditional economy on the island of Sumba in Indonesia, has pointed out that personalism is profoundly connected to contemporary economic orders. Our understandings of human beings as individuals defined by "freedoms" within which the motives on which personalism is centered develop, are closely linked to our understanding of the openness of the entire world to being valued in monetary terms, where prices are set in a negotiation among individual desires and rationalities. The idea that items can be assigned prices is closely related to the idea that words can be assigned meanings (in fact, baptismal ideology, which credits such assignments to some authority, works in both contexts). And of course the right and capacity of individuals to transact in markets are among the central "freedoms" that we recognize. That is, personalism is part of a broader "representational economy." Yet personalism, as Keane (2002) has suggested, is in constant crisis. This crisis occurs not merely because the personalist requirement that words, belief, and reality should match is routinely flouted at every level of private and public life. The crisis emanates as well from the fundamental nature of linguistic signs as conventional and public. I mentioned in Chapter 3 the work of Butler (1997), who followed Derrida (1988) in observing that speech is by its very nature repeatable for any purpose, and thus is intrinsically detachable from any autonomous, individual site of belief or commitment. Bakhtin (1981) convincingly argues that no level of private commitment permits speakers to fully purge their words of the traces of history and the voices of others. Personalism and referentialism require defense from such heresies, which might undermine the representational economy in which meanings and markets are connected.

The ongoing crisis of personalism requires that those who live most fully within the representational economy which it anchors – which includes such dimensions of contemporary thought as the possibility of rational choice, the possibility of authentic belief, and the possibility of valid assertions about the value of money (Keane 2002, 2007)[5] – must find occasions to defend and reinscribe it. The persons who benefit most from this system have been, for several hundred years, White elites. Accusations of racism against sports heroes or major politicians provide occasions for them to reassert the forms of common sense that are most valuable to them. These public figures exemplify the personalist ideal, seeming to possess agency and freedom of the highest and most complete type. Thus, any challenge to their control of the truth, or to the validity of their beliefs, or to the sincerity of their intentions, invites the probing of all of these major dimensions of personalism. The constant core of the inner self, the coherent propositional, affective, and intentional states of that self, and the degree to which meanings emanating from these match the world, can become natural once again as they are backgrounded as "mere" presuppositions in debates over charges of racism and the categorization of racist utterances as "gaffes." These debates show clearly the complex intertwining of White racism with other large-scale structures of White culture and history.

# Chapter 5

# Covert Racist Discourse: Metaphors, Mocking, and the Racialization of Historically Spanish-Speaking Populations in the United States

## Introduction: What is Covert Racist Discourse?

Slurs and gaffes are salient forms of racist talk for White Americans, rendered visible within widely shared linguistic ideologies and the ways that these intersect with the folk theory of racism. Critical approaches to White racism invite us to look for other racist discourses that are invisible to these ideologies and to the folk theory. And indeed, we can find them. I illustrate these "covert racist discourses" with a way of speaking that Whites do not understand as racist, but which works to reproduce negative stereotypes of people of color, in this case, members of historically Spanish-speaking populations in the United States. I call this covert racist discourse Mock Spanish (Hill 1993a, b, 1998, 2001, 2005b).

By "covert" and "invisible" I mean "for Whites." Latinos/as have indeed noticed Mock Spanish and related forms of Spanish used by Whites, and objected to them. I discuss examples of such objections here, drawn from published material, from personal communications from colleagues, and from interviews. However, Whites, who are usually quite guarded about public race talk (Bonilla-Silva 2003), use Mock Spanish without any of the usual hedges. Consider an example of a Mock Spanish utterance:

(1)   Does CIM Stand For "Consider It Mañana"? (Strassman 1992).

The sentence in (1) was the title of a lecture on "Corporate Information Management" presented at the Department of Defense on September 22,

1992. It seems very unlikely that the speaker would have hedged the title with the expression, "I'm not a racist, but I'm going to talk about whether CIM stands for 'Consider it mañana'." This frame, "I'm not a racist, but . . . ," discussed by van Dijk (1993), provides a good test for whether an utterance is covert racist discourse or not. If the frame works, the utterance is visibly racist in the ways shown in Chapters 3 and 4. If it does not work, but analysis can show that racist meanings must be conveyed by the phrase, we have encountered covert racist discourse. In this case, much evidence shows that the choice of "mañana" to lighten up the title in (1), make it a bit of a joke, requires that those who "get" the joke have access to a stereotype of speakers of Spanish as lazy procrastinators (Hill 2005b).

Another kind of evidence that this language is covert and invisible as racist is the absence of public reaction. The Mock Spanish tag line "Hasta la vista, baby" was made famous by Arnold Schwarzenegger in the 1992 film *Terminator II: Judgment Day*. In the film the utterance is not a sincere farewell, since Schwarzenegger says it as he blows his enemy into a million pieces with an enormous automatic weapon. The phrase is so catchy for Whites that Schwarzenegger has used it repeatedly in his own campaigns and when campaigning for other Republican candidates, and it has been borrowed by Democratic candidates as a reliable applause line. But the pleasure of the phrase requires access to a negative stereotype of Spanish speakers as treacherous and insincere, the kind of people who would tell you politely "Until we meet again" and in the next instant blow you away. But in the dozens of times I have heard the phrase, I have never heard anybody frame it with "I'm not a racist, but . . ."

## The Spanish Language in the United States

Since Mock Spanish is directed against Spanish speakers, to understand it in context we must briefly review their history in the United States. A community of speakers of Isleño Spanish (originating primarily in the Canary Islands) became citizens when their lands were incorporated by the Louisiana Purchase in 1803. The language is still spoken in southern Louisiana, although it is moribund (Campbell and Muntzel 1989; LeStrade 2002). Statehood for Florida and Texas in 1845 brought more Spanish speakers into the union. After 1848, with the conquest of the enormous Mexican territories that make up the southwestern United States and California, Spanish became the nation's most important language after English. Article IX of the Treaty of Guadalupe Hidalgo guaranteed Mexican citizens of the conquered territories full rights in the United States, in the language seen in (2).

(2)   "The Mexicans who, in the territories aforesaid, shall not preserve the character of citizens of the Mexican Republic, conformably with what is stipulated in the preceding article, shall be incorporated into the Union of the United States, and be admitted at the proper time (to be judged of by the Congress of the United States) to the enjoyment of all the rights of citizens of the United States, according to the principles of the Constitution; and in the mean time, shall be maintained and protected in the free enjoyment of their liberty and property, and secured in the free exercise of their religion without restriction."

Unfortunately, these guarantees proved to be largely meaningless, since until the post-Civil War Reconstruction amendments to the US Constitution, American citizenship was restricted to "Free White Persons." Indians were not permitted to become citizens until 1924. Many Mexicans in the new territories were thought (correctly) to have "Indian blood." Menchaca (1993) has documented the legal struggles undertaken by this population. Menchaca (1995) and Sheridan (1986, 2006) review the theft of their land, water, stock, and other forms of capital and labor opportunities over 150 years, leading to the marginalization of Mexican American populations into the nearly caste-like status that can be observed in much of the region today.

In addition to the old populations, today immigration from all over the Spanish-speaking world has contributed an enormous diversity of Spanish-language ways of speaking and Spanish-heritage communities to the American scene. Unfortunately, this diversity is seldom recognized by Whites, who understand populations of Spanish-language heritage within the homogenizing framework that Zentella (1995) has called "chiquita-fication." Thus populations originating in countries as diverse as the Dominican Republic, Guatemala, and Colombia are assimilated to the system of White stereotypes originally developed around Mexican Americans.

The same racism that permitted Mexican Americans to be stripped of material resources also marginalized the Spanish language, as Spanish was either ignored or actively proscribed. Although after 1924 Mexican Americans were all citizens, the bilingual public health and safety announcements, voter informational materials, and ballots required by law today did not appear until the late 1960s and early 1970s, and court interpretation remains a hit-or-miss affair. First-language Spanish was forbidden in public schools, with students suffering draconian punishment for speaking it. Against enormous odds, some Spanish-language mass media including newspapers, radio, and theater survived, but the language was for many years quite absent from public space, which was defined as White and English-speaking. The same racist attitudes that led Mexican Americans to be evaluated as backward, superstitious, treacherous, and dirty were reflected in evaluations of their language, assigned a place as illiterate and ungrammatical "border Spanish" which was thought to hold its speakers back from the benefits of the full modernity that could be obtained through English.

### The Official English movement

Pressure against Spanish never really ceased, and during the last two decades it has again intensified. Organizations like US English, ProEnglish, and English First have funded dozens of state-level initiatives as well as campaigns for federal legislation to make English the "official" language of government. Employers, often supported by the courts, have tried to create English-monolingual workplaces.[1] Public schools are retreating to English-only policies in many districts, with opportunities for publicly funded bilingual education now sharply restricted in California and Arizona and threatened in several other states. The right of students to speak their home language even in the halls and on the playground is under attack in some districts (Reid 2005; Crawford 1992a, 1992b, 2000, 2004 reviews the Official English movement and the fight against bilingual education).

While labels like "English First" suggest a concern for the well-being of the English language, those who advance official-English policies cannot rationally be worried about the status of the language. English is unquestionably the most important international language today. And indeed the organizations most actively involved in advancing the officialization of English and restrictions on the use of other languages give minimal attention to efforts such as funding innovations in English-language instruction, prizes for English-language works of literature, or institutes that will encourage the study of English and English-speaking culture in other countries. Instead, it seems clear that their motives are merely exclusionary. However, their efforts have framed the debate over language politics in the United States. Those who wish to defend US Spanish both as a national resource for all Americans and as a heritage for historically Spanish-speaking communities are constantly forced to expend their energies in struggle within this framework.

Beyond the political promotion of "official" English, explicit attacks on Spanish are part of everyday practices among Americans of English-language heritage across a wide front. In the previous sentence, I wrote "Americans of English-language heritage" rather than "White Americans," my usage in previous chapters, because African Americans have often joined in attacks on Spanish and its speakers. They vote heavily in favor of Official English legislation, and the limited materials to which I have access suggest that African American elites, like middle-class Whites, are heavy users of Mock Spanish. I have not included attention to African American attitudes here, because my data are very limited. But many African Americans may share with Whites negative attitudes about Spanish.

Informal pressure against Spanish is a ubiquitous fact of American life. For instance, at a website that offers a wide range of paraphernalia expressing right-wing political views, one can purchase for $15.00 an antiimmigrant t-shirt that says "OK, you snuck in. Speak English." To get a sense of the company one might keep wearing such an item, another shirt in the site's small inventory bears an image of a Confederate battle flag with the slogan "Ban illegal immigration, not Southern heritage."[2]

Objections to the public use of Spanish extend even to details of orthography and pronunciation. Sociologist José Cobas, a faculty member at Arizona State University, reports a long struggle, still unsuccessful, to make the university's bureaucracy place the acute accent over the "é" in his given name in official correspondence and documents (José Cobas, personal communication, July 15, 2004). The journalist Aly Colón reports that he resorted to inserting an accent mark by hand on his byline so that his surname would not read like a body part (Wides-Múñoz 2006).[3] Pronunciations are also hotly contested, with Whites often insisting on "hyperanglicized" versions of Spanish personal and place names. Peñalosa (1981) early identified this practice as emanating from White racism. LouisorWhite and Valencia Tanno (1994) documented the struggles of Spanishheritage newsreaders on Los Angeles television stations to be permitted to pronounce their own names in Spanish. While such pronunciations are now quite common, they remain marked and objectionable for many Whites. I have been present when Whites have ridiculed, with exaggerated "r"-rolling and other parodic strategies, the pronunciations that two Latina television newsreaders in Tucson, Lupita Murillo and Barbara Grijalva, use for their names. The choice of /tuk′son/ vs. /′tuwsan/ for the city's name is politically charged, with Whites insisting on the latter pronunciation even though it leads to inevitable misspellings (we all regularly get mail addressed to "Tuscon"). Our airport code is TUS, a not-unexpected victory for the Anglo pronunciation.[4]

The rejection of Spanish as a language that is valid in public space is evident as well in gross grammatical errors in public notices of all types. Peñalosa (1981) noted signs posted over the sink in public restrooms that read "Wash your hands/Lave sus manos" (Spanish *Lavarse las manos*, or perhaps *Lávese las manos*). Peñalosa commented that it was astonishing to see three grammatical errors in three words, but exactly the sign that he critiqued is still easy to find nearly 30 years after his observation. An astonishing example of ungrammatical public Spanish greets drivers entering the United States from the Mexican side of the border at the Mariposa Crossing between Nogales, Sonora, and Nogales, Arizona. As they reach the inspection area, they encounter a huge sign reading "All vehicles must stop/Todos vehiculos deben pararse." The Spanish translation is grossly ungrammatical and unidiomatic, as well as misspelled, and especially entertaining to many speakers of local Spanish who argue that *pararse* means "to stand up," not "to stop," which for them is simply *parar*. Humorous examples abound: A school in California sent out a reminder letter to parents who had been asked to sign what in English is called a "permission slip." The reminder message called this item "Un resbalón parental de permission." The word *resbalón* does not mean "slip" in the sense of "permission slip," but refers instead to skidding, sliding, or, most humorously, a moral lapse. Thus *un resbalón parental* can mean something like "a parental sexual misstep."[5] All of these examples come from parts of the country where literate Spanish speakers could have easily been asked to proofread them. The signal that is sent (and received by Spanish speakers) is that their language is not taken seriously enough to require consultation with them.

Many Whites object to bilingual health and safety postings in any context. Predictably, they are objects of parody. In the 1980 comedy film *Airplane*, as the catastrophe begins, warning lights come on over the seats, with the "bilingual" message seen in (3).[6]

(3)    "No smoking
       El no a you smoko
       Fasten seatbelts
       Putana da seatbeltz"

Informal pressure against Spanish in the United States includes a ritualized linguistic routine: On overhearing someone speaking a foreign language, one aggressively confronts them and insists "This is America! We speak English here!" (Urciuoli 1996). In April 1998 I heard this line when I had to change planes in the Dallas-Ft. Worth Airport. The terminals in the airport were connected by an automatic tramway, and each exit was announced in both English and Spanish over a public address system. On my tram that day were a dozen teenagers chaperoned by two well-dressed adult couples. When the first announcement in Spanish came on, one of the men said loudly and indignantly, "This is America! We speak English here!" Of course Dallas-Ft. Worth is an important international airport, with a huge amount of traffic in and out of Latin America. Apparently, this gentleman would have preferred to have foreign visitors miss their flights than to have Spanish on the airport's public address system.[7]

A shocking instance of this routine occurred on my own campus. On March 3, 2006, Mauricio Farah G., of the Human Rights Commission of Mexico, was an invited speaker at a colloquium of the Latin American Studies Program at the University of Arizona. While the organizers of the colloquia apparently assumed that people specializing in Latin American

Studies will understand Spanish, university functions are open to the general public. Mr. Farah reported his experience as follows:

(4)  "Empecé agradeciendo, en español, la invitación que me permitía estar allí.
     Los gritos seguían: 'This is America!'"
     [I began in Spanish with thanks for the invitation that had permitted me to be present. The outcry followed: "This is America!"]

Mr. Farah was shouted down by several members of Border Guardians, a small anti-immigration group headquartered in Tucson. They proudly report this bit of activism on their website (Border Guardians' Victories! 2006). Mr. Farah received an apology from the President of the University of Arizona, and spoke again in March 2007; on that occasion, the Center for Latin American Studies provided a translator (which could easily have been done during the previous year, had the Border Guardians requested one rather than shouting down the speaker).[8]

A staple of anti-Spanish rhetoric is that hearing Spanish makes "Americans" feel like aliens in their own country. A clichéd expression of this feeling is objection to the message on many automatic telephone answering systems, "Press 'One' for English." A Google search on this sentence on August 8, 2007, produced an astonishing 438,000,000 hits! An amateur recording in a country-music style of a song with this title was a YouTube hit during the Summer of 2007, when the US Congress was considering an immigration bill that, in the view of its opponents, granted "amnesty" to "criminals." Objection to "Press 'One' for English" is now a hardy perennial of right-wing talk-radio ranting.

A moral panic was precipitated in the Spring of 2007 by the release of a recording of a Spanish-language arrangement of "The Star-Spangled Banner," the US national anthem, under the title "Nuestro Himno." Recorded by a number of leading Latino and Latina recording artists, this was an exceptionally beautiful arrangement, both musically and in the poetry of its language. However, it was greeted with passionate opposition. Even President Bush, who has boasted of his ability to speak Spanish, observed that

(5)  "I think the national anthem ought to be sung in English, and I think people who want to be a citizen of this country ought to learn English and they ought to learn to sing the national anthem in English" (Bush: Anthem Should Be Sung in English 2006).

Some observers of the panic pointed out that "The Star-Spangled Banner" has been translated into many immigrant and Native American languages.

President Bush himself had sung the anthem in Spanish, backed by a "Viva Bush" mariachi band from his home state of Texas, when campaigning in Mexican American communities (Candidate Bush Would Sing the Star-Spangled Banner in Spanish at Hispanic Festivals 2006).

Even a single word in public Spanish can trigger an indignant reaction. In a game against the New York Yankees on May 5, 2006, the Texas Rangers celebrated the Cinco de Mayo holiday with uniforms that read "Los Rangers." This use of *los*, the masculine plural definite article, falls entirely within the overlapping ranges of Booster Regionalist Anglo Spanish (linking Texas to a romantic Hispanic heritage) and Mock Spanish appropriations of Spanish morphology. But when the right-wing commentator Michelle Malkin posted a picture of the uniform with the offending Spanish definite article, correspondents on her blog were outraged:

> (6)  "I understand the Rangers wanted to do something innocuous to recognize a holiday celebrating historical and cultural pride. But the politically correct selectivity here is telling. While it's considered a celebration of 'diversity' to acknowledge the military sacrifices of another nation's heroes, it's considered racist to acknowledge the military sacrifices of one's own. Case in point: Can you imagine if someone proposed changing the Rangers' jerseys to 'Confederate Rangers' to celebrate Confederate Heroes' Day? Oh, and I'm sure I'll be labeled a racist for pointing out the double standard."[9]

In summary, formal and informal pressure to exclude Spanish from public space in the United States is intense and takes many forms. As Urciuoli (1996) has pointed out, Whites are comfortable with the language only in contexts like ethnic festivals and Mexican-themed restaurants. At the same time, however, Whites use a great deal of Spanish in the registers of Regionalist Anglo Spanish and Mock Spanish reviewed below. This simultaneous suppression and appropriation suggests strongly that what is at stake is White privilege, their right to control the symbolic resources of Spanish and shape these to their own purposes.

Even the fiercest advocates of Official English and the proscription of Spanish deny that they have a racist agenda.[10] They argue that they are patriots, insisting on English and objecting to Spanish because national unity requires a single language, and because they want immigrants to learn English so that they can enjoy the full measure of success that America offers (Woolard 1989). However, once we start looking for it, obvious racist language targeting members of historically Spanish-speaking populations[11] is easy to find. Santa Ana (1999, 2002) showed that the language of journalism in the *Los Angeles Times*, a newspaper considered to have a centrist or moderately liberal editorial perspective, is demonstrably organized within a culture of White supremacy. Texts about immigration in the newspaper in Santa Ana's large sample were replete with very negative metaphors, the most frequent being IMMIGRANTS ARE ANIMALS.[12] After I read Santa Ana's work, I started watching for these racist metaphors, and found that they were astonishingly frequent. Two recent examples were uttered by politicians addressing national audiences. On October 18, 2005, the Secretary of Homeland Security, Michael Chertoff, made the statement in (7):

(7)　"We are moving to end the old '**catch–and–release**' style of border enforcement, increasing removals by tens of thousands a year" (Mann 2005).

Chertoff refers to a technique in recreational fishing, where a fisherman takes the fish off the hook and throws it back in the water, and uses this to criticize a practice whereby immigration agents would arrest undocumented immigrants and, if they were not wanted for any crime, release them with a ticket requiring them to appear for a deportation hearing at a later date.

In a second case, Senator John McCain of Arizona, a candidate for the Republican nomination for the presidency in 2008, was twitting an opponent. Mitt Romney of Massachusetts, a well-groomed suburban businessman and former governor, had attempted to project an image as a "man's man" by insisting that in his youth he had "hunted small varmints . . . rodents and rabbits." Romney had employed a landscaping firm to care for his yard that used undocumented Guatemalan immigrant workers, giving McCain an opening to attack him by producing an especially ugly image of Guatemalans as proliferating "rodents and rabbits."

(8)　"Maybe he [Romney] can get out his **small-varmint gun** and drive those Guatemalans off his yard" (Roston 2007).

Santa Ana follows Lakoff (Lakoff 1987; Lakoff and Johnson 1980), arguing that IMMIGRANTS ARE ANIMALS is a constitutive metaphor "that reproduces a view, with all the entailments, and most importantly the political and social consequences to disparage human beings. Its dominant use thus sustains the racist world view" (Santa Ana 1999:217). To say that a metaphor is "constitutive" means that it creates our understanding rather than merely elaborating it. The abstract frame IMMIGRANTS ARE ANIMALS is productive, permitting speakers to draw on their entire experience of animals, as prey, as domestic, as food, as fighting animals, as sexual creatures, in order to create fresh utterances.

Constitutive metaphors of this type seem to be invisible. Santa Ana points out that the various usages derived from IMMIGRANTS ARE ANIMALS are prosaic; they do not stand out, but reinforce the "conceptual linkage" between IMMIGRANTS and ANIMALS at a level below conscious awareness. Santa Ana (1999:217) observes of the *Los Angeles Times* that

> Rather than explicitly legitimating racist practices and power relationships, in these political contexts the newspaper merely reflects the embodied basic values of the American political order that subjugates immigrants to other citizens.

That is, these metaphors have remained invisible because they reflect the foundational role of racism in White American worlds. They are visible only to people who are outside that system, or who are victims of it, and to careful scholars like Santa Ana. Thus these metaphors, like Mock Spanish, exemplify covert racist discourse (and they do not appear in the frame "I'm not a racist, but. . . ."). But, unlike Mock Spanish, once noticed these metaphors are visibly repulsive and clearly racist, filling the same semantic role that "squaw" occupied from the seventeenth century to suggest that Indian women were closer to does and mares than to women. Santa Ana's work strongly supports the central claim of the critical theory of White racism, that racism is built into the very foundations of White American culture, shaping unreflecting thought, speech, and behavior among those who share it.

## Mock Spanish: Covert Racist Discourse and Indexicality

"Mock Spanish" (Hill 1998, 2005b) is a set of tactics that speakers of American English use to appropriate symbolic resources from Spanish. In Mock Spanish, Spanish loan words like *macho* "male," *cerveza* "beer," and *mañana* "morning, tomorrow," expressions like *hasta la vista* "until we meet again," and even a few morphological elements such as the Spanish definite article *el* and the masculine singular suffix -*o* are assigned new pronunciations, new meanings, and new kinds of cultural value (Agha 2003) in American (and even international) English.

Mock Spanish works to create a particular kind of "American" identity, a desirable colloquial persona that is informal and easy going, with an all-important sense of humor and a hint – not too much, but just the right non-threatening amount – of cosmopolitanism, acquaintance with another language and culture. At the same time that Mock Spanish helps to constitute this identity, it assigns Spanish and its speakers to a zone of foreignness and disorder, richly fleshed out with denigrating stereotypes.

Like the IMMIGRANTS ARE ANIMALS metaphor, Mock Spanish has passed unrecognized as racist among Whites. I suspect that its function in White racism remains covert partly because it works by indexicality, a semiotic process that is not highlighted in White American linguistic ideology. This chapter will show how this indexicality works. First, though, I locate Mock Spanish within a wider range of appropriations of Spanish-language resources into American English.

## Mock Spanish in context: Forms of Anglo Spanish

Spanish-language loan words appear in English by the late sixteenth and early seventeenth centuries. Early examples include "peon," from *peón* "peasant," and "grandee," from *grande*, a title of nobility – and, of course, "race," from *raza*. Throughout the history of this borrowing, loan words of Spanish origin have been especially susceptible to odd phonological developments and to pejorating semantic change. "Grandee" illustrates both of these. The usual patterns of anglicization should yield /grænd/ or /ˈgrændiy/ (illustrated, for instance, in the anglicizations of the toponym "Rio Grande"), but "grandee" is hyper-foreignized, with unusual stress on the last syllable, a treatment that is also common for Spanish surnames like "Pérez," pronounced /pəRˈɛz/. It is also slightly pejorative; to call someone a "grandee" is usually not a compliment (and of course "peon," although it exhibits normal phonological anglicization, is negative in Spanish but an insult in English).

The American English pronunciations of Spanish-origin place names are of special interest. These are often "hyperanglicized," suggesting that speakers are at pains to avoid anyone thinking that they might be speaking Spanish. A good example of hyperanglicization is the treatment of Spanish-origin stressed 'a' as /æ/. Place names with Spanish *San* "saint, holy" are almost invariably realized as [sæn], even though first-language English permits [an] as in "mañana," or [hwan] from Spanish "Juan." An example noticed by Peñalosa (1981) is [ˈsæn ˈpiydrow] "San Pedro" (California) instead of [ˈsan ˈpeydrow], which would be a normal anglicization. The more important the place name, the more likely it is to be hyperanglicized. Two interesting cases where White pronunciations are hyperanglicized are "Tucson" and "Los Angeles." In English the first is pronounced /ˈtuwsan/, where Spanish is /tukˈson/. English /ˈlas ˈændžələs/ "Los Angeles" is of interest because the pronunciation /las/ for "Los" is almost invariant in this place name, where other California and southwestern place names often exhibit /lows/. Place names can be subjected to further modifications, as in clipped "San Antone" from "San Antonio" (Texas), or clipped and boldly mispronounced "San Berdoo" from "San Bernardino" (California), or merely boldly mispronounced as in /Rə'fəRiyow/, the official pronunciation of the city of Refugio (Texas).

Several varieties of American "Anglo Spanish" can be identified (Hill 1993a; "Anglo" is the term used in the US Southwest for English speakers). "Cowboy Anglo Spanish" is the nineteenth-century source of words like "adobe," "lariat," "corral," "mustang," and "buckaroo," along with many other loan words associated with the technology and culture of open-range cattle herding and its associated landscapes ("mesa," "arroyo"). Cowboy Anglo Spanish overlaps with Mock Spanish and contributed several items to its vocabulary (Hill 1993a). Cowboy Anglo Spanish is notable for the phonological strangeness of many of its lexical items. "Buckaroo," from *vaquero* "cowboy," like "grandee," exhibits hyper-foreignization (see Cassidy 1978 and Wentworth 1942 for discussion of this item). "Dalleywelters," a technique of roping stock where one end of the lasso is looped around the saddle horn (from Spanish *¡Dále vuelta!* "Give it a turn"), is a case of "hyperanglicization," where the pronunciation seems to be exaggeratedly distant from the Spanish source. The lexicon of Cowboy Anglo Spanish suggests that those who borrowed these words into English did not speak Spanish well. For instance, "lariat," from Spanish *la reata*, treats the definite article and the noun as a single word, which is a symptom of very restricted language contact. Cowboy Anglo Spanish does not attest to a golden era of bilingualism in the Old West. Instead, it provides evidence that those who spoke it were working hard to distance themselves from the Spanish language and members of its heritage community.

While a few Cowboy Anglo Spanish items persist in specialized vocabularies in some parts of the United States, it has largely passed out of use in its core areas (Sawyer 1959, 1975). It survives mainly in frozen forms that are periodically reinforced by use in films, such as "tough hombre," and in words that were recycled into Regionalist Anglo Spanish and Mock Spanish.

"Regionalist Anglo Spanish" has at least two varieties. The most obvious is "Booster Regionalist Anglo Spanish," which appears especially in California and the Southwest. It shows up by the 1880s as these regions began to market themselves to tourists and potential residents by drawing on the presence of Spanish-speaking and Indian heritage communities to create new regional images (e.g. Gutiérrez 1989; Thomas 1991). The recruitment of these symbolic resources, which seems so natural today (although not to everyone, as we shall see), was by no means a foregone conclusion. Indians and Spanish speakers were throughout these regions the victims of ferocious discrimination, and these symbols were often adopted only reluctantly by White boosters. Wilson (1997) has described Santa Fe, New Mexico, as a "reluctant tourist town" where the Anglo business leaders would have preferred to market the city as modern and up-and-coming. However, when they realized that wealthy easterners came to Santa Fe in search of spiritual inspiration from Indians, they began to promote the "Pueblo" architecture which has for many years been required for all construction in the city. Until late in the twentieth century the New Mexico Spanish-speaking community felt quite left out of the Santa Fe tourist boom, and to this day may be more threatened than benefited by it (Rodríguez 1987). But "Spanishness" along with Indianness is important in marketing Santa Fe and New Mexico. The public linguistic landscape of Santa Fe is so Spanish that local tourist and real estate marketing materials often include glossaries to aid newcomers (Hill 1993a). In Tucson real estate developers embraced Spanish nomenclature only in the 1960s, with the curious result that the older parts of the city, which have the highest percentage of Spanish-heritage residents, have streets with English names (or numbers), while the new developments on the edges of the city, which are heavily White, have Spanish street names and subdivision names. Villott (2000) found in Tucson an almost perfect correlation between average household income by US Census tracts and the ratio of Spanish to English street names: the wealthier the neighborhood, the more Spanish street names it has.

Booster Regionalist Anglo Spanish, like public Spanish informational signage, is inattentive to standard Spanish grammar and orthography. For instance, I have encountered "Buenas dias" (Spanish *Buenos días*) on a breakfast placemat at a Mexican-themed restaurant in Las Cruces, New Mexico. A recent October produced a newspaper advertisement from a Tucson jewelry store, announcing a sale celebrating "La dia de muerte" (Spanish *El día de los muertos*).[13] Ungrammatical street names and subdivision names in Tucson led to protests from local Spanish speakers, and for the last 15 years or so all such names have had to be cleared for Spanish grammar and spelling by an officer of Pima County.

A sub-variety of Regionalist Anglo Spanish is the use by individuals of a few Spanish items to signal a regional identity as an "old timer" in the Southwest. I believe this to be largely a masculine practice. It includes sincere, as opposed to mocking, uses of Spanish greetings and other expressions. An example appeared in an e-mail that I recently received from a White male colleague. The e-mail, which was a sincere expression of thanks for a favor, bore the subject heading *Mil Gracias*. Such usages are surely appropriations (see Chapter 6), but they suggest positive images of Spanish speakers as warm and courteous, in contrast to the Mock Spanish usages of the same items that I will discuss below.

Spanish words are often recruited to lend apparent authenticity to journalistic reports on Spanish-heritage populations, often without any attention to Spanish grammar, and these also overlap with Mock Spanish. For instance, a *New York Times Magazine* article on the influence of Latinos on US Catholicism was entitled "Nuevo Catholics," assimilating the Spanish word to English grammar by leaving out number agreement (Rieff 2006). An article in *Time* magazine on Mexican politicians campaigning among immigrants in the US was entitled "Don't stop thinking about mañana," a play on the words of the famous Fleetwood Mac song, "Don't stop thinking about tomorrow," which President Clinton had used as campaign theme music (Katel 2001). This usage crossed the line into Mock Spanish in a recent article in the *Washington Post* travel section for Sunday, December 3, 2006 (Lyke 2006) under the Mock Spanish headline "No crowds? No rush? In Mexico, no problemo." The article included phrases like "gorgeous pescado" and "mongrel perro." None of these "Spanish" words challenged monolingual speakers of English, since they are all familiar from Mock Spanish or transparent in context. But they invite English-speaking readers to think of themselves as worldly and cosmopolitan.

As we might expect from the previous discussion, even in regions where Booster Regionalist Anglo Spanish is very common, we encounter objections from English speakers to Spanish in this function. But opposition to Booster Regionalist Anglo Spanish and related usages does not come from a recognition of its grammatical errors or objection to it as appropriation or theft. Instead, complainants find it un–American and alienating, reflecting, not a claim by Anglos on Spanish-language symbolic resources in order to legitimize their regionalist *bona fides*, but politically correct catering to immigrants. I have already discussed the case of the "Los" on the uniform shirts of the Texas Rangers at their Cinco de Mayo ball game. Another example occurred recently in Tucson, when the *Arizona Daily Star* decided to rename their Sunday travel section with a classic bit of Booster Regionalism, ¡Vamos!, complete with double exclamation points. On March 4, 2007, the paper kicked off the new name with the following remarks from the Reader Advocate:

(9)   "Today's Accent section has a new name – ¡Vamos! – that nicely fits its new mission to give readers a sense of what it's like to live here. ¡Vamos!, pronounced VA-mos, is Spanish for 'let's go,' 'Come along with us.' It's the *Star*'s way of saying, 'Come, let us show you . . . ,' Features Editor Maria Parham said. . . . I'm eager to hear your thoughts on ¡Vamos!. In the meantime, let's go" (Kornmiller 2007a).

Only two weeks later, the Reader Advocate had to confess that "Those who called to criticize the section all focused not on the content or its organization but on the name – ¡Vamos!" (Kornmiller 2007b). Among the comments reported were those in (10):

(10)   "A terrible, terrible decision to use a Spanish name for a general interest section. What in the world were you people thinking?" As one (online) commenter put it: "What's next? 'Tacos' for the food section?" (Kornmiller 2007b).

The Reader Advocate was pushed into a very unusual explicit (albeit partial) statement of the functions of Booster Regionalist Anglo Spanish, in (11):

(11)   "The *Star* mixes languages every day, just as many Southern Arizonans do . . . Editors saw ¡Vamos! as an extension of a line that is already blurred, and blurred mostly by English speakers for their own purposes, which is to give what they're doing a sense of place. That was the editors' goal with ¡Vamos!" (Kornmiller 2007b).

## A brief history of Mock Spanish

The oldest token I have identified of an item that is today Mock Spanish is "peon," pronounced ['pijan], first attested in 1634, according to the Oxford English Dictionary.[14] In the United States Mock Spanish appears early. A jail could be called "calaboose," a bold mispronunciation of Spanish *calabozo*, by 1792 (DARE I:508).[15] "Adios" appears as a hostile dismissal by 1837 (DARE I:13). "Vamos" as a command meaning "Get out of here!" (usually "vamoose") appears by 1900 (Parker 1902, cited in Bagley 2002:67; Parker reports the utterance from an incident in southern Utah in 1857). But the full flowering of Mock Spanish is not evident until the middle of the twentieth century. Gray et al. (1949) report a rich array of Mock Spanish forms among English-speaking students at the University of Arizona. These include bold mispronunciations in salutations such as "hasty lumbago" and "buena snowshoes." Raymond Chandler's mystery novel *The Long Goodbye* (1953) attests an example from the same period. No Mock Spanish appears in Chandler's earlier books, but in *The Long Goodbye* an evil doctor threatens to beat up Chandler's detective Philip Marlowe. As Marlowe beats a retreat, "Dr. Vukanich" says, "Hasta luego, amigo. Don't forget my 10 bucks. Pay the nurse" (Chandler 1981[1953]:131).

Coinciding with the rise of the Official English movement, Mock Spanish exploded in the 1980s and 1990s in every type of media, from major Hollywood film and television productions to minor sites of mass reproduction such as t-shirts, greeting cards, and dog dishes (Hill 1993a, b). Mock

Spanish from this period until today has become an important resource for American English speakers. It lends colloquial flair to every level of usage, from everyday talk to dialogue in films and television shows to political oratory at the highest level. It is a staple of humor in films, and especially in television cartoons aimed at children.[16] Also during this period, probably influenced by Hollywood films and American television, Mock Spanish spreads around the English-speaking world; I have identified examples from Scotland, Ireland, England, and Australia. Mock Spanish appears everywhere in the United States; I have collected anecdotes from every region, and Breidenbach (2006) assembled a rich collection of tokens from English speakers in South Carolina from about 2000.[17]

## Tactics of appropriation in Mock Spanish

Mock Spanish borrows Spanish-language words and suffixes, assimilates their pronunciation to English (often in a hyperanglicized or boldly mispronounced form), changes their meaning, usually to make them humorous or pejorative, and uses them to signal that the moment of English-language speech or text thus embellished is colloquial and informal. Mock Spanish can accompany lexicon located at the extremes of vulgarity, but it can also lend a tone of American authenticity, of being a "real person," to speech in quite formal contexts.

The core vocabulary of Mock Spanish is probably no larger than 100 words.[18] Occasionally new forms enter from popular culture. For example, in the early 1990s Camel cigarettes were advertised on billboards in Latino-dominant neighborhoods with a picture of the character Joe Camel and the caption *Un tipo suave*, "a cool guy." A tip jar bearing the handwritten label "El tip-o suave" turned up on the counter of Bentley's Coffee House, near the University of Arizona. Ricky Martin's 1999 hit song "Livin' la vida loca" contributed this expression, as in a recent *New York Times* article on undergraduate drunkenness which reported that campuses are addressing "la vida loca with in loco parentis" (Freedman 2007). However, very few such new expressions have appeared during the nearly two decades that I have studied Mock Spanish; most of its vocabulary is attested from the 1950s or even earlier. Mock Spanish is used primarily by monolingual speakers of English, who are not able to draw freely on Spanish vocabulary for useful new words.

Four major tactics reshape Spanish loans into Mock Spanish. In semantic pejoration, Spanish words of neutral or even positive meaning are moved down into a semantic space that ranges from the merely jocular to the deeply negative and insulting. In this space expressions of leave-taking, like "Adios" and "Hasta la vista," become insults and threats. Mock Spanish

**Figure 2**    Semantic pejoration in Mock Spanish.

"Adios" is especially rich. It can be used to constitute a claim of an authentic "old-timer" identity and a stance of southwestern warmth. But insulting usages are very common. For example, an *Arizona Daily Star* column published February 1, 1993, reflected the attitude of the community that it had been betrayed:

(12)  "When Alaska Airlines said adios to Tucson yesterday, it pointed to the tough problem of keeping Southern Arizona connected to the nation's hard-pressed air travel system" (Ducote 1993).

The word appeared in the meaning "Goodbye and good riddance" in the astonishing context of an advertisement for a training course for human resources professionals:

(13)  "Sexual Harassment Training in Spanish – Adios to Lawsuits."[19]

A bus-bench advertisement for a Tucson pest-control firm, seen in Figure 2, declared "Adios, cucaracha" to passers-by in a fancy upscale Anglo neighborhood; "Cucaracha" is also part of Mock Spanish vocabulary.

A *New York Post* editorial for December 21, 2006, observed that New York State comptroller Alan Hevesi was about to plead guilty to a felony under the headline "Adios, Alan."[20] In my collection is a nationally marketed Hallmark greeting card in the "Shoebox" line (on recycled paper) that bears a little figure in serape and sombrero saying "Adiós" (complete with accent mark). Inside, the card reads

> (14)    "That's Spanish for sure, go ahead and leave your friends, the only people who really care about you, the ones who would loan you their last thin dime, give you the shirts off their backs, sure, just take off!"

Spanish-language terms of address and titles are useful as insults. These include "amigo," "Señor," "Señorita," and "Compadre." Another widely used product of semantic pejoration is "nada," which in Spanish means, simply, "nothing," but in Mock Spanish means "absolutely nothing, less than nothing." The Sony Corporation during 2007 ran an advertisement in upscale publications (I saw it in the *New Yorker*) showing a well-dressed businessman wearing his expensive headphones in a crowded and noisy airport waiting area over the legend YADDA YADDA NADA, meaning that absolutely no unwanted sound will penetrate the headphones. Spanish words for money like "dinero" or "pesos" imply that the items thus priced are bargains. An especially rich play on this usage of "pesos" appeared on a Taco Bell cup acquired by José Cobas's teenaged son:

> (15)    "One Grand Prize Winner will win a Million Pesos (That's $93,000 amigo) And become El Presidente of Taco Bell! Thousands will WIN INSTANTLY! Cash Prizes from 100–10,000 pesos ($9 to $939)!" (José Cobas, personal communication, May 22, 2006).

Another example attests to the internationalism of Mock Spanish as well as its presence in elite contexts. An offer of a cut-rate subscription to the upscale British literary magazine *Granta* came in an envelope that bore the invitation "Carpe dinero!" Other famous pejorated items include "macho," which in Spanish includes the simple meaning "male" and need not imply masculine excess. Again, the *New York Times* provides an example, from an editorial criticizing the state of American politics:

> (16)    "Republican presidential candidates are still playing *¿Quien es mas macho?* [sic] Mitt Romney and Rudolph Giuliani are in their cardboard tough-guy armor, bickering about 'sanctuary cities' and who used to treat his immigrant constituents more harshly" (Is it Fixed Yet? 2007 [editorial]).

"Mañana," which in Spanish means "morning" or "tomorrow" and need not connote procrastination or laziness, conveys only this pejorated sense

**Figure 3**   Euphemism in Mock Spanish.

in Mock Spanish (Hill 2005b). All Spanish words that appear in Mock Spanish are targets for semantic pejoration. They need not necessarily be insults, but they cannot be in any way formal or serious.[21]

Rodríguez González (1995) confirms Mock Spanish semantic pejoration. For instance, he points out that the Spanish suffix -*ista* in English, in contrast to -ist, nearly always conveys a negative stance. Hence, "Peronist," a neutral usage, compared to "Peronista," a negative label. Recent examples include "Clintonista," a not-very-thoughtful ally of former President Clinton, or "fashionista," a slavish follower of fashion.

The second tactic for constructing Mock Spanish is euphemism. Spanish words that are insulting, lewd, or scatological in Spanish are substituted for vulgar English words. "Loco" for "crazy" dates from 1887 (DARE III:396). Scatology is illustrated in the use of the Spanish nursery word "caca" as a euphemism for English "shit." A coffee cup in my collection, shown in Figure 3, was purchased at a nice gift shop near the University of Arizona several years ago. It bears the inscription "Caca de toro," and might be used on a desk in a place of employment where English "Bullshit" would be unacceptable.

**Figure 4**    Borrowed Spanish morphology in Mock Spanish.

For several years a bumper sticker reading "Caca pasa" (for English "Shit happens") was ubiquitous in Tucson. A usage that is especially offensive to Spanish speakers is "cojones" (pronounced /kə'howniyz/), and sometimes spelled as "cajones" (Spanish for "boxes"; Spanish speakers find this hilarious). Speaking in 1996 as US Ambassador to the United Nations, former Secretary of State Madeleine Albright used the word in an address to the Security Council, arguing that a Cuban pilot who had shot down a spy plane from Florida had shown "not cojones, but cowardice" (Gibbs 1996). *The Economist*, the upscale British weekly magazine addressed to the international Anglophone business community, once featured on its cover an image of US President George W. Bush with an arrow pointing to his crotch bearing the legend "No cojones on Palestine and Israel" (*The Economist*, April 3–9, 2004).

The third tactic for constructing Mock Spanish is to add Spanish morphology, especially the definite article "el" and the suffix "-o" (although other suffixes, such as "-ista," noted above, occasionally appear), to English words. The most common example is "No problemo," from English "No problem." The Spanish word is *problema*. Figure 4 shows this usage in a beer advertisement: Corona beer is "The Drinko for Cinco."

A second example of "-o" suffixation is "mucho," as in "Sell mucho book-os," overheard in the University of Arizona bookstore. "Mucho" (pronounced /ˈmuwtšow/), accessible because it is clearly related to English "much," is the only adverb available in Mock Spanish; Spanish *muy* almost never appears. For instance, Spanish grammar absolutely requires *muy macho*, not Mock Spanish "mucho macho" as in (17).

(17)  "The yacht used to be called 'Bouy Toy,' so named by its former owners, a gay couple, according to sources at the Capitol Yacht Club. Apparently, the fellas down at the marina kind of razzed ol' Duke, a former 'top gun' fighter pilot, about the gay-themed name. And apparently, Cunningham couldn't take it. He changed the boat's name from the sweet-and-saucy Bouy Toy to the **mucho macho** Duke-Stir in December 2004, according to Coast Guard records" (Marshall 2005).

"Mucho macho" appears to be a fixed expression; it is attested as well in (18), from a *New York Times* film review headline:

(18)  "For Fun, a Mucho Macho Black Hero" (Kerr 2002, reviewing *Undercover Brother*).

A recent addition to the universe of "-o" suffixed Mock Spanish items is the website www.eurocheapo.com, using the association between Spanish and cheapness to market a site that helps the user find travel bargains in Europe.

The use of "el" is illustrated in the name of a screensaver from the early 1990s, an electronic aquarium called "El Fish." This was a pun on "Electronic Fish," but it worked nicely since something called "el fish," within the semantically pejorated universe of Mock Spanish, is something less than a real fish. "El" and "-o" are often found together, forming locutions like "el cheapo" and "el foldo," as in (19), from a blog commentary on the Iraq war.

(19)  "So the generals have done the big el-foldo [*sic*] and are signing on to the McCain escalation plan."[22]

The "el . . . -o" frame can be used for any reference that the speaker or writer wishes to locate within a jocular colloquial register, and suffixation with "-o" can proliferate through an utterance or text, as in this example from the personal ad section of the student newspaper at the University of California at San Diego:

(20)  "Don Thomas! Watcho your backo! You just mighto wake uppo con knee cappo obliterato. Arriba!"[23]

The frame "numero X-o" is especially productive. "Numero Uno" is of course common, but constructions like "numero Two-o" and "numero Eleven-o" also appear.[24]

The last major tactic for Mock Spanish is hyperanglicization and the closely related tactic of bold mispronunciation. All Mock Spanish tokens are anglicized; one cannot speak Mock Spanish except in a broad American English accent. Some phonological adaptations in Mock Spanish represent merely normal anglicization to the English sound system. For instance, anglicized Spanish "d," as in "San Diego" or "adobe," is a stop /d/ or a flap /D/, not a spirant /ð/, and is alveolar, not dental. Vowels change their qualities to fit the English canon. Thus Spanish "e" in final position, as in "adobe," becomes /iy/ rather than /ey/, since English does not have /ey/ in unstressed word-final position in native vocabulary. Under stress, it remains /ey/, as in [how'zey] "José" – a pronunciation which provides the Mock Spanish fixed expression "No way, José."

However, many Mock Spanish words – and some important words that are not really Mock Spanish, such as place names of Spanish origin – are not merely anglicized, they are hyperanglicized or boldly mispronounced. In normal anglicization, Spanish-origin stressed "a" is approximated with English /a/ (as in "father"), as in Mock Spanish words such as "caca," "mañana," and "Hasta la vista, baby." However, in hyperanglicization we encounter /æ/, as in the joke "Grassy-Ass" for "Gracias" (diversely realized in images on humorous greeting cards; see Figure 5), or /bæn'diyDow/ (where /D/ is an alveolar flap) "bandit."

Bold mispronunciation, a subclass of hyperanglicization, is quite old; for instance the pronunciation of Spanish "o" as Mock Spanish /uw/ rather than /ow/ is attested in "calaboose" and in Cowboy Spanish items like "vamoose" from *vamos* and "buckaroo" from *vaquero*. Today this tactic yields bilingual puns like "Fleas Navidad," which shows up every year on humorous Christmas cards with pictures of dogs, and that hardy perennial "Moo-cho" with a picture of a cow. The opposite treatment is "Much Grass" from "Muchas gracias." A whole set of jocular leave-takings formed with "hasty" as a bold mispronunciation of "hasta" uses this technique: "hasty lumbago," "hasty banana," etc.

A specialized development of bold mispronunciation is parodic imitation of a Spanish accent in English. Such parodies were a staple of comedy routines in the 1940s and 1950s. Today, however, they are more visible as racist than are other forms of Mock Spanish. They have more in common with the intentional mockery that Ronkin and Karn (1999) labeled "Mock Ebonics" and Chun (2004) called "Mock Asian" than does Mock Spanish, which does not explicitly make fun of Spanish. However, examples of parodic imitation can be found. The example in (19) is reproduced exactly (although in black and white instead of color) from the "South of the

**MUCHO GRASSY ASS**

**Figure 5** Hyperanglicization and bold mispronunciation in Mock Spanish. The hair appears as green in the original.

Border" website, advertising a tourist trap on the state line between North Carolina and South Carolina:

(21) "BUENS DIAS, AMIGO! pedro VER' GLAD YOU COME!! pedro got 112 meelion amigos, who stay weeth heem, opp teel now all satisfy come back, send frans . . . thees make pedro ver' HAPPEE . . . like for frans come back all time . . . pedro hope YOU make 112 meelion and wan happee amigos! you come back soon, too, yes?"[25]

This example, which appears with a stereotyped image of "Pedro" wearing white pajamas, a striped serape, and an enormous sombrero, would probably be judged to be racist by many Whites as well as by Latinos. However, other examples are less obvious. In (22) we see a brief passage written in support of a congressional candidate by a left-wing blogger who calls himself "¡El Gato Negro!."

(22) "Some of joo may remember Coleen Rowley as one of the only peeples een the FBI who was focused on the future 9–11 highjackers. She weel breeng much needed security experience to her new job as Congresswoman. But eef joo theenk that she ees a one-issue candidate, I invite joo to go to her website and read her position on unplanned pregnancy,

she could teach the 'abortion ees icky' crowd a theeng or two. *Amigos*, thees *tres señoras* need jour help een retaking the Congress for *las Democratistas*, and stopping the steenky, corrupt Republi*culo* agenda right een eets' tracks ¡*Vamanos!*" (¡El Gato Negro! 2006).

¡El Gato Negro! is probably from a Spanish-speaking community (although not necessarily a fluent speaker of the language). I suspect this because of the bilingual pun "Republiculo," combining "Republican" with *culo* "ass," which is much more sophisticated than most Mock Spanish coinages. So this case may exemplify what Chun (2004) called "legitimate mockery," mockery by speakers licensed as insiders. Another case of this type is the controversial nationally syndicated column "Ask a Mexican." The author, Gustavo Arellano, uses a rich vocabulary of Spanish and English vulgarisms. I read these as attempts at reappropriation (see discussion in Chapter 2). However, such efforts risk being read as self-hatred (Navarro 2007).

## Indexicality and the Multiple Functions of Mock Spanish

Mock Spanish has multiple functions. It constructs a light, jocular, humorous stance. "Stance" (Ochs 1996) is a term used today in sociolinguistics for the speaker's positioning or alignment, both affective and "epistemic" (that is, in reference to the truth or likelihood of an assertion) in regard to her utterance. Mock Spanish also constitutes an identity, signaling that the speaker possesses a desirable colloquial persona that is peculiarly "American." At the same time, Mock Spanish locates "Spanish" – as a language – as marginal, disorderly and "un-American." It covertly reproduces negative stereotypes of the Spanish language and Spanish-language-heritage populations. Finally, it asserts control over the symbolic resources of Spanish, which it reshapes in the interests of Whiteness. These functions are accomplished almost entirely by the semiotic process known as "indexicality."

Indexicality is one of the three major relationships between the sign and its object – what the sign stands for – that were distinguished by the nineteenth-century American philosopher C. S. Peirce (Parmentier 1994). The others are the "iconic" and "symbolic" relationships. An indexical sign or index is grounded in its object – that is, connected to it and recognized as a sign for it – by proximity, contiguity, or necessity. Examples of Peircean indexes are a weathervane, which indexes the direction of the wind, smoke, which indexes fire, or symptoms such as hives or fever, which index physiological disorder or illness. Iconic signs are grounded in their objects by resemblance; for instance, a map resembles the territory for which it stands.

Symbols are grounded by convention: the word "cat" is a sign referring to the animal because the English-speaking community is committed to this denotative value for the sound sequence /kæt/ and the orthographic sequence "cat."

Peirce's idea of indexicality was adapted in linguistics by Jakobson (e.g. 1971) and his student Silverstein (e.g. 1976, 1979) in order to investigate words like "this, that," "here, there," "yesterday, today, tomorrow," the pronouns "I" and "you," and tense markers. Jakobson called such words "shifters," because they change their meaning depending on the context in which they are uttered. For instance, to assign reference to temporal expressions like "now" or "yesterday," or tense markers like "will," we must know when the utterance in which they were used occurred. If I say on September 16, 2007, that "Yesterday I went to a nice party," we know that the party took place on September 15, 2007. Similarly, to assign reference to "this," "that," "here," "there," we must know where the utterance occurred. To assign reference to "I" or "you," we must know who was speaking, and to whom. Thus, in Peircean theory, these words are "indexical," ineluctably linked to their contexts.

Silverstein (1976) distinguished these "referential indexicals" from "social indexicals." A particular language, or a particular class or regional dialect of a language, can function as a social indexical that signals an identity as "speaker of X" or "person from Y." Where there is language conflict, as between English and Spanish in the United States, the social indexicality of language choice may be very complex. For instance, the city of "Tucson" is exactly the same place whether it is called /tuk'son/ or /'tuwsan/, but in saying /tuk'son/ the speaker signals her Chicana identity, a commitment to her right to speak this word in Spanish, and her primordial claim to the place and its resources.

Silverstein (1976, 1979) points out that social indexicals are "creative": they produce or entail their context, rather than being determined by it. The identity indexed by /tuk'son/ – "politically conscious Chicano/a asserting the public validity of Spanish pronunciation and primordial claim to place" – is not an element in nature that can be assigned a "referential index." Instead, it is precisely projected by the speaker saying /tuk'son/: upon this pronunciation, the context of situation includes that dimension of identity, that political stance. In contrast, the pronunciation /'tuwsan/ indexes several possible stances and identities, such as, "I am not a Spanish speaker," or "I am a member of a Spanish-heritage community, but I am no radical, so I am not going to make trouble by asserting my linguistic heritage in a contested pronunciation of this place name." In yet another option, the local Spanish slang name for Tucson is *La Tusa*. To use this name indexes yet another identity, as a *barrio*-oriented *cholo*. For instance, a Tucson low-rider club bears this name. Since this name is largely unknown to the English-speaking community, it functions primarily to signal an identity as an insider among others who would also use the name.[26]

Silverstein (1979) observed that social-indexical functions can become the objects of "metapragmatic awareness," where speakers develop views on appropriate usage and can discuss these. However, usages can have some functions that are accessible to metapragmatic awareness, but others that are not. Users of Mock Spanish exhibit this kind of split in metapragmatic awareness. Most English speakers are aware in a general way of the positive functions of Mock Spanish in enhancing White identities, but oblivious to its negative functions of denigration, marginalization, and racist stereotyping.

## Visible functions of Mock Spanish: Positive indexes of identity and stance

English-heritage speakers and even members of Spanish-heritage communities often volunteer that Mock Spanish expressions are funny and cute. English-heritage speakers, questioned about using a Mock Spanish item, will suggest that they used it because they have "picked up a little Spanish." This rationalization is at least 50 years old. Gray et al. (1949) argued that Anglo University of Arizona students who used expressions like "Hasty lumbago" did so because they had grown up in the border region and knew Spanish. Thus the positive indexicality of Mock Spanish, of a light, colloquial stance, possession of a sense of humor, and a cosmopolitan identity, is accessible to speaker awareness.

The positive indexical function of Mock Spanish in creating a light stance and a desirable colloquial persona is not only available to metapragmatic awareness, it is so important in this function that to be able to use Mock Spanish is a vital part of the rhetorical skill set of someone who aspires to a prototypical "American" identity.[27] A canonical example that demonstrates this function appears in the film *Terminator 2: Judgment Day* from 1992. In the film Arnold Schwarzenegger plays a hero machine, a "Terminator," who has been sent from the future to defend a child, John Connor, who will grow up to save humanity by defeating an army of evil machines. Consider the following dialogue, which occurs as John Connor and his mother are fleeing the forces of evil in a car driven by Schwarzenegger as the "Terminator."

> (23)  *Mother.* Keep it under sixty-five. We don't want to get pulled over.
>  *Terminator.* Affirmative (in machine-like voice, with German accent).
>  *John Connor.* No no no no no no. You gotta listen to the way people talk! You don't say "Affirmative," or some shit like that, you say "No

problemo." And if somebody comes off to you with an attitude, you say "Eat me." And if you want to shine them on, you say "Hasta la vista, baby."

*Terminator.* Hasta la vista, baby (still in machine-like voice).

*John Connor.* Yeah, later, dickwad. And if someone gets upset, you say "Chill out!" Or, you can do combinations.

*Terminator.* Chill out, dickwad (in machine-like voice).

*John Connor.* That's great! See, you're gettin' it!

*Terminator.* No problemo (in nearly normal voice).

In this dialogue the famous tag "Hasta la vista, baby" is introduced for the first time. In his final utterance in the scene, the Mock Spanish tag "No problemo," the Terminator's voice sounds fully human for the first time in the film. That is, it is through the use of Mock Spanish that Schwarzenegger's Terminator moves from being a machine, a symbol of fascist foreignness amplified by his German accent, to being a sympathetic protagonist who talks "the way people talk." The English vulgarisms that accompany the Mock Spanish in this little language lesson – "Eat me," "dickwad" – suggest the range of the register of colloquialism constituted by Mock Spanish.[28]

In *Terminator 2: Judgment Day*, the Terminator becomes, not merely human, but "American." This use of Mock Spanish to construct an explicitly "American" voice appears in other films as well. In 2006, the film *Talladega Nights: The Ballad of Ricky Bobby* was an enormous hit for the comedian Will Ferrell. The DVD of the film, which appeared in time for Christmas, was heavily marketed as appropriate family entertainment for the holiday season. Ferrell played Ricky Bobby, a NASCAR racing champion who hits hard times when his preeminence is challenged by Jean Girard, a French driver from the Formula One circuit. The character of Girard parodied the anti-French sentiment that had exploded in 2003 when the French refused to endorse the US invasion of Iraq. Jean Girard is not only French, effete to the highest degree, in contrast to Ricky Bobby's down-home style, he is gay! (This antithesis of all that is "American" is played to over-the-top perfection by the great comedian Sacha Baron Cohen.) Ricky Bobby's first confrontation with Jean Girard comes in a bar when the French driver switches the jukebox from country music to cool jazz. As Ricky Bobby reaches back to punch out the French interloper, he says "Welcome to America, amigo." Another plot twist is that, in despair over his failures on the track, Ricky Bobby breaks up with his best buddy Cal Naughton. In the last moments of the film, Ricky and Cal reunite. Mock Spanish plays a key role in this moment of tender all-American male homosociality. Cal's track nickname is "Magic Man," and Ricky announces that finally he, too, has picked a perfect nickname: It is "El Diablo," which

Ricky asserts "is like Spanish for a fighting chicken, with the claws, and the beak!"[29] This clever touch, which shows that Ricky, typical of Mock Spanish users, knows nothing at all about Spanish, is part of the film's satire of NASCAR-centered "Americanness," and the film's use of Mock Spanish, appearing at pivotal moments in plot transition, is very telling.[30]

Mock Spanish nicknames are an important index of a certain kind of American masculinity. President George W. Bush is famous for giving nicknames to friends and subordinates, and many of those that have been published are Mock Spanish. Among those recorded are "Pablo" for his first treasury secretary, Paul O'Neill, "Camarones" for Carl Cameron, a correspondent for Fox News, and "El Grande Jorge" for Congressman George Miller of California.[31] At his 56th birthday golf outing July 6, 2002, Bush wore a baseball cap with the embroidered legend "El Jefe," and joked to reporters that the expression was "French." Another Mock Spanish nicknamer is right-wing radio personality Rush Limbaugh, who often refers to himself as "El Rushbo." The most elaborate Limbaugh nickname is probably "El loco poco Dicko" for former Democratic congressional leader and presidential candidate Dick Gephardt.[32]

The use of Mock Spanish is certainly not restricted to the political right. The late columnist Molly Ivins, who was far to the left in American political terms, called Bush "El Chico" and employed Mock Spanish to humorous effect in many of her essays. Ivins constructed a regional identity as a down-to-earth Texan, but Mock Spanish usage can be heard even from New England, as in another example from the political left, from the *Boston Globe*'s columnist Ellen Goodman, in (24):

(24)    "But the sexier and racier question dominating the early chatter [about possible Democratic presidential candidates for 2008] is the possible mano-a-womano, black-and-white matchup that could be offered with Hillary Clinton or Barack Obama atop the national ticket" (Goodman 2006).

Mock Spanish is available to convey a down-to-earth colloquial stance not only in everyday interaction, but in the highest levels of public life. Mock Spanish is always good for a laugh, for showing that, even in a formal context like Ellen Goodman's *Boston Globe* op-ed on the Democratic presidential candidates, the writer is serious, but not so serious that you wouldn't like her. When Ambassador Madeleine Albright said "cojones" in front of the Security Council of the United Nations, she was transformed from a double-chinned dowager with a formidable bosom, the stuff of Marx Brothers caricature, to a tough, savvy, all-American broad who could be promoted with confidence to the exalted position of Secretary of State. President Bush's Mock Spanish nicknames are part of his image as a likeable fellow. And for at least two decades scriptwriters have drawn endlessly on Mock Spanish tags to create characters like John Connor in *Terminator 2: Judgment Day* and Ricky Bobby in *Talladega Nights*, who resonate as "real people" for an American audience.

## Mock Spanish and negative indexes of racist stereotypes and marginalization of Spanish

If Mock Spanish is such a useful tool in creating stances and identities that many Americans find enjoyable and positive, what could possibly be wrong with it? Indeed, should we not think of Mock Spanish as making a continual display of the importance of the contribution of Spanish to the American language, and as showing American openness to and respect for this linguistic heritage? Metapragmatic discourses by Whites about the functions of Mock Spanish often include this notion, that Mock Spanish is a symbol of our diversity, or of the speaker's respect for Spanish language and culture. Regrettably, it is easy to show that this is very unlikely, but to do so is a scholarly exercise that cannot be accomplished within the terms of the folk theory of racism and personalist-referentialist linguistic ideologies. I have never met a speaker from an English-language heritage who suggested that anyone might object to Mock Spanish, or who believed that using Mock Spanish might be a way to reshape and control the Spanish language, or who was willing to admit that Mock Spanish might play a part in denigrating and marginalizing Spanish and its speakers. English-heritage Americans are more likely to find such a proposal to be not merely ridiculous, but profoundly threatening. Several years ago I gave a talk about my work to the Chicano Studies Program at the University of Arizona. A reporter from the student newspaper, the *Arizona Daily Wildcat*, wrote up the talk in a short piece (Schechter 2000). Letters to the editor vigorously attacked what they believed my ideas to be, and the entire staff of the *Wildcat* joined in an editorial denouncing my work as divisive and "just go[ing] too far."[33]

So, what is the evidence for the negative functions of Mock Spanish? First, Mock Spanish associates the Spanish language irrevocably with the non-serious, the casual, the laid-back, the humorous, the vulgar. "Spanish" is available for joking and for insult; it cannot lend gravitas or sophistication. Compare, for example, a case of "Mock German": the marketing of an expensive computer keyboard, intended for programming specialists, under the name "Das Keyboard" (überGeeks only!).[34] Here, the German definite article "Das" is intended to convey fine engineering and high-tech credibility. It is unimaginable that such a product could be called "El Keyboard." "El Keyboard" would be a bargain-basement item marketed to people who need a product that is no more than basic, or, at best, a way of joking about something familiar and not terribly special.[35]

Mock Spanish, with its relentlessly anglicized and even hyperanglicized and boldly mispronounced phonology and pidgin grammar, assigns native Spanish fluency to the realm of the "un-American." To pronounce Spanish place names or the names of public figures with any approximation of native Spanish-language phonology is to risk being accused of being stuffy, effete, p.c., even ridiculous. A *Saturday Night Live* television skit called "NBC News Employees" that aired on November 10, 1990, made this very clear.[36] The skit included the Latino actor Jimmy Smits. All the Anglo characters make themselves ridiculous (I make this judgment from having shown the skit many times in talks and to classes – and also from a line given to the Smits character: "If you don't mind my saying, sometimes when you take Spanish words and kind of over-pronounce them, well, it's kind of annoying") by insisting on phony-sounding hyper-foreignized pronunciations of everyday Spanish names like "Nicaragua," "San Diego," "Broncos" (the Denver football team), and names for Mexican food. A running joke involves the name of Smits's character, Antonio Mendoza, who keeps insisting that he prefers that his name be pronounced just /mɛnˈdowzə/, and not /menˈdoθa/ or /menˈdosa/. I take this as an important part of the construction of a desirable identity for the Smits character, who is displayed in the skit as the only person present who is unpretentiously comfortable with an all-American voice. In contrast to this proscription against accurate Spanish pronunciation by Whites, we have seen that a Spanish speaker who insists on such pronunciations, even one who pronounces his or her own name with Spanish phonology (as do many Latino and Latina newsreaders on television), is heard as making a highly marked political gesture.

Another indication that Mock Spanish indexes racist stereotypes is that it often appears accompanied by highly stereotypical and offensive images of "Mexicans" (as in the "South of the Border" website quoted in (21)). It is common in anti-Spanish contexts such as anti-immigrant websites. On one such site, a picture of Congressman Tom Tancredo (R–Colorado), among the most vitriolically anti-Hispanic members of the US Congress, a person who described the city of Miami as "third-world," is captioned with the words in (25):

(25)    "Tom Tancredo is America's '*Numero Uno* Point Man!' in Congress on Illegal Immigration!" (italics and extra exclamation point in original).[37]

On another such site, a "Gringo dollar" is pictured; the idea is to print it out and send it to the Republican National Committee. The presidential image on it is George W. Bush, alongside the legend "Gringo de Mexico."

The denomination is "00 Nada pesos." Across the base of the fake bill is written "Secure America's borders. Stop catering to illegals. Then we'll send American dollars."[38]

Mock Spanish, with its utter neglect of Spanish grammar and its distancing from Spanish phonology, creates a linguistic space for what I have called "orderly disorder" (Hill 1998). This space is "orderly" because it is part of a larger, cultural order where Spanish has been assigned a non-serious function, and disorderly because in it Spanish loses the grammatical constraints indigenous to it. Within this space, even bilingual messages involving health and safety that are required by law are likely to be grossly ungrammatical. A dramatic illustration of such orderly disorder was identified by Barrett (2006), who conducted research in an Anglo-owned Mexican restaurant where Anglo servers spoke a Mock Spanish-influenced pidgin to Spanish-speaking kitchen staff. One tactic of the English speakers was to use Spanish words from which Spanish syntax and morphology were stripped, such as "Could you *hablar por telefono* and see if he can *trabajo*?" (Barrett 2006:180, 185). Even written communications to Spanish-speaking staff used this kind of language. The resulting misunderstandings, which at best compromised the efficient running of the restaurant and at worst led to lapses in sanitation, were invariably blamed on the Spanish speakers.

One case in my files of such Mock Spanish-influenced usage arguably led to the death of an American citizen. In April 2001, a Peruvian military pilot shot down a suspected drug-smuggling plane, only to discover that he had accidentally killed an American missionary and her infant daughter. Accompanying the Peruvian flight was an American spotter plane; one member of the spotter crew tried to stop the Peruvian from firing by radioing these words: "Are you sure it's a bandido?" (Kelley 2001).[39]

The "orderly disorder" of Spanish is taken for granted and even appreciated by English speakers, who think of themselves as "knowing a little Spanish." An important contributor to this opinion is the fiction that "Spanish is easy" (the collocation "Spanish" and "easy" returned 89,900,000 Google hits on August 12, 2007; see Schwartz 2006 for additional discussion). Spanish is by far the most studied foreign language in the United States, with three times the number of students of its nearest competitor, French. This sense of empowerment over Spanish among Whites contrasts with the most acute anxiety among Spanish speakers about English, as documented by Urciuoli (1996). Urciuoli's respondents believed that they must never mix the two languages, that even a slight Spanish accent in English is discreditable, and that to code-switch by using Spanish and English expressions in the same sentence (a practice which decades of linguistic research has shown is an important dimension of linguistic order in US Spanish bilingual communities) suggests ignorance of English. This contrast, between the casual disorderliness of Spanish as used by English speakers to construct a White public space, and the hypervigilance over linguistic boundaries within that space required for Spanish speakers, strikingly exemplifies the way that practices associated with Whiteness can become unmarked and unnoticeable, while very similar practices associated with Color become the object of intense monitoring (Hill 1998).

Finally, the connotations conveyed by the semantic pejoration of Mock Spanish vocabulary items constantly reproduce and reinscribe vulgar racist stereotypes of the Spanish language and people of Spanish heritage. To find "mañana" entertaining, one must have access to the stereotype of laziness. For "adios" and "hasta la vista" to function as brush-offs or hostile threats, one must have access to the stereotype of treachery and duplicity, of superficial politeness and friendliness that is really only a thin veil for vicious motives. An ad for a sale at an upscale Tucson furniture store with the headline "Contemporary and Southwestern dining, for pesos!" makes sense only if speakers understand goods priced in pesos to be especially cheap, since obviously the meaning is not literal. The store would never have accepted Mexican currency, which is almost impossible to exchange in Tucson.[40] Other Mock Spanish expressions index stereotypes of dirt, disorder, and sexual looseness. These effects, like the humorous colloquial stance projected by Mock Spanish, are the product of social indexicality. In these cases, however, we see not only the creative indexicality of stance projection, but what Silverstein (1979) has called "presupposing" indexicality, in that the jokester who uses the Mock Spanish words and expressions humorously presupposes the negative stereotypes as background. However, the usages not only reinforce the stereotypes by presupposition, they can also create or entail them, making them available to people who did not have them in mind.

We can exemplify this function by showing how Mock Spanish reproduces the stereotype of Latin political corruption by using Mock Spanish political titles like "el presidente" and "Generalissimo." "Generalissimo El Busho" is a favorite insult of the left-wing cartoonist Ted Rall, who dresses President Bush in an absurdly over-decorated military uniform with huge epaulettes and a high-peaked military cap covered in braid and insignia, as seen in Figure 6.

In order to "get the joke" of Rall's insult – indeed, to understand that it is an insult – one must have access to the stereotype of the overblown, inauthentic, and corrupt military dictator who rules over a Latin American "Banana Republic." We can be sure that the stereotype plays a role in the usage, because explicit statements of this stereotype occasionally surface. For instance, in March 2001, the editors of the leftist magazine *The Nation* suggested that "Mr. President" was not a good title for George W. Bush, since he had not been elected (he was installed by a 5–4 decision of the US Supreme Court). They ran a contest in which readers were invited to

**Figure 6** "Generalissimo El Busho": Entailing racist stereotypes in Mock Spanish. Rall © 2003 Ted Rall. Reprinted with permission of Universal Press Syndicate. All rights reserved.

submit an appropriate title. Inevitably, "El Presidente" was suggested. *The Nation* editors commented, "A Banana Republican, of course."[41] The liberal blogger Kevin Drum used the header "Banana Republicans" for remarks about the politicization of the 2006 mid-term elections by the US Department of Justice.[42] Knowing the liberal politics of these writers, we can be sure that "Banana Republican" is an insult. In case we doubted our conclusion, a *New York Times* op-ed essay by Bill Keller, who deplored intemperate attacks on President George W. Bush, explicitly labeled the Spanish political word "junta" an "insult."

(26)  "I doubt anyone ever referred to his father as a 'chicken hawk' or to the first Bush administration as a 'junta.' These are insults, not arguments" (Keller 2003).[43]

A fascinating irony of the Banana Republic stereotype is that the original Banana Republic was not created by Latin Americans possessed by some essential instinct for Ruritanian misrule, but by Americans who in 1910 installed a corrupt dictatorship in Honduras to protect the interests of the

United Fruit Company. Similar American-assisted coups installed at least three other notorious military dictatorships: Rafael Trujillo in the Dominican Republic in 1930, Carlos Castillo Armas in Guatemala in 1954, and Augusto Pinochet in Chile in 1973. However, very few White Americans know this history. The "Banana Republic" stereotype is extraordinarily resilient, and it shapes relationships between the United States and Latin America at the highest level. Interestingly, these relationships are inflected not only by the presumption of corruption, but by the idea that Latin America is somehow a trivial part of the world that can be taken lightly, a position entirely consistent with the trivializing jocular stance constructed by Mock Spanish. Before the destruction of the World Trade Center on September 11, 2001, President George W. Bush, who as a former governor of Texas had some notion of the importance of US relations with Mexico, put Latin American policy high on his agenda. This initiative, however, was interpreted by critics as revealing Bush's lack of gravitas. The remarks in (27), by Maureen Dowd of the *New York Times*, were typical:

(27)   "W.'s advisers tried to make him look more impressive in his first forays into diplomacy by keeping the big world leaders at bay and letting him hang out with lesser leaders he could talk to in Spanish. So now we have a whole new alliance with Central and South American countries simply because W. feels more comfortable at what *USA Today* dubbed 'amigo diplomacy'" (Dowd 2001).

The stereotype of the "Banana Republic" continues to make sense to Americans for a variety of reasons. Explicit statements of the stereotype occur in what Myers (2005) has called "race talk" among intimates. Woolard (1989) reported that the stereotype of the corrupt Latino politician strongly influences supporters of the campaign to make English an official language. Its resiliency is, I believe, at least partly due to the constant use of forms like "el presidente" as jokes and insults in Mock Spanish, where White Americans simultaneously construct themselves as humorous, delightful, all-American, and "knowing a little Spanish," while projecting a very negative image of the Spanish-speaking world, its language, and its citizens.

In the vast majority of cases of Mock Spanish usage, the stereotypes are entirely implicit, projected by indexicality. To call President Bush "Generalissimo El Busho" can only be funny if we have access to the Banana Republic stereotype. Otherwise, it would simply make no sense. Since American English speakers do find expressions like "Generalissimo El Busho" funny, inviting jokesters to repeat it often (Ted Rall even has a section on his website where "Generalissimo El Busho" paraphernalia can be purchased), the Banana Republic stereotype is made more real.

Technically, in Peircean terms, the relationship between "Generalissimo El Busho" and the proposition "Latin American politicians are corrupt, phony, and incompetent" is not exactly one of index and object. In Silverstein's (1979) terms, the proposition is an entailment or creation, a projection, constituted by expressions like "Generalissimo El Busho." Since the phrase exists in English, speakers who share referential linguistic ideology must assume that it stands for some object in the world. That is, it is what Peirce called a "dicent" or "dicisign," where a sign of another type is "apprehended as" an index (Parmentier 1994). Both "Generalissimo El Busho" and the stereotype of the Banana Republic are really symbols, signs grounded in their objects by convention. The convention of the Banana Republic emanates from the culture of White racism, within which the stereotype is a kind of truth. In American English the expressions "Generalissimo" and "El Presidente," which are titles of respect in Spanish, are very difficult to use with a straight face. They carry a very heavy burden of history, of the voice of White racism, which evokes and reinforces the fictional property of the world, the Banana Republic, that is White racism's creation.

The creative indexicality of Mock Spanish expressions – the ways that they invite hearers to make negative inferences, to become aware of stereotypes to which they might not have paid attention – occurs because the pressures on interlocutors to make sense of Mock Spanish are quite intense. Mock Spanish is a very important tactic of colloquial American English and its registers of jocular intimacy. To stand apart from it, to refuse to make the inferences and "get" the jokes, to join in the fun, is to reject this mutuality and intimacy and its pleasures, to be divisive, and, finally, to be un-American.

## Why are the negative functions of Mock Spanish below the limits of awareness?

Silverstein (2001[1981]) suggested that one property of linguistic expressions which makes them accessible to consciousness is "unavoidable referentiality." Linguistic ideology takes the expressions of Mock Spanish to be "referential," to "mean the same" as the corresponding English words.[44] So "mañana" means "tomorrow" or "later." But if we admit indexicality to our analysis, we can see that the word projects many non-referential meanings. The first is a stance, which can be glossed something like this: "I am using this word because it is a humorous way to talk about delay, implying a bit of naughty laziness." The second is an identity, of which this description is an approximation: "In using this word, I signal that I am more than an uptight, sober, rigidly responsible White person, who is always on time.

I am a nicer, funnier, more interesting person than that." To enjoy the mutuality of the implicated stance, and to buy into the projected identity as a congenial interlocutor, one must be able to retrieve something like this: "The naughty laziness in my stance is like the laziness and irresponsibility of a Spanish speaker, someone who would, in the baptismal moment, have said *mañana* (the 'real' Spanish word)." The stereotype, "Spanish speakers are lazy," which would be visible to linguistic ideology as racist were it to be uttered in that raw form, is never spoken, so referential linguistic ideology finds no purchase. What could be wrong with a word that means "later" while showing that the speaker "knows a little Spanish"? Nor is the word "mañana" accessible as a slur or an epithet: there is certainly no overt hostility in the usage, so performative linguistic ideology finds no purchase either. Furthermore, the negative entailments of "mañana" are surely not intentional, in the usual sense. Indeed, should these entailments be explicitly expressed, users of those expressions might quite sincerely point out that they do not believe them. So these usages are invisible to personalist linguistic ideology. Even if they are pointed out, within the folk theory of racism, which requires racist intentions and beliefs, they do not count as racist. However, within the critical theory of racism, we can understand that such utterances are part of a collective project, in which negative stereotypes are constantly naturalized and made normal, circulating without drawing attention to themselves. By constant repetition in this covert form, they become part of the basic cognitive tool kit of White Americans, just like the metaphor IMMIGRANTS ARE ANIMALS. If we focus on individual beliefs and intentions, as the folk theory of racism insists, we completely miss the way in which these stereotypes work in a cultural system, living in interactional space created in mutual engagement, as people get jokes, apprehend stances, and orient toward identities.

I have suggested that the negative entailments of Mock Spanish expressions are invisible because these expressions work as social indexicals. However, the positive entailments of these usages are visible to Whites, in spite of their non-referential properties. Thus, the analysis presented above is not completely satisfying. I suspect that an important reason, in addition to its non-referentiality, that the negative indexicality of Mock Spanish is invisible is because this is actively repressed. The positive stances and identities entailed in Mock Spanish support the project of White virtue. But the negative entailments, the racist stereotypes, undercut that project, and undercut it in a way that is both unintelligible within the folk theory of racism and deeply threatening. Mock Spanish is not redneck ranting. Most Whites encounter it almost daily, use it themselves, and certainly have heard it from public figures and characters in entertainments that they admire and enjoy. The suggestion that this everyday way of being funny might simultaneously be racist simply lies outside the regime of truth and sanity. It is frightening and dangerous, an attack on White virtue at the most basic level.

## Latino/a reactions to Mock Spanish

I have called Mock Spanish a covert racist discourse, because its racist functions, in reproducing negative stereotypes, are invisible (or at least deniable) for Whites. However, Mock Spanish is visible as racist to many Latinos and Latinas. While the Puerto Rican sociologist Clara Rodríguez (1997) reported that when she first heard Mock Spanish, she was baffled by it, the sociolinguist Fernando Peñalosa (1981), working in southern California, identified the racist functions of hyperanglicization and bold mispronunciation of Spanish loan words as long ago as the 1970s. Spanish speakers object to the use of offensive words like *caca* and *cojones* in public English, and many also object to the ungrammaticality of expressions like "No problemo," and mis-spellings like "Grassy-Ass," as showing disrespect for the language.

In 1997 Dan Goldstein and I conducted interviews with 11 Anglos, 1 African American, and 12 Latino/a subjects, who were asked to look through a scrapbook of examples of Mock Spanish, Booster Regionalist Spanish, and bilingual announcements. They were invited to comment in any way that they wished on the examples (Hill and Goldstein 2001). We encountered some diversity among our 12 Latino and Latina subjects. A few thought that some Mock Spanish usages were cute and funny. Several expressed sympathy for Anglos who had to struggle with words that might be difficult for them to pronounce (none suggested that Anglos were cosmopolitan people who knew some Spanish!). Others thought the scrapbook examples were simply dumb, empty, and meaningless. Two young men recognized that some of the usages might be offensive, but that they "didn't let it bother them." But several respondents, ordinary people all, not scholars, reported that they found the usages demeaning, disrespectful, and racist. Some examples are given in (28–31).

(28)    "Muchos smoochos"? [on a greeting card with an image of Snoopy]. These playing on words, sometimes these are very demeaning. I don't know, I have a hard time with that."

In (29), a man responds to an example of a political advertisement with the headline "Don't let Congress say Adios to Mining Jobs," over a picture of a man in a hard hat leading two small blond boys away from a gate labeled "closed." This respondent objects to linguistic appropriation (see Chapter 6):

(29)    "It's a double message, adios and, a, a, a white uh, uh male adult with
        two uh white kids, um, what a double message. What a co-, covert way
        of once again, uh, playing with people's minds."

Two men objected to the pejoration of the word *macho* in its Mock
Spanish usage, as in (30):

(30)    "That whole word in itself was totally bastardized. It used to have an
        entirely different meaning, which had nothing in reference to how much
        you would drink, or what–, how many women you could, you know,
        what was your conquest. Basically a, a macho, a, Machismo was a very
        comprehensive person that could communicate, uh, that could show his
        emotions and express them; once it crossed the border it changed its
        whole definition to being sarcastic, egotistic, narcissistic. I'm gonna drink
        you under the table and how many women can I–."

One woman, after looking at the entire scrapbook, volunteered a com-
prehensive critique of the materials she had seen:

(31)    "Some of those you just kinda hafta be real careful, because you, you,
        you know you get somebody to read it and because they're using maybe
        one or two Hispanic words in there or something like that, you think,
        oh, you know, they're kinda, they're nice, they're uh, they, they like
        our people or whatever, and then all of a sudden underneath it you can
        see a real message of, you know, hate or dislike or, or, or being really
        um uh, discriminatory towards, towards the Hispanics, and so you kinda
        have to take 'em with a grain of salt."

## Conclusion

White speakers of American English, when confronted with the proposal
that Mock Spanish presupposes and reproduces racist stereotypes, vigorously
reject this idea. Surely no racism is intended by such ordinary, and even
entertaining and delightful, usages, which liven up television and cinematic
dialogue, provide a resource for entertaining political commentary from all
points of view, and are frequently heard in everyday conversation. And
many examples of Mock Spanish do seem to be entirely benign to the
unreflecting overhearer. Consider the following exchange, which I noted
down on a Sunday morning in March 2001 in the Elk City Cafe in
Redway, California. Both speakers were obviously Anglos, and all apparently Spanish words in the exchange were uttered with normally anglicized
phonology.

(32)   *Counter server* (female): How's it going?
       *Customer* (male): Oh, mas o menos.
       *Server:* Not so bueno, huh?

It is certainly wrong to accuse these speakers of intending a message of racist denigration. However, I hope to have shown that this innocuous bit of chit-chat is part of a much larger system of White racism and its discourses. This little exchange has played a part in naturalizing, in making normal and commonsensical for the speakers and those Whites who overheard them, the idea that if Spanish is to be "American," it cannot sound like Spanish, and it cannot be serious. To become American, Spanish words must be transformed into light talk like (32), or into jokes and insults. Furthermore, if we think for a moment, we realize that a Spanish-speaking counter server and customer, exchanging very similar sentiments in real Spanish, would have been vulnerable to censure with the "This is America" routine, which any White customer present (this café, located on the main highway through town, was a White-dominated space) might have initiated. In fact, it is highly likely that, had the server been a Latina, she would have received explicit instructions from her manager not to speak Spanish in the serving area of the restaurant, for fear of making White customers uncomfortable. Indeed, it is highly likely that had she been a Latina, she would not have been a server at all; she would have been backstage, washing dishes and mopping the floor (Barrett 2006).

In summary, even these friendly folks in the Elk City Cafe on a sunny Sunday morning participated, through unreflecting everyday practice, in the reproduction of White racism as a cultural system. I hope to have made clear that the cultural projects of White racism work through diverse devices. Spanish and its speakers are assigned to the lower, colored levels of the racial hierarchy, and material and symbolic resources are appropriated from them for the purposes of Whites. The many kinds of pressure, formal and informal, against the Spanish language in the public arena also function to accomplish these purposes, as do explicit slurs and the utterance of stereotypes. But the unending repetition of unmarked appropriations of Spanish, from the banal Sunday-morning conversation in the Redway Cafe to the prose of *New York Times* opinion pieces and the high dudgeon of White diplomats, must also be a very important part of the White racist project, and may be especially important and useful precisely because it is covert. However, as I have tried to show, these usages are not covert and invisible to Latinos and Latinas. Instead, they are felt as demeaning, as degrading, as disrespectful, as an audible, visible, and unpleasant effect, albeit a less important one than material oppression and the threat of violence, of living in a racist society.

# Chapter 6

# Linguistic Appropriation: The History of White Racism is Embedded in American English

## Introduction to Linguistic Appropriation

The constitution of White privilege, achieved by recruiting both material and symbolic resources from the bottom of the racial hierarchy, Color, to the top, Whiteness, is one of the most important projects of White racist culture. Linguistic resources are among its targets. Students of language contact label the shift of resources across language and dialect boundaries with neutral terminology like "loan words" and "borrowing." But when we approach the problem from the perspective of critical theories of racism, we can understand some linguistic borrowing as a kind of theft. I label these borrowings-as-theft with the term "linguistic appropriation." In linguistic appropriation, speakers of the target language (the group doing the borrowing) adopt resources from the donor language, and then try to deny these to members of the donor language community. They attempt this denial through formal legal prohibition and informal monitoring and censure, as we saw in Chapter 5. But they also achieve it indirectly, by reshaping the meaning of the borrowed material into forms that advance their own interest, making it useless or irrelevant, or even antithetical, to the interests of the donor community. This reshaped meaning may then be imposed on donor speakers.

The control of meaning in linguistic appropriation uses techniques that are well known from advertising and propaganda. In linguistic appropriation words are commodified and become property, with their meanings and uses determined by their owners. To impose these meanings and uses, speakers of the target language must dominate speakers of the donor language. The dominant group must control the institutions through which linguistic resources circulate, such as markets, media, schools, and the legal system. It must also control both formal and informal mechanisms through which the linguistic behavior of the donor population can be regulated. White racism in the United States exhibits this kind of dominance. One of the implications of this model of linguistic appropriation is that it must involve elites, people with the wealth and power to enforce the reorganization of the linguistic universe. Such a conclusion is consistent with the critical theory of White racism, but not with the folk theory, which restricts racism to marginal and backward individuals.

Theorists of cultural dominance of the type called "hegemony" (e.g. Bourdieu 1991; Crehan 2002 [for the ideas of Antonio Gramsci, to whom the modern sense of the term is usually attributed]; Williams 1977) have emphasized that it is never complete. Contradictions, lapses, and interstices in which counter-hegemonic projects can develop are always present, and both residues of older systems and emerging alternative hegemonies may exist alongside dominant cultural formations. The processes of linguistic appropriation are no different, so the shift of linguistic resources may never be absolute. Furthermore, while linguistic appropriation is like theft, it is not exactly like boosting a wallet or hot-wiring a car. The material nature of linguistic materials, which live in intersubjective cultural spaces and in personal mental spaces, are resistant to theft as usually understood. But linguistic appropriation includes processes that look surprisingly like theft, and they are so labeled by victims.

Loan materials that fit the definition of linguistic appropriation have been recruited into mainstream White American English mainly from three sources: American Indian languages, African American English, and US Spanish. I begin with an example involving US Spanish that attracted national attention in December 2005. Zach Rubio, a student in a Kansas City high school, was suspended for a day and a half for speaking Spanish in the school hallway. He reported the conversation that led to the suspension as follows:

(1)   "He's like, '¿Me puestas un dólar?' . . . So I'm like 'No problema'" [He's like, "Loan me a dollar?" . . . So I'm like, "No problem"] (Reid 2005).

The utterance that Mr. Rubio reports, "No problema," is a so-called loan translation or "calque" from English "No problem." "No problem" is part of a large family of English idioms that delete expletive "there" and the verb "is/are" to create examples like "No worries," "No dice," "No way," and "No gas today." Spanish as spoken by native speakers who are not influenced by English does not possess such an idiom; such speakers require the verb *hay* "there is/are" in expressions such as *No hay problema*. The bilingual Mr. Rubio used a loan-translation of English "No problem," except that he used the correct Spanish gender suffix -*a*, rather than Mock Spanish "-*o*." I have never heard of a student being censured for saying "No problemo," a Mock Spanish expression that is ubiquitous in colloquial English (Google returned 906,000 hits). However, Latino identity, final "a" instead of "o," and perhaps a few other phonetic details, cost Zach Rubio a suspension. Although the punishment was eventually rescinded, it was considered by his family to be an attack on his civil rights serious enough to take to court. This case illustrates linguistic appropriation and looks very much like theft. Mock Spanish "No problemo" is freely available to Whites, at the same time that Mr. Rubio was punished for saying "No problema." And Zach Rubio's experience was by no means an isolated incident, but was instead quite typical of practices that are in play all over the country every day. What got this particular case into the national media was that Mr. Rubio and his family decided to fight back. Most victims of linguistic appropriation suffer in silence.

I have borrowed the term "appropriation" from Marxist theory. Marx (for instance, in *Capital*) used the word for the process through which capitalists, owners of the means of production, collect the value of the work of the workers, who do not control these means. The term appropriation has been borrowed into cultural studies and cultural anthropology, where it has been productively generalized from material appropriation to the case of symbolic appropriation. Examples have been identified especially in the arts and in music. Perhaps the best-known illustration is the theft by White impresarios and musicians of musical styles and even specific compositions by African Americans. This tradition of symbolic appropriation created some of the most important symbolic wealth of "American" – that is, White American – culture, from nineteenth-century minstrelsy to ragtime and jazz, through rhythm and blues and rock and roll to the current international fad for hip-hop music (Hall 1997). This appropriation had, of course, important material economic consequences, generating immense wealth for White entrepreneurs and artists who interpreted African American compositions, while leaving their creators in poverty and obscurity. This was possible because Whites controlled the institutions within which the symbolic resources of African American music could be converted into material resources: media markets, distribution networks, and legal and governmental institutions that enforce contracts, copyrights, and trademarks. African American musicians were marginal to these systems, and kept there by Jim Crow racism.

Like the symbolic appropriation of African American music, the linguistic appropriations discussed in this chapter add value to an "American" identity – one that is prototypically White. Speakers use appropriated words and ways of speaking to make claims on a wide range of desirable qualities:

learned, cosmopolitan, regionally grounded, cool, hip, funny, street-smart, tough, masculine, laid-back, rebellious, etc. However, at the same time, the project of appropriation denigrates and marginalizes members of donor groups. Mock Spanish, discussed in Chapter 5, illustrates this process. Spanish-language origin materials are reshaped in Mock Spanish to constitute desirable stances and positive identities for White speakers, while at the same time accomplishing the covert reproduction of racist stereotypes of Hispanics.

The case of Mock Spanish also shows how linguistic appropriation can work to exclude people from symbolic resources. Linguistic appropriation is accompanied by informal everyday mechanisms through which dominant, borrowing groups monitor and regulate the speech of subordinate, donor populations, restricting or denying their access to symbolic resources which they once controlled. These mechanisms may be taken up and internalized by members of these populations, as shown by Urciuoli (1996) in her discussion of high levels of linguistic self-consciousness and self-monitoring of language use in the Puerto Rican community of New York City. Alongside linguistic appropriation we also find formal legal institutions that accomplish such monitoring, such as the high school rules that suspended Zach Rubio for speaking Spanish.

## Native American Languages and White Linguistic Appropriation

Linguistic appropriations from Native American languages and ways of speaking are part of a larger body of practices that have reshaped Native American symbolic materials to serve White American identity during the entire history of the United States. This project of national identity construction has been accompanied throughout its history by the extreme marginalization of actual Indians, including genocidal warfare and the seizure of almost all their lands and property, as well as the proscription of their languages (Deloria 1998).

Linguistic appropriation from American Indian languages began in the seventeenth century with the incorporation into English of loan words from the Eastern Algonquian languages spoken along the Atlantic seaboard at the sites of the earliest English colonies. Along with "squaw," discussed in Chapter 3, well-known examples include "papoose," "wigwam," "moccasin," "wampum," "pow-wow," "skunk," "moose," "pecan," "succotash," "hominy," and "tomahawk." These words, from languages like Powhatan, Massachusett, Narragansett, and Delaware, in most cases (although not in the case of "squaw" or "papoose," which belong to the system of animalizing racial labels discussed in Chapter 3) labeled items of culture and nature that were exotic to the English settlers. However, from the earliest date of their appearance it is evident that the words were more than merely convenient labels for these novelties. These words had an elevating force, contributing to new and valued identities for Europeans. Early voyagers to North America used them to claim an identity as scholars of exotic languages, knowledgeable about the New World and its resources. This is evident from their publication of these words in works of "general history," where they are deployed as a form of knowledge along with descriptions of landscape, flora, and fauna. Cutler (1994) points out that such works often boast of the amount of vocabulary that the author has acquired.

As disease, White attacks on their communities, and invasions of their land decimated the indigenous populations of eastern North America, new Indian-language loan vocabulary largely ceased to enter American English. However, the seventeenth-century loans remained extremely useful in the creation of a uniquely "American" English-speaking voice. Perhaps the most extreme example is Henry Wadsworth Longfellow's great bestseller of 1855, *The Song of Hiawatha*. The vocabulary from the Algonquian language Ojibwa, and from other languages (the name "Hiawatha" comes from an Iroquoian language), in the work is so extensive that Longfellow, to assist his readers, felt it necessary to append to his epic poem a 130-item "Vocabulary."

The place names that Whites used to create an "American" landscape are an important site of appropriations from Indian languages. For many White Americans today, these are the only American Indian words that they are aware of. Some place names, like "Massachusetts," "Chatahoochee," or "Tucson," are borrowed from languages spoken by the people who actually lived where the names appear. However, what Bright (2004) calls "transfers," names that appear in regions where the source language had no history, show up early in the nineteenth century. These transfers demonstrate that borrowed Indian place names had become fully assimilated to a White project of making meaning. This included the reshaping of the meanings of the names in order to create useful local mythologies. Bright cites as an example Pasadena, California, from Ojibwa *basadinaa* "valley" (Bright 2004:370). The city's official website observes that the word has "been interpreted to mean 'Crown of the Valley' and 'Key of the Valley,' hence the adoption of both the crown and the key in the official city seal."[1] Another example is "Ahwatukee," a sprawling southern suburb of Phoenix, Arizona. Local boosters claim that this name is from a Crow Indian word that means "House of Dreams."[2] This translation is, of course, made much of by the local real estate and resort industry. However, Bright (2004:26) points out that the only Crow-language word that makes sense as a source is *awahchúhka* "flat land, prairie."

These place names exemplify appropriation not only because their meanings are reshaped for White purposes. In itself, such reshaping cannot be accused of being part of the project of White racism, since meaning change is common in linguistic borrowing. But in the case of appropriated American Indian place names, at the same time that these spread across the map of the United States as labels for White communities, the original Indian place names were lost. The geographic knowledge of Indian experts, and the languages in which it was encoded, became nothing more than signs of savagery. Official maps converted landscapes that were dense with indigenous names into trackless wastes, or replaced Indian names of places with new ones that better served White interests.[3] Indian place names, if they survived at all, lived in the White world in inaccessible scholarly publications that added value only to academic careers. The Phoenix area has bogus "Ahwatukee," but, as pointed out in Chapter 3, when a new name was sought for the offensively labeled "Squaw Peak," no records of the Akimel O'odham name of the mountain could be found.

Native American awareness of heritage has begun to focus on place names. Currently, mapping projects are under way in many communities to recover place names in indigenous languages. Basso (1996) is an exceptionally thorough treatment of the meaning of place names among the Western Apache; Webster (2000) outlines efforts to recover place names by Mescalero Apache. Samuels (2001) shows how Britton Goode, a Western Apache elder, actively contested the meanings of place names in Arizona, arguing that Apache etymologies should replace those offered by Whites for names such as "Tucson."

Alongside the embellishment of Indian words with romantic myths is another important semiotic process, which Peter Whiteley (2003) calls "flattening." Whiteley illustrates this with the English word "kachina," borrowed from Hopi *katsina*. *Katsinam* (the Hopi plural form) in Hopi religious practice are sacred beings "who may manifest themselves as rain clouds, as protagonists in sacred narratives, and as personated actors in masked ritual dramas" (Whiteley 2003:718). However, "kachina" in White usage refers primarily to the carved dolls that represent *katsinam*. These are made as gifts to young girls by their senior male relatives, but since the early twentieth century they have also been made for sale to tourists. The Hopi name for these dolls is *tiihu*, plural *tithu*. However, this name is hardly known to Whites, so Hopis inevitably have to use "kachina" for the dolls when transacting with White buyers. Many young Hopis have absorbed something of this "flattened" sense of the term. Thus, argues Whiteley, White usage effectively functions to deny to Hopis a part of their cultural heritage, as the term "kachina/*katsina*" is "drastically evacuated of meaning" (Whiteley 2003:718).

Neither romanticized Indian place names nor flattened loan words like "kachina" can be said to denigrate Native Americans. However, these exist alongside other reshaped Indian loan words that convey highly negative stereotypes of Indians. Thus "squaw," a harmless Massachusett word meaning "young woman," had by the early nineteenth century become a slur (Bright 2000). By the beginning of the eighteenth century, the stereotype of the "wild Indian" shows up as an entailment of borrowed Indian words. Gangs of ruffians in the British Isles were called "Mohocks," after an Eastern Algonquian insult that was used as the label for an Iroquoian group (Cutler 1994:53). At the Boston Tea Party, the rioters wore war paint and spoke "ugh-peppered pidgin English" (Deloria 1998:32). White Americans borrowed political language to convey denigrating images. "Mugwump," from a Massachusett word for "war leader," was used in the mid-nineteenth century to jeer politicians who were said to have their mug on one side of the fence and their wump on the other. Chinook Jargon, a Native American trade language spoken along the Columbia River, contributed "muckamuck," which appears by 1856 in the expression "high muck-a-muck" or "high mucketymuck." These jokes project a pejorative stereotype of Indian political leaders as foolish and inauthentic, and are very similar in function to Mock Spanish "el presidente" and "Generalissimo" discussed in Chapter 5. Other insults developed early as well. "Podunk," a loan from Natick Algonquian "boggy place," came to mean "irredeemably provincial and marginal." "Siwash," ultimately from French *sauvage* by way of the Chinook Jargon word for "Indian," was taken up by the writer George Fitch, who used it as the name for a fictional small college. To joke that a school is "East Siwash" is to locate it in the lowest spheres of American academia.[4]

A humorous voice that simultaneously makes Whites funny and delightful and Indians primitive and savage uses expressions like "ugh," "heap big," and the "-um" suffix. Cutler (1994) traces such forms to the early nineteenth century, especially to the Leatherstocking novels of James Fenimore Cooper. Cutler observes that some of these "Indianisms" may be authentic translations, such as "firewater," "iron horse," "forked tongue," "Great Spirit," "peace pipe," "red man," "warpath," "war paint," and "medicine" (in the sense of magical power). However, others, such as "paleface" and "happy hunting ground," were probably invented by Whites to "sound Indian." Meek (2006) has found that English-speaking Whites can easily produce tokens of this parodic voice such as "Me smoke-um peacepipe" and "How!" accompanied by a raised hand, along with phrases such as "many moons" and "happy hunting ground." Meek argues that the register is perpetuated in what she calls "Hollywood Indian English," which she has found in dozens of recent films and television programs. She gives an example from the 1997 film *Con Air*, where the parodic "Indian" voice that is widely recognized as racist talk is given to an African American character (played by Dave Chapelle) speaking to an Indian (Meek 2006:93).

(2)   "Pinball" Parker (Dave Chapelle) (looking at unnamed Indian man):
                                                What's up Cochise?
    (lowers voice pitch)                        How! (raises hand)

In this example, Pinball Parker is not being friendly, since in the very next bit of action he sprays gasoline on the Indian man and sets him on fire. In spite of the fact that this kind of usage is so overtly offensive that it can be used to convey the repulsive character of Pinball Parker in *Con Air*, Meek has found that it is frequently assigned to Indian characters in films. Thus in a 1994 film, *Maverick*, the distinguished Nez Perce leader Chief Joseph is given lines like the following, which index a stereotype of stupidity and primitiveness (Meek 2006:96).

(3)   a. "But much wampum needed."
     b. "Injun shot by white man's weapon not reach happy hunting ground."

Relevant for the model of linguistic appropriation proposed here, Meek (2004) found that even some Native Americans accept the "Hollywood" portrait of Indian English as accurate, and join in denigrating their own local forms of language. Parodic "Indianisms," so common in mass media, are probably a factor in the rejection by many Native American children of their heritage languages as embarrassing and unsuited to the identities that they desire. Such rejection is not universal, but it has been widely reported by researchers and suggests the power of White semiotic projects, spread through national media, to impose meanings within Native American communities. Many Indians feel this deeply, and may resent even the scholarly linguistic study of their language, feeling that it is a form of theft.[5] I have heard many times, from members of a community whose members treat me well and appreciate my work, statements like "You've taken our language," "You have our language." A telling (and true) story that has circulated for many years in the Southwest involves a very distinguished linguist who had learned to speak a local Indian language, and was conversing in it on the sidelines at a dance. He was assaulted by a drunken local man who threatened him with a knife, crying, "You white people have stolen every single thing we ever had, and now you're stealing our language."

## African American English and White Linguistic Appropriation

Bonfiglio (2002) has pointed out that "standard" American English has in part emerged through active distancing from African American usage. Yet, somewhat paradoxically, African American language and culture have at the same time been crucial sources for the construction of an authentically "American" identity among Whites. Roediger (1991) has pointed out the role of minstrelsy, blackface performance in supposedly "Negro" styles, in the assimilation of the Irish in the nineteenth century, when some of the best-known performers in this tradition were Irish Americans. Rogin (1995) shows how performers like Al Jolson used blackface and minstrelsy to erase and obscure their Jewish identities and become fully "American." These cultural appropriations are paralleled by a rich history of linguistic appropriation. African American English has provided an endless source of new materials, both lexical and grammatical, for mainstream White American English. Writers like Mark Twain drew heavily on stereotypes of African American English, and Gubar (1997) showed how a kind of talk called "dis-'n-dat" became the voice of White elites in the Jazz Age of the 1920s. Today, forms appropriated from African American English permit Whites to claim many desirable qualities, especially preferred forms of masculinity. These include toughness, urban "street-smarts," and especially "cool," a sort of sexy, edgy unflappability that has a very high value in contemporary American popular culture. Geneva Smitherman (1998:206) has pointed out that the ability to maintain one's "cool" probably originated within African American culture to stay out of trouble and survive in a world of lynch mobs and police brutality. However, in White popular culture "cool" has been flattened into a fashionable aesthetic of the self.[6]

Smitherman (1998), taking a very generous view of White linguistic appropriations from African American English, argues that African American words "cross over" into White English because Whites, like Blacks, suffer alienation and desperation, and the "dynamism and creativity" of the Black lexicon meet their needs as well. However, borrowings from African American English are well attested at the highest level of elite White society, where "alienation and desperation" may exist, but are surely not due to economic deprivation. In the *New York Times* for August 12, 2005, the lead article in the "Escapes" section was about White families who follow a way of life long traditional among upper-income New Yorkers: Mothers and children spend the summer vacation on the Jersey Shore, while the fathers work weekdays in Manhattan and commute down to their vacation homes on weekends. In one of these happy families, the elementary-school-age children (who are pictured in the article, playing in the surf) are reported to have a produce stand in their front yard where they sell vegetables from their garden. The name of the stand is "We Be Growin" (Strom 2005: D7). "We Be Growin" is immediately recognizable to White Americans as a borrowing from African American English. The "g-drop" in "Growin," which in written English signals a non-standard register, and especially the presence of "invariant be," a shibboleth of "Mock Ebonics" (Ronkin and Karn 1999) reveal this source. On August 11, 2007, the *New York Times* published another account, of a family so prominent that the story began with a photograph of them on the front page of the newspaper. Their summer home in Southampton is called "Da Crib." The young daughter of the house is quoted in (4), contrasting this name with a more conventional Hamptons style:

(4)   "'You know, like how Pop-Pop has Ocean Grove or whatever?' Serena said. 'And we have Da Crib.' Pop-Pop is A. Alfred Taubman, the former chairman of Sotheby's" (Konigsberg 2007).

Like "We Be Growin," "Da Crib" is obvious as an African Americanism because of the hip-hop inflected spelling of "the" and the use of African American Vernacular English "crib" for "home, home place." "Da Crib" is the name of a hip-hop music company, which features a drawing of an old-time rural southern house with a big porch on the home page of its website. Clearly, the *Times* reporter, Eric Konigsberg, and his editors found the usage delightful; not only is it singled out for mention in the story, but it is used as a title on the front page: "Summer Rituals: Grilling at 'Da Crib'."

African Americanisms like "We Be Growin" and "Da Crib" are ubiquitous today in White American English. These inflect the speech of White youth at every social level and in every part of the United States (cf. Bucholtz 1999; Cutler 2003). Only last weekend, I was working in my front yard in Tucson when a young White man, perhaps in his late teens, walked by, punching in a number on his cell phone. When his callee picked up, I overheard him say "What up, girl?"

African Americanisms also appear in the speech of White adults of all ages, and are used to make adults seem more youthful and in tune with the latest styles in popular culture. I remember my octogenarian grandfather, 60 years ago, using "copacetic," which Smitherman (1994) identifies as of African American origin. Watching the 2004 Summer Olympic Games, I was startled to hear Bob Costas, a fiftyish White broadcaster hosting NBC's coverage, offer "props" to his producer for his hard work. "Props," from more general African American "propers" (Smitherman 1994:185), probably ultimately from "proper respect," has today moved out of the Black hip-hop world to become so widespread in White American English that even someone Costas's age can use it.

**Figure 7**    Aaron McGruder's *Boondocks* satirizes the appropriation of African American language and stereotyping imagery of African American men. The Boondocks © 2005 Aaron McGruder. Distributed by Universal Press Syndicate. Reprinted with permission. All rights reserved.

African American English is especially common in advertising aimed at youthful White audiences. Such advertising frequently draws on an image that Mary Bucholtz (1999) has labeled "hypermasculinity," an idea of physical power and danger, simultaneously attractive and threatening, that is iconically associated with Black men and very damaging to them. Such advertising reproduces this very negative image while simultaneously bleaching and reshaping the language, draining it of specific content in favor of the flattened aesthetic of cool. An example comes from a MacDonald's advertising campaign from January 2005, when the fast food chain placed on the Internet "banner ads" that ran across the top of a number of youth-oriented websites. The African American cartoonist Aaron McGruder satirized these in his brilliant *Boondocks* comic strip. In his April 12, 2005, strip the first panel shows McGruder's character Huey, a deeply hip and knowledgeable 10-year-old, staring at his computer screen and observing that "McDonald's is trying to appeal to a young urban demographic." The next panel, labeled "actual McDonald's ad," shows a man of ambiguous racial identity holding a hamburger and saying, "Double Cheeseburger – I'd hit it," using an African Americanism that at the time meant "have sexual intercourse with."[7] In the next panel, Huey says, "I think they're a bit confused," and his little friend Michael Caesar says, "Can you even do that with a cheeseburger?"[8] McGruder continued his attack on McDonald's for months. A July 22, 2005, strip has his character Huey say: "Know what it'd take for McDonald's to be cool? A bouncer outside the door, a V.I.P. section, and thirty-dollar cheeseburgers."[9] The last strip in the McDonald's series, on July 23, 2005, is seen in Figure 7. Huey sighs in exasperation at the sight of a huge McDonald's billboard (which I believe was invented by McGruder, but which is not at all far off real examples) with a stereotypical Black "gangsta" in an aggressive pose, waving a handgun and using a Mock-Ebonics version of street language.[10]

Smitherman points out that, like McGruder's character Huey, many African Americans see appropriation of African American usages as a kind of theft, because in their view "Whites pay no dues, but reap the psychological, social, and economic benefits of a language and culture born out of struggle and hard times" (Smitherman 1998:218). Most pertinent for our model of linguistic appropriation is Smitherman's point that "When a term crosses over into the White world, it is considered suspect and is no longer *dope* in the Black world" (Smitherman 1998:222). The May 27, 2005, *Boondocks* strip makes this point: it opens with a panel that reads, "Cease and desist using a slang word when you hear the following people say it": the choices were Paris Hilton (a White celebrity who personifies "rich White girl" vapidity), McDonald's, and Old People.[11]

Appropriations from African American English obviously are intended to recruit desirable qualities to White speakers. However, while they lend to White people a "cool" identity, they simultaneously index dangerous negative stereotypes. These stereotypes of African American males mean that the extraordinary rates of violence in African American communities and the incarceration of a very high percentage of African American men are considered by many Whites as merely consequences of their essential nature. Thus these remarkable statistics, unique in the world, stimulate no re-evaluation of public policy or White attitudes. Furthermore, just as seemingly benign loans from American Indian languages coexist with the racist excesses of "Hollywood Indian English," loans from African American English in everyday use in White speech coexist with overtly racist attacks on African Americans and their language. Ronkin and Karn (1999) documented an explosion of parodic websites illustrating "Mock Ebonics."[12] Many of these sites are vulgar and racist to the highest degree, advancing the most vicious stereotypes of African Americans.

African American English is the single most important source for new slang (and, eventually, unmarked everyday colloquial usage) in White American English. Yet White authorities and ordinary people scorn and abuse it in every possible way. African American English is widely regarded as a disorderly form of "slang," to be discouraged at school and on the job. A recent study showed that job seekers with recognizably African American first names like "Lakisha" and "Jamal" are 50 percent less likely to be selected for contact and interview than are applicants with "White" names like "Emily" and "Greg" (Bertrand and Mullainathan 2003). While African American attitudes and linguistic ideologies are complex (Morgan 1994), some African Americans have themselves internalized this understanding of African American English, and understand it only as a corruption of White varieties. However, while appropriations from African American English clearly can be understood as a sort of word-by-word sequence of thefts, the African American case contrasts with the Native American situation.

Native American languages have made important contributions to American English, but they are seriously endangered, and enjoy very little institutional support at any level. In contrast, a very well-established system of counter-hegemonic socio-cultural formations keeps African American English lively and dynamic. Furthermore, increasing African American economic control over some media sectors, especially within the hip-hop world, may permit the use of formal mechanisms, such as enforcement of copyright, to resist appropriation. In spite of persecution – and perhaps because of it (Labov 2007) – African American English is probably here to stay.

## US Spanish and White Linguistic Appropriation

Although Spanish is by far the most important minority language in the United States, it is often represented today as so very much an "un-American" language that it is astonishing to find, as shown in Chapter 5, that Spanish loan words are an important resource in contemporary colloquial American English. Regionalist Anglo Spanish, especially Booster Regionalist Anglo Spanish used in marketing real estate and tourism in the Southwest and California, and Mock Spanish as well, can be understood as forms of linguistic appropriation. Within Mock Spanish, the meanings of Spanish lexical items are reshaped to serve White purposes. As discussed in Chapter 5, Mock Spanish works through dual indexicality to elevate the White speaker as a person with a delightful sense of humor and a cosmopolitan access to foreign languages, while at the same time parodying Spanish speakers as lazy, dirty, insincere, undependable, politically corrupt, and hypersexualized. Extremely hyperanglicized forms like "Buena snow-shoes," common in Mock Spanish, simultaneously draw on Spanish for humor while actively distancing the speaker from the Spanish-speaking communities in which *Buenas noches* might be heard. Furthermore, the proliferation of Mock Spanish coexists with both informal and formal efforts to sharply restrict the use of Spanish among members of its heritage populations in the United States.

Spanish is, of course, a world language, and the Mock Spanish use of "adios," "nada," "compadre," "mañana," "cerveza," "el presidente," and similar locutions hardly threatens these lexical items in the usage of citizens of Spanish-speaking countries. However, the constant repetition of these and similar Mock Spanish forms at every level of the American mass media and continually in everyday talk convey the message that Spanish is not a serious language. Spanish in the bilingual classroom, where it is still permitted, is seen only as a crutch for those who do not speak English adequately, and not as a form of discourse that deserves cultivation and development. Zach Rubio, the student suspended from high school in Kansas quoted in (1), had clearly internalized this constraint; he observed that while he thought it was fine to speak Spanish in the hall with a friend, he would never speak Spanish in the classroom, where he had been taught that it would be disruptive and inappropriate (Reid 2005). When politicians speak Spanish, they are understood only as pandering to their base, not as developing serious ideas before an important public (Woolard 1989). Whites often see Spanish-language media merely as a way that corrupt cultural brokers make money off the Latino population, and not as an alternative public sphere with its own contribution to civic life and to the arts. Just as African American English is widely condemned as a degraded slang, Spanish as spoken in communities in the United States is denigrated by Whites as an inferior corruption of an idealized standard often called "Castilian." Zentella concludes that the impact of these pressures indeed threatens the use of Spanish in the US.

> the net effect of dialect dissing, Spanglish bashing, the Hispanophobia that insists that only English be used in the schools and workplaces, and the "Mock Spanish" spoken by Anglos that makes fun of Spanish speakers . . . is the promotion of language shift. Latin@s who end up convinced that their Spanish is bad or *mata'o* ("killed"), and that "real Americans" are English monolinguals, rush to adopt English and eventually do kill off their Spanish.
>
> (Zentella 2002:331)

Among linguistic appropriations from Spanish can be found examples of what Whiteley (2003) called "flattening," as in his example of "kachina." This is evident from a recent campaign that the Univisión television network ran in order to attract advertisers. The climax of this campaign was a full-page advertisement, which I encountered in the Business Section of the *New York Times*. The ad read as in (5):

(5)    THE BIG FOUR ARE NOW THE BIG FIVE. ¿COMPRENDE? (*New York Times*, Friday, May 27, 2005, p. C6).

Mock Spanish "¿Comprende?" is a word that generations of Mexican Americans have associated with racist bosses.[13] In this usage, the wide range of meanings of the Spanish form is flattened into the narrow Mock Spanish sense, where ¿Comprende?, pronounced /kəmˈprɛndiy/, is a contemptuous threat.

Finally, as pointed out in Chapter 5, linguistic appropriations of Spanish into diverse forms of American English exist side by side with formal legal attempts to constrain the use of Spanish, such as laws in support of "Official English" and against bilingual education which have passed in many states.

As with appropriations from American Indian languages and African American English, appropriations from Spanish do meet resistance from members of Spanish-heritage communities. José Cobas's protest to Univisión about its use of Mock Spanish "¿Comprende?" in advertising is only one of many letters of protest that Professor Cobas has initiated. Almost as soon as I began working on Mock Spanish, I heard from Spanish speakers about their efforts to resist it. After I spoke at the University of California-Irvine in 1994, Professor Raúl Fernández shared with me a copy of a letter he had written to the *Los Angeles Times*, protesting the use of Mock Spanish "cojones" in a film review.[14]

Booster Regionalist Anglo Spanish and Mock Spanish frequently co-occur with imagery that is offensive to members of Spanish-speaking communities. Especially common is the image that Mexicans call "El Pancho," the figure shown asleep with his sombrero pulled over his eyes, often leaning improbably against a saguaro cactus. I have found "Pancho" figures for sale in Tucson on little ceramic flower pots, on greeting cards, on Christmas gift wrap, and even on concrete tiles intended for flooring local patios. While the Spanish-speaking population in Tucson deplores the grammatical lapses in the local version of Booster Regionalist Anglo Spanish, they usually tolerate it. But this tolerance does not extend to "Pancho" imagery. One case of the juxtaposition of a "Pancho" with Booster Regionalist Anglo Spanish text led to a successful effort on the part of local Spanish speakers to change these usages. In 2002, Pima County and the City of Tucson initiated a program to encourage the use of alternative modes of transportation. The centerpiece of the program was a week of public events, called the "Clean Air Fiesta." The brochure for the first year of the program, shown in Figure 8, was widely distributed locally. Every employee of the University of Arizona received a copy and there were piles of them in banks, supermarkets, and the lobbies of civic buildings. It read "Clean Air Fiesta/Give your Car a Siesta."

The text in the brochure was rich with Mock Spanish, complete with iconic upside-down exclamation marks, as in the following examples: "¡Hola amigos! Celebrate clean air at downtown's El Presidio Park"; "Call 884-RIDE for RideShare information. ¡Muy bien!"; "pedal your bike to work or school today . . . ¡Fantástico for our air!"; "¡Arriba! ¡Arriba! Grab your sneakers, let's get walking!"; "¡Hay Caramba! Nearly 70% of Tucson's air pollution is created by motor vehicles."

But the inexcusable feature of the brochure for the "Clean Air Fiesta" campaign was that, as part of the festive imagery on the cover, seen in Figure 8, there appeared a "Pancho" – a little car lying on its back,

CLEAN AIR
FIESTA

GIVE
YOUR CAR     MARCH 22 –
A SIESTA     APRIL 7
             2002

WALK THERE, BUS THERE, BIKE THERE,
NET THERE, RIDE SHARE

**Figure 8**    This stereotyping image, a "Pancho" in the form of a sleeping car, is associated with an instance of Booster Regionalist Anglo Spanish. It drew objections from Latino/as in Tucson in 2002.

sombrero over its radiator grill, saying "zzzzZ." Many members of Tucson's Hispanic community were profoundly offended. Sylvia Campoy, Director of the Equal Opportunity Office for the City of Tucson, initiated a campaign to recall the brochures, posters, and t-shirts that displayed the sleeping car. Campoy was quoted in the *Arizona Daily Star* as saying that "It is a stereotypical depiction . . . it is a negative stereotype." Anglo city officers defended the program in the usual rhetoric; Beth Gorman, program manager for the Pima County Department of Environmental Quality, said that the image was "meant to honor Tucson's Hispanic heritage" (Davis 2002). Latino public officials took sides, with their reactions ranging from acceptance, through "there are bigger things we should be focusing on," to the outraged reaction of Campoy and many of her colleagues (Portillo 2002).

In March 2003, the "Clean Air Fiesta" took place again, with a new brochure. While the admonition to "Give Your Car a Siesta" was retained, the Pancho car was gone, replaced by a folkloric dancer in a colorful costume. Furthermore, except for "fiesta" and "siesta," the text of the brochure was entirely in English without even a whisper of Spanish, and no upside-down exclamation points. In April 2005, the Spanish had completely disappeared: The slogan "Clean Air Fiesta/Give Your Car a Siesta" had become the "Clean Air Fair: Join the Clean Air Fair for Healthier Air," and the colorful brochure included flowers and butterflies with only a faint hint of Mexican folkloric style and no Spanish in its sober list of events. In 2006 and 2007, the website for the "Clean Air Fair" had no Spanish content.[15] It was clear that objections from Tucson's Spanish-heritage community had reshaped the use of language and imagery during the history of the campaign.

## Conclusion

Linguistic appropriation in the United States has been historically an important tool of White racism, dating back to the simultaneous elevation of early English explorers as men of learning and the denigration of Native Americans as animalistic savages in the seventeenth century. And linguistic appropriations remain an important tactic for White racist culture. Linguistic appropriation within White racism aims to control the linguistic resources of subordinated populations, permitting these to survive only to the degree that they are useful, in the form of substantially reshaped and reorganized meanings, for White projects. These include the constitution of White virtue and the creation of White privilege, simultaneously with the denigration and stereotyping of members of the communities in which the appropriated forms originate.

Like other kinds of hegemonic projects, White American linguistic appropriation is not total. Some Native Americans continue to understand their indigenous languages and their local forms of English as important resources for their communities, although White projects and rhetorics may pose a problem for efforts at language revitalization (Errington 2003; Hill 2002). Speakers of African American English draw on a deep well of creativity to produce new expressive forms. Many US Latinos/as honor their Spanish-language heritage and work to develop it. But these successes operate within a powerful field of constraints imposed by White domination over linguistic resources. The concept of linguistic appropriation can clarify exactly how these constraints work, and how they might best be interrupted and counteracted to permit the full expression of American linguistic diversity.

# Chapter 7

# Everyday Language, White Racist Culture, Respect, and Civility

## Above-Ground White Racism and the Evidence of Language

White racism lives in the minds of American Whites in a curiously misapprehended shape. Most of them understand it as a peripheral part of America's past that does not require much attention. The kind of celebratory history of the United States that most White Americans are exposed to in school glosses over the extraordinary truths: nearly 250 years of slavery, more than 100 years of White terrorism and Jim Crow, 300 years of genocidal warfare against American Indians, repeated pogroms against Mexican and East Asian Americans, and the blinding, mind-boggling contradictions of American leadership – that many of the framers of American democracy, men held in nearly universal reverence by White Americans, owned Black slaves, and that the majority of White American leaders since the Civil War, at every level and in every social field, have been White supremacists and segregationists. This literally white-washed history makes it impossible for most White Americans to think seriously about how racism might live in the very foundations of their traditions: for instance, in strange aberrations like the role of the Electoral College in presidential elections (Epps 2007), or in the absence of any provision for the legal movement of labor in the so-called North American Free Trade Agreement (in sharp contrast with the Schengen Agreement that shapes the free movement of labor within the European Community), or the "right-to-work" laws in the former slave states that make American labor unions weak and marginal. Nor do they realize how this history lives in their talk, where to say "American" can be shown to evoke an image of a White man, uninterrupted by the legal stipulations of citizenship in the Fourteenth, Fifteenth, or Nineteenth Amendments to the US Constitution.

White historical amnesia exists alongside active inattention to the vividly visible racial stratification of contemporary American society, including the astonishing levels of imprisonment of African American men, for whom the United States is a carceral dystopia. Should Whites somehow be forced to notice racial disparities in wealth, education, and opportunity, well-documented traditions of rationalization permit them to blame the people of color who are its victims, since venerable stereotypes of laziness, improvidence, sexual license, dirt, and stubborn ignorance are always ready to hand.

Unfortunately, a good deal of recent scholarship on White racism, while acknowledging its continued existence, does not fully capture its realities. For instance, much scholarship suggests that White racism today lives "underground," expressed subtly in a chilly climate and in "benign neglect," rather than in beatings and lynchings and verbal muggings with slurs and epithets. It is true that upstanding White citizens no longer pack sandwiches to attend lynchings. Yet news of racial violence and racist threats against people of color arrives daily. I write this as the morning paper reports an epidemic of threats against people of color using the ugly symbol of lynching, the hangman's noose. News that White kids in Jena, Louisiana, had threatened Black kids by hanging nooses in a tree on the local high school grounds in the Spring of 2007 was easily assimilated to the "Ku Kluxer," "Redneck" stereotype of the folk theory of racism. But a noose hung on the door of a Black professor at Columbia University Teachers' College in New York City does not fit the folk theory so easily. Nor can it be assimilated to the "chilly climate" scenario, where people of color are merely left out of informal social moments like after-class drinks or the Saturday afternoon tennis game. A noose means only one thing: it is a White on Black death threat. And that is how the New York police understood it, assigning the matter to their hate crimes unit (Gootman and Baker 2007).

The linguistic landscape revealed in this book hardly supports any claim that White racism has gone underground. The underground dimensions of White racist language are, indeed, important, and in Chapters 5 and 6 I have discussed several types of covert racist discourse. Linguistic anthropologists trace to Franz Boas and Benjamin Whorf their understanding that cultural ideas are most effectively encoded in discourse precisely when they are organized below the level of metalinguistic and metapragmatic awareness, in unassailable presuppositions that are almost never made explicit. In Chapter 5 on Mock Spanish and in Chapter 6 on linguistic appropriations, I showed how racist stereotypes that date back hundreds of years can persist in this "underground" form. But I have also tried to show that one reason that covert racist discourse remains underground is that Whites actively resist acknowledging its existence. Furthermore, covert racist discourses have authors, influential Whites who appropriate new linguistic resources from ways of speaking associated with people of color, and reshape these to serve their own purposes.

But racist and racializing stereotypes do not live only in covert racist discourse. They appear as well in highly visible and overt racist talk and text, at the highest levels of American society, and in the most elite media. Indeed, when it came time to finish drafting Chapters 3 and 4, on slurs and gaffes, I discovered that the last couple of years had brought a positive embarrassment of riches. Between the Spring of 2003, when I first drafted the chapter on Senator Trent Lott's notorious December 2002 statement in support of racial segregation, and Fall 2007, as I prepared this book for submission, so many new moral panics over racist utterances had occurred that it was difficult to select which to mention. I had to set aside rich materials on Senator George Allen of Virginia, on Don Imus, on Michael Richards, on Senator Joseph Biden of Maryland (who remarked on February 7, 2007, that Senator Barack Obama was "the first mainstream African American who is articulate and bright and clean" [Thai and Barrett 2007]). Each one of these incidents produced, day after day, the overt inscription of ugly stereotypes, in the most explicit language, in every medium of information and entertainment. And this is to say nothing of the incidents that never moved beyond the campus of the University of Arizona or the local news here in Tucson. The astonishing moment when thugs from the "Border Guardians" shouted down an invited speaker, a representative of the government of Mexico, in a scholarly colloquium at the University of Arizona (mentioned in Chapter 5), was reported only in the local papers.

In summary, much of the everyday language of White racism has not gone underground. Instead, it circulates in the full light of day. Every slur, every stereotype in its repertoire receives frequent exposure and publicity. While Chapter 3 shows that people are most likely to utter explicitly racist statements in their own voices when they are protected by anonymity, and while scholars like Myers (2005) and Picca and Feagin (2007) have suggested that explicit racist talk circulates most freely when interaction is "backstage," moral panics around gaffes repeat explicitly racist words, provide them with immense publicity, and attach them to famous names in an elaborate discourse of motives. In summary, the analyses presented here suggest that, while White racist language has its subtle side, much of it is not subtle at all, and it is not underground. Instead, it is posed in the spotlight, wrapped in red, white, and blue.

## White Racist Culture as a System of Contradictions, Erasures, and the Intersubjective Creation of Meaning

Alongside the assertion that White racism has moved underground, a good deal of recent scholarship centers on so-called "structural racism" or "institutional racism." The recognition of structural racism, which foregrounds the racist impacts of formal policy in government, banking, criminal justice, education, and other institutional domains, was an important step forward from an exclusive focus on individual bigotry. The theory of White racist culture illustrated here aims to enlarge our understanding of racism once again. I have advanced a rather simple theory of how White racist culture is organized in such a way that White racism can persist, and yet be deniable or even invisible to those who participate in it. I recognize two basic components that make possible this deniability and invisibility, the folk theory of racism and several linguistic ideologies. These interlock in such a way that Whites can misapprehend the workings of their world and erase its many contradictions. And, since this misapprehension and erasure benefits them, preserving their illusions of virtue and their genuine privileges, both material and symbolic, there is little incentive to critique or challenge it.

The folk theory of racism, outlined in Chapter 1, is crucial to White misapprehension and erasure. The folk theory takes "race" for granted as a basic biological category, holds that people naturally aggregate at every social level along racial lines, and sees "racism" as what happens when backward and marginal individuals believe that some races are inferior to others, and act on these beliefs. Alongside the folk theory of racism, several linguistic ideological complexes are important. Referentialist ideology sees the principal function of language as the exchange of information and the enlargement of our knowledge of the truth. The words of language are thought to be linked by history to this task, and people should know the truth and choose the words that best represent it. The conduit metaphor suggests to us that the meanings in words pass unproblematically from speaker to hearer, so that the truth is easily shared.

While referentialist ideology understands meaning as residing in words, personalist ideology sees individual intention as the most important source of meaning. Even though the meaning of words is thought to be unproblematic, established at historical moments of authoritative baptism, personalist linguistic ideology holds that we cannot really know what a person's words mean until we assess her beliefs and intentions. Finally, performative ideology holds that language is powerful, that it can have material effects in the world, including hurt and comfort to individuals.

None of these linguistic ideologies is in itself racist. While I have suggested that linguistic ideologies are saturated with political interests, in the broad sense these particular ideologies are probably neutral in reference to the cultural project of racism. Indeed, all of these ideologies encompass important insights, and genuine advances in our understanding of the nature of language and speech have been produced by adapting the frameworks for thought that they provide. But, taken together with one another and with the folk theory of racism, these neutral understandings lead us away from productive anti-racist analysis, and towards the reproduction of White racist culture. The folk idea of race as a biological category obscures the way that race is a social-cultural and, especially, a political-economic category, and leads us into fruitless debate about whether disparities are due to "race" or "class." The idea that racists are marginal and backward obscures the role of elites in the perpetuation of White racism. The folk-theory notion that "people prefer to be with their own kind" reproduces the understanding of "kind" as "race" with unspoken precision. Furthermore, it makes all forms of discrimination morally equivalent, and obscures again the way that political and economic dominance are required in order to accomplish the projects of White racism, and are not available to people of color. The idea that racism is a matter of individual belief, together with the referentialist ideology of words and the conduit metaphor, obscures the way that racism is perpetuated through indexicality, in the intersubjective spaces where meaning is negotiated and inferences are made without ever being made explicit. This intersubjective space, the site where culture is made public and exchanged at every level of interaction, including the most quotidian, is neglected by scholarship on institutional racism with its focus on policy.

Thus referentialist and personalist ideologies are neutral in regard to racism, but the forms of common sense that they make possible draw us deeper into the traps set by the folk theory. The folk theory of the racist as ignorant, backward, and marginal makes ordinary Whites intensely resistant to recognizing the racist history and content of common expressions in their own language. The debate over "squaw" in Phoenix in 2003 and 2004 made clear that they draw on the folk theory and on referentialist and personalist understandings about the meanings of words in order to justify their resistance. The moral panics around gaffes, with their important metacultural role in perpetuating stereotypes, are driven by personalist and referentialist ideologies working together. Personalist linguistic ideologies require us to evaluate a speaker's beliefs and intentions before assigning meaning to her words. Referentialist ideology requires that we get this exactly right, so that we can be sure exactly what kinds of truths we are hearing, or whether we are hearing lies. Personalist ideology admits to motives, like joking and light talk, that suspend the referentialist connection between core beliefs and the truth of words. The semiotic play that this suspension provides opens up opportunities for creativity that include social life's greatest pleasures. Yet in a White racist culture, it also licenses speakers to assign the blame for the pain inflicted by racist utterances to their "over-sensitive" victims. Curiously, performative ideology, which makes slurs visible as racist language and should work as well to make salient the hurt felt by victims, is seldom invoked by Whites. The folk theory of racism, which admits only Ku Kluxers to be racists, always permits the claims of White virtue to trump a claim of injury on the part of a person of color.

The interlocking workings of the folk theory of racism and the diverse dimensions of linguistic ideologies outlined above make it possible for White Americans to rationalize and erase the racism that permeates and shapes their world. There is nothing special about such processes: this is, in fact, how all cultures work. The task of cultural analysis is to penetrate the contradictions and inconsistencies that underlie the seeming coherence and validity of our worlds. When these worlds turn out to be damaged and damaging, as is the case in a cultural world centered on White racism, cultural analysis can help us understand how to change them.

## Respect, Civility, and Equality: Interrupting the Everyday Language of White Racism with Foundational American Values

In Chapter 4, I introduced the idea of "social alexithymia" (Feagin 2006), Hernán Vera's term for White Americans' curious lack of empathy for the feelings of people of color. We can now see that this lack of empathy involves a chain of reasoning that goes something like this: "I am a good and normal mainstream sort of White person. I am not a racist, because racists are bad and marginal people. Therefore, if you understood my words to be racist, you must be mistaken. I may have used language that would be racist in the mouth of a racist person, but if I did so, I was joking. If you understood my meaning to be racist, not only do you insult me, but you lack a sense of humor, and you are oversensitive." Notice that this entire chain of reasoning makes the speaker the sole authority over what her words shall mean. But this exclusive control is merely the common sense of personalist logic, and it is very hard to interrupt common sense.

But White Americans do share other values that are not consistent with this kind of common sense. Most of them claim that they believe strongly in respect for others, in civility in communicative exchange, and in the equality of all human beings. If they truly believe in the principle of equality, then respect and civility must be extended to everyone, regardless of race. Under these values, the claim of an interlocutor or an overhearer or an audience member that a word or a sentence caused pain should enjoy equal status with the claim of a speaker that no harm was intended. The usual civilities of everyday life should prevail: The speaker should acknowledge respect for the claim of pain, apologize, and discuss how to avoid any repetition. The constant repetition of the idea that anyone who calls language "racist" and objects to it is "oversensitive" or "angry" or "divisive" violates this norm of civility and mutual respect among fellow citizens. The only possible explanation for this violation is that those who commit it believe that people of color somehow do not deserve full citizenship, civility, and respect. And even under the folk theory, such a belief is racist. Indeed, from the point of view of the critical theory of racism, the victims of racism have special qualifications to detect and name it. Van Dijk (1993:18) argued that "knowledgeable minority group members" are our surest guides to where racism is active. People of color have produced some of the most profound thinking about racism, and, while they pick their battles carefully, letting much that is offensive pass by without objection, both in small acts of everyday rejection and in deliberate public manifestations by entire communities, they have been active in resistance. When I have talked to people of color about "covert racist discourse," I often find that they have understood this concept, in an informal way, since childhood. Among Whites, the idea of "linguistic appropriation" is a concept encountered, if at all, during a university education. Among African Americans, it is a commonplace of everyday understanding. So, not only do people of color deserve civility and respect as fellow citizens, they deserve the attention of anti-racist Whites as knowledgeable experts in the analysis of White racism, which is surely one of the greatest challenges faced by American society.

Along with accusations of "oversensitivity," the media ritual of the moral panic over "gaffes" should cease. I have followed these affairs for about a decade. Their terms are rigidly formulaic. The exchange of blame and excuse is utterly predictable, with Harvard-educated *Washington Post* columnists and middle-western talk radio hosts alike invoking the same hackneyed formulas, knotting up once again the frayed ends of the folk theory of racism and the personalist rhetoric of motives to return to the same tired conclusions about decent people who somehow slipped. It is time to simply hold people responsible for their words. If victims claim that those words were hurtful and damaging, that alone should carry blame and bring appropriate punishment. Arguments about whether or not speakers are racist are not useful, and function largely to reproduce White racism's central ideas.

What about the covert racist discourses? While I have quite self-consciously stopped using Mock Spanish, sacrificing a useful resource for an enjoyable kind of light talk, I am not optimistic that others will follow my example. There is probably no way to purge the American language of the various forms of Anglo Spanish, and there is certainly no way to shame rich White kids out of trying to talk like poor Black kids, no matter how silly they sound. But in matters of public usage, basic respect and civility should be the rule. If a community wishes to honor its Hispanic or Native American or African American heritage – by naming a charity walk, a festival, a street, a shop, or by developing a museum exhibit or a historical tour route, or by adopting a preferred architectural style – attentive (rather than merely *pro forma*) consultation with leaders in the communities closest to that heritage should be a given. Such celebrations are an opportunity as well to fund work by heritage-community artists, and to involve young people who might otherwise be alienated in useful and remunerative work. Otherwise, there is no honor, there is only erasure and appropriation, usually accompanied not only by hurt and anger and further alienation, but also by silly mistakes, distortions, and the flattening of language and history that produces the homogenized world that many White Americans themselves claim is objectionable.

These are very simple ideas for interrupting the everyday language of White racism. They require Whites and people of color to respect one another, to talk to one another long enough to listen to objections, to deliver apologies, and to consult about simple questions of representation and compensation. Small exercises in common courtesy are a start in interrupting the processes that I have described in this book. But nobody should think that even such a minimal intervention will be easy. As the materials in this book have illustrated, courtesy and respect unfortunately cannot be taken for granted. While the efforts of ordinary people to change how they interact are very important, people in authority especially need to make this change, to substitute the rituals of blaming and making excuses with rituals of apology and difficult negotiations toward increasing mutual understanding. I believe that Americans of good will of all colors desire change, so perhaps, once they are able to recognize where common sense today leads them astray, the probability of accomplishing change will grow. With effort, the everyday language of White racism that I have treated in these chapters may join slavery and official segregation as a part of American memory.

# Notes

## Chapter 1   The Persistence of White Racism

1   The table does not include figures for "Asians," which are obscured by the structure of the 2000 US Census. Figures for Native Americans are also not included, since these populations are so small that the statistics are often not very useful.

2   Except as otherwise noted, statistics are from the *2007 Statistical Abstract: National Data Book* (US Census Bureau 2007). Tables cited are as follows, and numbers in Table 1 are from the most recent year in the cited table: Table 2.4 Educational Attainment by Race and Hispanic Origin: 1960–2005; Table 54 Marital Status of the Population by Sex, Race, and Hispanic Origin; Table 62 Family Groups with Children under 18 by Race and Hispanic Origin: 1970–2005; Table 613 Unemployed and Unemployment Rates by Educational Attainment, Sex, Race, and Hispanic Origin: 1992–2005; Table 677 Money Income of Families – Median Income by Race and Hispanic Origin in Current and Constant 2004 Dollars: 1947–2004; Table 685 Per Capita Money Income in Current and Constant (2004) Dollars by Race and Hispanic Origin: 1967–2004; Table 692 Persons below Poverty Level and below 125% of Poverty Level by Race and Hispanic Origin:1960–2004.

3   Orzechowski and Sepielli (2003).

4   Home Ownership by Race and Ethnicity of Householder 2007.

5   Health, United States 2006.

6   For Whites and Blacks: Miniño, Heron, and Smith (2006). Infant mortality statistics are also from this source.

7   Arias (2007). Data for Hispanics are controversial due to the problem of possible misidentification. See note 11.

8   The Sentencing Project. Statistics State by State 2007.

9   The disparity for household net worth has apparently widened slightly since 2000, the most recent date for this statistic made available by the US Census Bureau. In 2005, households headed by a White householder had a median net worth of 105,100 dollars, while households headed by a Black householder had a net worth of 8,900 dollars (Gouskova and Stafford 2007). This source does not break out Hispanic-headed households.

10   The statistics offered in *The Bell Curve* are almost certainly invalid. For a careful critique, see Fischer (1996).

11   The census figures for many dimensions for Hispanics (obviously, a diverse population) have been the object of considerable controversy. The US Census figures for Hispanics suggest that, in spite of high rates of negative factors such as poverty and incarceration, this population enjoys higher life expectancy and lower infant mortality than Whites. Some scholars have suggested this "Hispanic paradox" is the result of cultural factors that promote good health, such as supportive family structures. Others, however, have argued that the flaw lies in the statistics themselves, and especially in the sampling strategies and ways of categorizing people that lies behind them (cf. Smith and Bradshaw 2006).

12   Critical Race theorists have made detailed discoveries about the way racial practices are deeply embedded in the workings of the law (e.g. Crenshaw, Gotanda, Peller, and Thomas, eds. 1995 and Delgado and Stefancic, eds. 2000). Social scientists have conducted rich explorations of both institutions and everyday life that show how racism is practiced in taken-for-granted routines (Bonilla-Silva 2003; Feagin 2006; Feagin and Vera 1995; Omi and Winant 1994; Smelser, ed. 2001 – to cite only a few highlights in an enormous literature). Anthropologists have provided general theory (e.g. Fleuhr-Lobban 2006; Gregory and Sanjek, eds. 1994; Harrison 1995; Smedley 1993; Spears, ed. 1999; Stoler 1995, 1997; Williams 1989), and work on specific racisms and racial ideas around the globe (Bashkow 2006; Crapanzano 1985; Goldstein 2003; Lancaster 1991; Sheriff 2001; Stoler 2002). Psychologists have explored the structures of self-construction and the forms of denial that create certain kinds of sensitivities about race, and suppress others (Hirschfeld 1996; Kovel 1970; Steele 1997). Philosophers have explored the forms of reasoning that underlie racist logics (Goldberg 1993). Historians have shown how, at key moments in American history, forms of attention to race were shaped toward what we find today (Blight 2001; Hartman 1997). Critics have explored the expression of racism in fine arts and letters (Gates, ed. 1986; Morrison 1992). This will give a sense of the multi-disciplinary range of the literature, which probably no single person can dominate. A number of good readers are available in the general theory of race and racism, e.g. Back and Solomon, eds. (2000). Useful histories of racism include Fredrickson (2002) and Miles (1989). And, of course, the great classic discussions of the contradictions of racism in the United States are Du Bois (1986) and Myrdal (1944).

13   As I write these final revisions in the Fall of 2007, Justice O'Connor's opinion, for all its faults, seems positively enlightened in comparison to the absolute rejection of racial criteria in the assignment of educational resources expressed by the majority of the US Supreme Court in *Parents Involved in Community Schools v. Seattle School District 1 et al.* (551 US 2007, decided June 28, 2007). This "colorblind" opinion holds that any denial of resources to a White student in the name of maintaining racial balance in public schools is on the same moral plane as was the racial segregation addressed in the famous 1954 decision, *Brown v. Board of Education of Topeka*, 347 US 483 (1954).

14   Sparks and Jantz (2002) take this position, attacking the famous pioneering work of Franz Boas on the plasticity of head shape. For a reply, see Gravlee, Bernard, and Leonard (2003).

15  Recent work in human genetics is summarized in a special supplement to the journal *Nature Genetics* 36, No. 11S (2004), entitled "Genetics for the human race." The journal is the site of choice for following the major debates. For instance, Kahn (2005) has an exemplary discussion of how the popular press distorts findings in medical genomics to fit the folk theory of racism.

16  This opinion is, of course, shared by the most highly placed African American in the United States, Supreme Court Justice Clarence Thomas. In his concurring opinion to Parents Involved in Community Schools v. Seattle School District 1 *et al.* (551 US 2007, decided June 28, 2007), Justice Thomas repeatedly asserts that the US Constitution is "colorblind," so that only extremely compelling concerns make permissible any racial basis for the allotment of government resources such as schooling in a particular school or school program. I assume that Justice Thomas chose to ignore Article I, Section 2, with the notorious "three-fifths" clause, or Article IV, Section 2, which deals with fugitive slaves.

17  I prefer to capitalize Black and White, but this is almost never seen in newspapers or magazines. In fact, I have had copy-editors for scholarly journals who were preparing my work for publication correct this usage, changing these words to lower case.

18  US Census 2001.

19  Indian bands in California that have become relatively wealthy by running gambling casinos are overwhelmed with applicants for enrollment (Leroy Miranda, personal communication, April 2003).

20  The "Other" is a technical term in psychoanalysis. The "Other" is a product of the imagination, created in order to project doubts, fears, and moral ambiguities onto an object thought to be as different as possible from the self, where these feelings and tendencies in fact originate. By projecting dirt onto an "Other," the self becomes clean. In projecting violence onto another, the self is made peaceful. Familiar examples of "Others" include Noble Savages, "terrorists," Barbarians, and the like.

21  Henceforth, I may not always write "White racism in the United States" or "White racist culture in the United States." However, unless I specify otherwise, that is the kind of racism I am talking about.

22  This quote can be found, for instance, at www.legis.state.ga.us/legis/1997_98/leg/fulltext/hr1139.htm; accessed February 14, 2004.

23  Housing Patterns 2000 (US Census Bureau).

24  Mortgage lending by private bankers was not regulated until the 1974 Equal Credit Opportunity Act, and rigorous enforcement of anti-discrimination laws did not really get under way until the late 1980s (Massey 2005). I have not seen the most recent figures, but it is well known that government agencies during the presidency of George W. Bush have not made enforcement of civil rights and anti-discrimination laws a high priority, so one must suspect that enforcement is currently lax to non-existent at the federal level.

25  The term "redlining" refers to the practice of financial institutions of using maps on which red lines were drawn around neighborhoods where lending was thought to be too risky. If a potential borrower needed financing inside a redlined area, the application was automatically declined.

26  For example, see discussion in *Hargraves v. Capital City Mortgage Corp.*, an early example of a court decision on "reverse redlining." Williams, Nesiba, and

McConnell (2005) found that even people of color who could qualify for prime home financing were likely to receive financing only through the sub-prime market, and predatory lenders, working in unregulated sectors of the finance industry, appear to be targeting minority communities. Sub-prime borrowers run a risk as much as ten times higher of losing their homes by foreclosure (Williams, Nesiba, and McConnell 2005). With the end of the housing bubble in 2006, minority communities are being gutted by bankruptcies and foreclosures, which of course lowers the property values of all owners in the community as foreclosed properties are sold at auction for fire-sale prices (Gonzalez 2007).

27    The key decision is the 1977 US Supreme Court ruling in *Village of Arlington Heights v. Metropolitan Housing Development Corp.*

28    In the instructions for fellows for the 2004–05 class, the list of "i.e.'s" disappeared entirely; perhaps someone had noticed the problem.

29    Charles (2003) uses more detailed figures to suggest that Hispanics are far less segregated than African Americans, and Asians are hardly segregated at all. Having lived in the Bay Area for a year recently, and knowing the cities of Los Angeles and San Diego very well, I find that this claim is not very revealing about facts on the ground. California cities all have their "Little Cambodias" and "Little Viet Nams" and "Koreatowns" where residential racial imbalance towards Asians is very obvious.

## Chapter 2    Language in White Racism: An Overview

1    An overview of the literature in discourse analysis can be found in Schiffrin, Tannen, and Hamilton (2001). In linguistic anthropology, landmark statements on discourse include Sherzer (1987) and Urban (1991). Foundational work in the study of the reproduction of racism in language has been carried out within the framework of "Critical Discourse Analysis" (CDA), including especially extensive work by van Dijk (1987, 1991, 1993, 1996, 1999), Wodak and her colleagues (e.g. Reisigl and Wodak 2001), and Blommaert and Verscheuren (1998).

2    To cite only one very famous example, in the UK, Australia, and New Zealand so-called "non-rhotic" varieties of English, where /r/ is not pronounced in pre-consonantal and syllable final position, are always prestigious (except among some communities in Scotland and Ireland which favor the prestige and venerable lineage of local rhotic varieties). In the United States and Canada, the varieties universally preferred as prestigious are rhotic, with /r/ pronounced in those positions. Even the sort of New England accent that is associated with high social status locally is often the object of teasing in other parts of the United States.

3    The language was a reference to the famous scene in Margaret Mitchell's *Gone With the Wind*, when the Black slave Prissy, who has pretended to know all about midwifery, confesses in a crisis, "I don't know nuthin' about birthin' no babies." The "aluminum tubes" reference was to the false claim, endorsed by Rice, that aluminum tubes found in Iraq were intended as parts for a nuclear reactor that

the dictator Saddam Hussein would use to enrich uranium for an atomic bomb. Under heavy attack, Danziger and the New York Times syndicate removed this cartoon, originally issued October 6, 2004, from his website.

4   By "core English-speaking world" I mean the UK, Ireland, Canada, the US, Australia, and New Zealand.

5   Several years ago, in the early 1990s (back far enough that I cannot retrieve it from their website – the hard-copy reference was lost in the accident mentioned in note 6), the well-known southwestern author Lawrence Cheek wrote an especially revealing and thoughtful column in the *Tucson Weekly*, which reflected on how racist stereotypes of Mexicans would somehow come to him out of the blue. One of his examples was looking at a roof that had been tiled crookedly, so that it would look "rustic," and saying out loud, "Looks like that tile was laid by a drunken Mexican." He wrote about how horrified he had been even to have had the thought, and wondered why it had occurred to him. One way is the inferences provoked by "cerveza," "vino," "borracho," and other elements in the Mock Spanish lexicon of boozing.

6   Unfortunately, a very large part of my collection of these items, dating back to about 1990, was lost in the Spring of 2007, when a temporary custodian, against the rules under which she was supposed to work, threw out a large box of files of Mock Spanish materials that was kept under my desk in my office at the University of Arizona. New materials continually appear, and I had already photographed and documented a few items in this collection. Nevertheless, this accident means that I cannot provide the detailed historical account that I had hoped to include in this book.

## Chapter 3   The Social Life of Slurs

1   In the same ruling, all place names with "Jap," an epithet for "Japanese," were also changed (Bright 2000).

2   A Google search on January 9, 2007, two months after the incident, returned 144,000 hits on <Kramer N-word>, 202,000 on <Michael Richards N-word> and 173,000 on <Michael Richards nigger>.

3   Celine Dion is a full-throated Canadian singer of top-40 pop ballads, of whom it can fairly be said that, at least in the African American sense, she has no soul at all.

4   Critical Race theory, which I spell with capital letters, is one school of the broader perspective, presented in Chapter 1, of the critical theory of race and racism, spelled with small letters.

5   Heumann and Church (1997) and Shiell (1998) include summaries of the major cases at prestigious institutions such as the University of Michigan, Brown University, the University of Wisconsin, and Dartmouth College.

6   Her term is borrowed from the work of Jacques Derrida (1988). Butler also refers to iterability as "citationality."

7   I owe much of the material in this section to the research reported in Bright (2000). Bill Bright was the director of my dissertation and a life-long friend and mentor. This chapter is dedicated to his memory.

8    The claim that the word comes from "Iroquois" (Mohawk is an Iroquoian language) was apparently first advanced by Sanders and Peek (1973), in *Literature of the American Indian*.

9    The first message board, during April 2003, was entitled "Piestewa Peak?", and ran at www.azcentral.com/message boards-Opinions & Viewponts-Piestewa Peak?. Beginning January 9, 2003, the message board, entitled "Piestewa or Squaw Peak?", ran at www.azcentral.com/message boards-In the News-Piestewa or Squaw Peak?.

10   I quote the message board postings exactly as they appeared, with the exception of using "/" for a hard return. I have in some cases reproduced only a single sentence from a message, where the rest of it deals with a completely different theme from the one at hand. Ellipses are in the original unless they appear in square brackets. I do not give the contributors' "handles" except when these are necessary to follow an exchange. Instead, I give the date and time of each posting. Since the message board accepted only one message at a time, this information permits the retrieval of individual messages.

11   In 2005 I had breakfast in a hotel in Salt Lake City next to a wall decorated with historic photographs that celebrated the local heritage. One of these bore the caption "Shoshone braves and a squaw."

12   Comparing the publicity received by the three female soldiers caught up in the incident in which Pfc. Lori Piestewa died speaks volumes about racial stratification in America. Pfc. Jessica Lynch is a delicate blond from West Virginia. Her poignant story received unprecedented coverage, and the US Army's publicity arm exaggerated her valor. Lynch took care to correct this once she knew of it, but still became "America's heroine." The other woman who survived the incident, Spc. Shoshana Johnson, is of Panamanian background and bilingual in Spanish (in the press, the dark-skinned Spc. Johnson was always referred to as an African American). Spc. Johnson received many honors, but most of these came from within the African American and Panamanian American community. A Google search on February 26, 2004, on the names of the three women tells the story: "Jessica Lynch" returned over 392,000 citations, "Shoshana Johnson" returned 47,800, and "Lori Piestewa" returned 9,220. Of course Piestewa was dead, so there was no coverage of events at which she appeared, although some events in her memory have been held, especially by Native Americans. African Americans did not fail to notice the difference in media attention and the lucrative opportunities that came to Lynch, but not to Johnson, and a brief and ugly controversy erupted when it was learned that Johnson had received much lower disability benefits from the Army (she was evaluated as having a 30 percent disability) than did Lynch (who was evaluated as 80 percent disabled). Many African Americans felt that the difference reflected racial discrimination (Wise 2003). The Army insisted that the evaluation of injuries was conducted by a Physical Evaluation Board with no reference to race (Douglas 2003).

13   Since the discourse around her fate often blamed her for it, we must note that Piestewa, a private soldier, was at no point responsible for the maneuvers of her unit, which included several officers and enlisted personnel who outranked her (Attack on the 507th Maintenance Company 2003).

14   Carmen, then a forty-ish M.A. candidate in bilingual education who took a class with me at Wayne State University, still remembered the pain and rejection she felt from this incident, which occurred when she was 6 years old.

15   Today all Hopis have first names and last names that they use in White-dominated institutions such as school attendance, birth registration, military service, voting records, and the like. The last names were adopted early in the twentieth century, and usually are the given names of senior men who were heads of families at the time. Although Hopi clan affiliation is matrilineal, these last names descend along male lines, just as they do among Whites. Thus Lori Piestewa's last name is the given name of a male ancestor from several generations ago. For Hopis it is obviously a male name: In the orthography used by *The Hopi Dictionary* (Hopi Dictionary Project 1988), the form is *pa-yes-t-iwa* "water-lying-resultative-stative." The name describes flat pools of water that lie on the desert after a rain: for Hopis, a beautiful and moving sight. Lori Piestewa probably also had a Hopi name, unique to her, given to her early in life by her father's sisters and evocative of some good or beautiful quality associated with her father's matrilineal clan (Whiteley 1992).

   Since each Hopi person has a unique given name, in a strictly Hopi sense Piestewa Peak is not named for Lori Piestewa, but for her male ancestor. However, Piestewa's mother has been quoted as saying that her daughter valued the family name, insisting on retaining it during divorce proceedings and saying "I want to die a Piestewa" (Reid 2003). The details surrounding Hopi naming did not become a public issue, and the chairman of the Hopi Tribe and Piestewa's family supported using it to name the peak. Permission by Piestewa's family, and support from Hopi leaders, to rename the peak with the "Piestewa" name, a family name of a type still felt by many Hopis to be a compromise with White custom, enlarged that compromise.

16   Indian casinos were a sore point for many who posted. In the United States, federally recognized tribes are sovereign nations and are not subject to many state laws. Recently many tribes, in the face of draconian budget cuts in Indian programs as the federal budget has shifted away from social initiatives, have drawn on this sovereignty to seek new revenues by setting up gambling casinos of a type that, off the reservations, are prohibited by law in most states. The National Indian Gaming Association listed 19 casinos in Arizona in 2003 (www. indiangaming.org/members/casinos.shtml, accessed March 11, 2004). But neither the Hopi Tribe (in which Pfc. Piestewa was enrolled) or the Diné (Navajo) Nation (on which she lived) run casinos; in both groups, tribal councils and popular referenda have ruled against them. Compacts with the state of Arizona regulate the number of slot machines a tribe may run, prohibit all table games except blackjack, and require the tribes to return a share of revenue to the state and to local jurisdictions. While the casinos are perceived to be very lucrative, only a couple of very small tribes have received genuine windfalls. Overall the per capita income for Indians in Arizona is far below that for other ethnic groups in the state, and casino income, while welcome, is far below what is required to address the many needs on the reservations. The casinos are extremely popular with Whites, not only for gaming, but because they offer excellent restaurants and first-class entertainment venues. However, other gambling interests, especially

the White-owned casinos at Laughlin, Nevada, on the Arizona state line and the state's horse- and dog-racing industries, have fought the Indian casinos and have spent a great deal of money to establish a widely held perception that the casinos give Indians an unfair advantage. Thus the casinos have become a focus for anti-Indian racism in Arizona, and this is evident in the discussion-board postings in the debate reviewed below.

17   Note that this contributor claims to be "1/4 Cherokee." My experience is that enrolled Indians usually introduce themselves more or less the way the contributor in (1b) does: "My familly comes from the Chicarilla [presumably the same as "Jicarilla," the Apaches of northern New Mexico], Picuris and Navajo Nations." Perhaps unfairly, I evaluate the "1/4 Cherokee" contributor as making a bogus claim.

18   Arizona is famous for Indians. However, Indians are a very small component of the population of the state. The 2000 US Census lists the population of Arizona as 5,130,632. The 255,879 persons counted as American Indians constitute approximately 5 percent of the total (Arizona ranks third, behind California and Oklahoma, for Indians as a percentage of the state's population). 160,820 Arizona Indians lived on one of the 22 reservations located entirely or partially within the state; 95,069 lived off the reservations. 33,489 of these lived in the city of Phoenix and its major suburbs, and constitute no more than 2 percent of the population of any local jurisdiction in the Phoenix area. Except for the Navajo reservation in the northeast corner of the state (which surrounds the Hopi reservation), Indians are not sufficiently concentrated in any state or federal legislative district to consistently elect Indian representatives. In summary, while readers of the *Arizona Republic*'s message boards for the Piestewa Peak controversy might conclude that Indians are a major political force in the state, this is not the case (Arizona Commission of Indian Affairs 2004).

19   Picca and Feagin (2007) document the intense elaboration of "backstage" contexts where White Americans today can enjoy deploying the most repulsive slurs in the exchange of racist jokes among close friends and family members.

## Chapter 4   Gaffes: Racist Talk without Racists

1   For example, see video at www.tmz.com/2006/11/20/kramers-racist-tirade-caught-on-tape/, accessed February 23, 2007.

2   Imus was fired and his show cancelled by CBS Radio on April 12, 2007, after a week-long moral panic that played out in exactly the same terms as those discussed in this chapter.

3   The second well-known mouth was Fox News Channel commentator Bill O'Reilly, who had said "wetbacks," a scurrilous word for undocumented Mexican immigrants, on his television show on Thursday, February 6, 2003.

4   This language was by no means original with Lott. Apparently, the same contrast between head and heart was invoked by the African American leader Jesse Jackson in apologizing for his famous "Hymietown" gaffe of 1983, when Jackson referred to New York City by that anti-Semitic expression.

5   To get a sense of how this "representational economy" is unified, think of how it is surely more comforting to think of the "full faith and credit" of the United States government as like the faith and credit of a person, than to think of it as a teetering pinnacle on a semiotic edifice built on constantly renegotiated forms of sociality.

## Chapter 5   Covert Racist Discourse: Metaphors, Mocking, and the Racialization of Historically Spanish-speaking Populations in the United States

1   For instance, *Gloor v. Garcia*, where the 5th Circuit Court of Appeals upheld an English-only workplace rule in 1990, and *Garcia v. Spun Steak*, where an English-only rule was upheld by the 9th Circuit in 1993.

2   www.illegalimmigrationbumperstickers.com/illegal_t_shirts, accessed January 5, 2007.

3   I thank Michael Walsh for forwarding to me this reference, which appeared on the Forensic Linguistics listserve.

4   The Spanish pronunciation is a better approximation of the source name, from the Tohono O'odham language. My interview materials (Hill and Goldstein 2001) suggest that the pronunciation /tuk'son/ is so charged that to use it indexes a strong commitment to Chicano activism, controversial in the local Hispanic community.

5   I am indebted for this example to Laura Cummings.

6   I am indebted to Benjamin Bailey for this example.

7   Precisely this attitude caused very serious problems at the Miami, Florida, International Airport for several years. Dade County, Florida, passed in 1980 a law that the county could not publish materials in any language other than English (Castro, Haun, and Roca 1990). This included information for tourists visiting the city from Europe and Latin America. Before the ordinance was repealed in 1992, several widely publicized violent robberies and even murders of European tourists – who took unlicensed cabs or who rented cars and got lost in dangerous parts of the city – occurred. Many observers suggested that the unavailability of tourist-informational materials in languages other than English might have played a role in these incidents. Multilingual informational brochures about transportation and safety practices for tourists are today available in the Miami Airport.

8   I have seen colleagues step forward to provide interpretation on numerous similar occasions. But a polite request for an interpreter is not the preferred style of Border Guardians.

9   michellemalkin.com/archives/005138.htm accessed May 7, 2006. One of the ironies here is that the Cinco de Mayo, which celebrates the victory of General Ignacio Zaragoza over the French forces of Napoleon III at Puebla in 1862, is not a very important Mexican holiday except in Puebla itself. In the United States, it is mainly an opportunity to sell Mexican beer to White people. Indeed, Cinco de Mayo advertising is a rich source of tokens of Mock Spanish (See Figure 4).

10    Although it is clear (and made explicit in the example in (6)) that people who object to Spanish are very aware that they risk being accused of racism. Materials reacting to the YouTube video "Press 'One' for English" often exhibited a "naughty" tone of pleasure in putting the forces of "PC" in their place. To take just one example from a blogger: *"Now here's one politically incorrect video for ya! Better check it out fast, before the ACLU and Mexican Consulate force You-Tube to take it down and have this musical couple locked up tight down in GITMO for 'Hate speech' and aggravated insensitivity!"* (Consent of the Governed 2007).

11    I use the rather clumsy term "members of historically Spanish-speaking populations" instead of "Latino/a" here in order to make the point that many such people do not speak Spanish. Martínez (2006) reviews the debates over the role of Spanish in Mexican American communities.

12    Capital letters are used to express the abstract underlying semantic structure of the metaphor. Specific realizations of it appear bolded in the examples.

13    Piney Hollow Ad, *Tucson Weekly*, October 10–October 16, 2005, p. 39.

14    Mock Spanish items are in English orthography, without acute accent marks. Real Spanish words are in italics.

15    Interestingly, the synonymous "hoosegow," from Spanish *juzgado*, is attested only from 1909 (DARE II:1090).

16    Mock Spanish in material for children exists alongside broad stereotyping mimicry of foreign accents. Lippi-Green (1997) includes a definitive chapter on this tendency.

17    Breidenbach (2006) includes usages and images from one of the most famous sites for Mock Spanish in the United States, the "South of the Border" shopping center in South Carolina, just south of the North Carolina state line on US Highway 301–501. Their website includes Mock Spanish as well as broad imitations of a Spanish accent, along with an offensive image of a stereotypical "Mexican," and uses the very unfortunate term "Pedroland" – given that "the Pedros" is today a racist slur for Latinos in the US Southeast (see www.pedroland.com/).

18    I had intended to provide a lexicon from my materials collected over nearly 20 years; this became impossible when they were lost through the custodial error at the University of Arizona mentioned in Chapter 2, note 6.

19    *The HR Edge*, Training Courses Available, Spring 2001. I am indebted to Bea Brown of the Southern Arizona Diversity Association for this example.

20    www.nypost.com/seven/12212006/postopinion/editorials/adios__alan_ editorials_.htm.

21    Spanish food terms are uniquely available to form colloquialisms, as with "the big enchilada," "the big taco" (both meaning "important person or event"), "the whole enchilada" (a very large and complete result of some action), "a few frijoles short of a burrito" (meaning "stupid," as in "a few bricks short of a load"), "hot tamale" (an attractive woman, especially a Latina), etc., along with the racist insult "taco bender" and its short form "taco" for "Mexican." The mayor of Scottsdale, Arizona, objected (in vain) to the name of a new chain restaurant in her town called "The Pink Taco"; she claimed the name referred to female genitalia. This was news to me, but it's an excellent example of semantic pejoration (Finnerty 2006).

22    digbysblog.blogspot.com/2006_12_01_digbysblog_archive. html#116689902380404624.

23   I thank Kathryn Woolard for contributing this example.
24   These usages are key to the "down-home style" of two Texas writers, the late political columnist Molly Ivins and humorist Joe Bob Briggs.
25   www.pedroland.com/, accessed August 12, 2007. I thank Carla Breidenbach for calling my attention to this remarkable place.
26   I am indebted to Laura Cummings for telling me about this place name variant. Observe that *La Tusa* reshapes the stereotypically English-language pronunciation of "Tucson" and may parody it.
27   Prototypical American identity is gendered as male, although women use Mock Spanish too. Mock Spanish use by African Americans is a very important phenomenon that illustrates its broader connotation of "Americanness" rather than merely of "Whiteness." Unfortunately, attention to this topic is beyond the scope of this chapter. Furthermore, in Tucson I do not have access to speakers or materials that would permit a careful study of the meaning of Mock Spanish for African Americans. A key text that drew my attention to African American usage is a novel by the African American writer Terry MacMillan, *How Stella Got her Groove Back*. In the novel Stella, a sophisticated African American professional woman, repeatedly uses Mock Spanish.
28   In the final Terminator film, *Terminator 3: Rise of the Machines* (2003), Schwarzenegger's Terminator character does not use Mock Spanish. When the John Connor character, who has become an adult, tries to elicit it from Schwarzenegger's character, he replies, "That was the other T-2–100." By the time of the final edit of the film, Schwarzenegger was already planning his campaign as a Republican for governor in a heavily Hispanic state where he ran as a "middle-of-the-roader" seeking cross-over Democratic votes. This suggests that Schwarzenegger's managers may have been aware that Mock Spanish did not necessarily go over well with Spanish-heritage audiences, who usually vote Democratic. However, bumper stickers and t-shirts reading "Hasta la vista, Davis" (the name of the recalled Democratic governor, Schwarzenegger's opponent) were widely available during the campaign.
29   This dialogue appears on a website dedicated to "Memorable quotes from *Talladega Nights*" (www.imdb.com/title/tt0415306/quotes).
30   In *Talladega Nights*, as in most Mock Spanish usages in film and television, Mock Spanish is used to construct a working-class voice. I am not at all convinced that this is authentic. In the early 1990s I was always able to find tokens of Mock Spanish on merchandise in gift shops and card shops oriented to middle-class shoppers, and I knew that the writers who were using it in newspapers and magazines were highly educated people. I collected many tokens in this period from PBS television shows like *Washington Week in Review* and *The McNeill-Lehrer Newshour*. In contrast, I was unable to find tokens at highway truck stops, which have extensive displays of goods intended for gifts of exactly the type that often have Mock Spanish captions in the fancy gift-shop context. One does hear Mock Spanish insults like "Pedros" and "taco-benders" on conservative talk-radio call-in shows (I am indebted to Margaret Smith for information on that point). The precise class association of Mock Spanish needs further research, but I am suspicious that it may be to a great degree an upper-middle-class and elite tactic.
31   www.nndb.com/group/750/000091477/, accessed December 31, 2006.

32    en.wikipedia.org/wiki/Jargon_of_The_Rush_Limbaugh_Show, accessed December 31, 2006.

33    "Mock Spanish not racist, just natural," *Arizona Daily Wildcat*, March 2, 2000. Electronic document at wc.arizona.edu/papers/93/110/03_1_m.html, accessed August 12, 2007. A former student, Dr. Tracey Duvall, did defend my work ("Mock Spanish misrepresented," Letters to the Editor, *Arizona Daily Wildcat*, March 6, 2002), but the *Wildcat* did not publish my four-line fax that simply gave the address of a website (now extinct) where those interested could read my work.

34    www.xoxide.com/das-keyboard.html, accessed December 28, 2006. I thank Eric Hill for calling my attention to "Das Keyboard."

35    Spanish is occasionally a source of model names for automobiles that do not appear to be jokes. Examples are Isuzu Amigo, the Ford Bronco, the GMC Caballero, Chrysler Cordoba, Honda del Sol, Lamborghini Diablo, Chevrolet El Camino, Cadillac El Dorado, Renault Fuego, Isuzu Hombre, Toyota Paseo, Kia Rio, Hyundai Santa Fe, Cadillac Seville, GMC Sierra, Hyundai Tiburon. This is the only case I have identified where Spanish words used in marketing are apparently intended to be entirely positive. These are part of a larger semiotic system of car names that is outside the scope of this chapter.

36    snltranscripts.jt.org/90/90enews.phtml.

37    www.illegalimmigrationbumperstickers.com/illegal_pics, accessed April 16, 2006.

38    The image can be found at The Write Idea Online, June 1, 2007, under the heading "Gringo de Mexico" (electronic document at writeidea.blogspot.com/2007/06/gringo-de-mexico.html, accessed August 9, 2007). The commentary under the image reports that it was part of a grassroots campaign that had produced a drop of 40 percent in revenues collected by the Republican National Committee from January 2007.

39    This was almost certainly pronounced [bæn'diyDow], which would be unintelligible to a Spanish speaker.

40    A Texas pizza chain, Pizza Patrón, reached out to Mexican customers by offering to accept pesos. News of this innovation in January 2007 triggered a national panic including death threats (blogs.usatoday.com/ondeadline/2007/01/pesosforpizza_c.html, accessed September 16, 2007).

41    "Name the President!" *The Nation*, March 26, 2001, p. 5.

42    www.washingtonmonthly.com/ accessed 070419.

43    For readers who may be uncertain of this point, *junta* is a perfectly ordinary Spanish word for a government entity. My son, who plays the viola in a symphony orchestra based in Valladolid in Spain, collects his paycheck from *La Junta de Castilla y León*, the governing body of the autonomous region. The English loan word has been pejorated to refer to some sort of undemocratic cabal, as when several colonels rule a country after a military coup. In the Fall of 2007, during a period of civil unrest and military crackdown in Myanmar, the word was consistently used for that country's military regime. The Mock Spanish association of the word was made clear in an editorial cartoon by Gary McCoy, who showed a heavily armed trooper shooting a hole in a peace sign represented as the dream of a Buddhist monk. The trooper was labelled "Junta *De* Myanmar" (my italics) (Gary McCoy.org/CagleCartoons.com, published in *Arizona Daily Star*, October 4, 2007, p. A7).

44    Agha (2007) has made this point about the naive apprehension of register, that it consists of words that "mean the same thing" as other words.

## Chapter 6   Linguistic Appropriation: The History of White Racism is Embedded in American English

1    www.ci.pasadena.ca.us/facts.asp, accessed August 17, 2005.
2    annmorgan.com/luxury/demographics.htm, accessed August 17, 2005.
3    Collins (1998) describes this process on the lands of the Tolowa in northern California.
4    An interesting question is whether these expressions continue to index "Indian-ness" for speakers of American English. They have intertextual resonances in syllable structure and other qualities of sound with the numerous Algonquian- and Siouan-derived place names that "sound Indian" to the American ear. However, this question requires further research.
5    For some examples, see K. Hill (2002) on resistance to the publication of a dic-tionary of Hopi, and Sims and Valiquette (2000:22), on a native speaker's (Sims's) distress about unauthorized work on her language.
6    An astonishing example of the completeness of linguistic appropriation from African American English, and its invisibility even to some scholars, is Stearns (1994). Stearns's book, *American Cool*, is a study of coolness in the sense of a muted and "reasonable" emotional style. The opening vignettes use examples that are clearly inflected with the African American usage, such as the character Joe Cool in the "Peanuts" comic strip and what Stearns calls "urban slang": "Be cool. Chill out" (Stearns 1994:1). However, there is no reference to African American language or culture in the book, and Stearns derives "American cool" entirely from high WASP style and sources. As seen in this chapter, upper-crust New Yorkers are among those Americans who borrow from African American style. That Stearns, who is obviously a good and careful scholar in his field, could miss very obvious phenomena like the notorious marketing of the "Kools" brand of cigarettes to African Americans shows the power of the forces that construct "American" culture out of "African American culture" and simply erase the latter.
7    "I'd hit it" to appreciate food is apparently now widespread. The blogger Atrios during August 2007 featured on his site digital photographs of beautiful sea food dishes that he had enjoyed during a vacation in Spain. Of a portrait of a plate of razor clams, one commentator remarked "I'd hit it" (atrios. blogspot.com).
8    www.livejournal.com/community/boondocks_comic/2005/04/13/.
9    *Boondocks*, July 22, 2005, www.livejournal.com/community/boondocks_comic/2005/07/22.
10   *Boondocks*, July 23, 2005, www.livejournal.com/community/boondocks_comic/2005/07/23.
11   *Boondocks*, May 27, 2005, www.livejournal.com/community/boondocks_comic/2005/05/27.

12    "Ebonics" is a term proposed for African American English by the Black scholar Robert Williams (1975) in his *Ebonics: The True Language of Black Folks.*

13    Carlos Vélez Ibáñez, personal communication (see Hill 1993a), José Cobas, personal communication, May 28, 2005. Professor Cobas asked me to join him in a letter to the officers of Univisión in protest against this ad. We faxed it to a long list of recipients including the then-president, Jerry Perenchio, but we never received an acknowledgment.

14    I do not know whether the letter was published. I suspect that it shared the fate of the several letters of protest that José Cobas and I have written, for which we have yet to receive replies.

15    The 2006 website can be found at www.pima.gov/deq/New/newsrelease/ CleanAirFair2006.html. The 2007 site is at www.tucsonaz.gov/cleanairdays/. The 2008 site, at www.cleanair.pima.gov/, also contains no Spanish of any kind.

# References

Abu-Lughod, Lila, 1990 The Romance of Resistance: Tracing Transformations of Power through Bedouin Women. American Ethnologist 17:41–55.

Accept, 1997 Electronic document. www.tigertales.com/tiger/accept042597.html.

Agha, Asif, 2003 The Social Life of Cultural Value. Language and Communication 23(3/4):231–273.

Agha, Asif, 2007 Language and Social Relations. Cambridge: Cambridge University Press.

Allen, Irving Lewis, 1990 Unkind Words: Ethnic Labeling from Redskin to Wasp. New York, Westport CT and London: Bergin & Garvey.

Allen, Mike and Jim VandeHei, 2002 Bid to Oust Lott from Leadership Considered. Washington Post, December 15:A1.

Alter, Tim, 2004 Why Whites Think Blacks Have No Problems. Electronic document. www.alternet.org/story.html?StoryID=11192if/.

Anchors, Sarah, 2004 "Squaw" Banished From Park. Arizona Republic, March 3. Electronic document. www.azcentral.com/php-bin/clicktrack/print.php/.

Applebome, Peter, 2002 Lott's Walk Near the Incendiary Edge of Southern History. New York Times, December 13:A22.

Argetsinger, Amy, 2002 Body Language of Political Winners Tells Its Own Story, Professor Says. Washington Post, January 15:C4.

Arias, Elizabeth, 2007 Estimation of US Life Tables for Minority Populations: Issues of Data Quality and Availability. Paper presented at the NAPHSIS/NCHS Collaboration: Past Successes and Future Challenges. Salt Lake City, UT, June 3–7, 2007. Electronic document. www.naphsis.org/NAPHSIS/files/ccLibraryFiles/Filename/000000000536/ARIASNAPHSIS2007FINAL3.ppt/.

Arizona Commission of Indian Affairs, 2004 Tribal Demographics. Electronic document. www.indianaffairs.state.az.us/tribes/demo.html.

Armour, Jody D., 2000 Race *ipsa loquitur*: Of Reasonable Racists, Intelligent Bayesians, and Involuntary Negrophobes. *In* Critical Race Theory: The Cutting Edge. 2nd edition. Richard Delgado and Jean Stefancic, eds., pp. 180–93. Philadelphia: Temple University Press.

Ask Dame Edna, 2003 Vanity Fair, February:116.

Attack on the 507th Maintenance Company, 2003 Electronic document. www.army.mil/features/507thMaintCmpy/AttackOnThe507thMaintCmpy.pdf/.

Austin, J. L., 1962 How to Do Things with Words. Oxford: Clarendon Press.

Back, Les and John Solomon, eds., 2000 Theories of Race and Racism: A Reader. London and New York: Routledge.

Bagley, Will, 2002 Blood of the Prophets. Norman: University of Oklahoma Press.

Bailey, Benjamin, 2000 Language and Negotiation of Ethnic/Racial Identity among Dominican Americans. Language in Society 29:555–582.

Baker, Nena, 2003a Rules Halt Name Change: Piestewa Peak Idea Must Wait At Least 5 years. Arizona Republic, April 10:B1.

Baker, Nena, 2003b Napolitano Seeks Ouster of State Official Over "Piestewa Peak." Arizona Republic, April 12:A1.

Bakhtin, Mikhail M., 1981 The Dialogic Imagination: Four Essays. Austin: University of Texas Press.

Balibar, Etienne, and Immanuel Wallerstein, 1991 Race, Nation, Class: Ambiguous Identities. London: Verso.

Barrett, Rusty, 2006 Language Ideology and Racial Inequality: Competing Functions of Spanish in an Anglo-Owned Mexican Restaurant. Language in Society 35: 163–204.

Bashkow, Ira, 2006 The Meaning of Whitemen: Race and Modernity in the Orokaiva Cultural World. Chicago and London: University of Chicago Press.

Bass, Gary, 2004 Department of Style: Word Problem. New Yorker, May 3:35–36.

Basso, Keith, 1996 Wisdom Sits in Places. Albuquerque: University of New Mexico Press.

Baugh, John, 2003 Linguistic Profiling. In Black Linguistics: Language, Society, and Politics in Africa and the Americas. Sinfree Makoni, Geneva Smitherman, Arnetha F. Ball, and Arthur K. Spears, eds., pp. 155–168. London and New York: Routledge.

Bernal, Martin, 2007 Letter Writer Needs to Open His Eyes to Latinos in Our Society. Tucson Weekly, July 26–August 2:6.

Berthold, Richard, 2004 Free Speech Protects, Offends. Daily Lobo, April 21. Electronic document. Lexis-Nexis.

Bertrand, Marianne, and Sendhil Mullainathan, 2003 Are Emily and Greg More Employable than Lakisha and Jamal? A Field Experiment on Labor Market Discrimination. NBER Working Papers Series, Working Paper 9873. Cambridge, MA: National Bureau of Economic Research. Electronic document. www.nber.org/papers/w9873/.

BET Interview with Sen. Trent Lott, 2002 Washington Post, December 17.

Bissinger, Buzz, 1997 A Prayer for the City. New York: Vintage Books.

Blight, David W., 2001 Race and Reunion: The Civil War in American Memory. Cambridge, MA: Belknap Press of Harvard University Press.

Blom, Jan-Petter, and John Gumperz, 1972 Social Meaning in Linguistic Structures: Code Switching in Northern Norway. In Directions in Sociolinguistics: The Ethnography of Speaking. Dell H. Hymes and John Gumperz, eds., pp. 407–434. New York: Holt, Rinehart & Winston.

Blommaert, Jan, and Jef Verscheuren, 1998 Debating Diversity: Analyzing the Discourse of Tolerance. New York and London: Verso.

Bobo, Lawrence D., 2001 Racial Attitudes and Relations at the Close of the Twentieth Century. *In* America Becoming: Racial Trends and Their Consequences. Volume 1. Neil J. Smelser, ed., pp. 264–301. Washington, DC: National Academies Press.

Bobo, Lawrence D., and Mia Tuan, 2006 Prejudice in Politics: Group Position, Public Opinion, and the Wisconsin Treaty Rights Dispute. Cambridge, MA: Harvard University Press.

Bonfiglio, Thomas, 2002 Race and the Rise of Standard American. Berlin and New York: Mouton de Gruyter.

Bonilla-Silva, Eduardo, 2003 Racism without Racists: Color-Blind Racism and the Persistence of Racial Inequality in the United States. Lanham, MD, Boulder, CO, New York, and Oxford: Rowan & Littlefield.

Border Guardians' Victories! 2006. Electronic document. www.borderguardians.org/index.php?option=com_content&task=view&id=40&Itemid=5/.

Bourdieu, Pierre, 1991 Language and Symbolic Power. Cambridge, MA: Harvard University Press.

Breathed, Berkeley, 2007 Opus (cartoon strip). Electronic document. www.salon.com/comics/opus/2007/07/22/opus/index.html?source=rss/.

Breidenbach, Carla Maria, 2006 Deconstructing Mock Spanish: A Multidisciplinary Analysis of Mock Spanish as Racism, Humor, or Insult. Ph.D. Dissertation, University of South Carolina.

Briggs, Charles, and John R. Van Ness, eds., 1987 Land, Water and Culture: New Perspectives on Hispanic Land Grants. Albuquerque: University of New Mexico Press.

Bright, William O., 2000 The Sociolinguistics of the "S-Word": *Squaw* in American Placenames. Names 48:207–216.

Bright, William O., 2004 Native American Placenames of the United States. Norman, University of Oklahoma Press.

Brightman, Robert, 1995 Forget Culture: Replacement, Transcendance, Relexification. Cultural Anthropology 10:509–546.

Britt, Donna, 2002 Lott's Words Repellent But Not Surprising. Washington Post, December 13:B1.

Brodkin, Karen, 1998 How Jews Became White Folks: And What that Says about Race in America. New Brunswick, NJ: Rutgers University Press.

Brown, Michael K., Martin Carnow, Elliott Currie, Troy Duster, David B. Oppenheimer, Marjorie M. Shultz, and David Wellman, 2003 White-Washing Race: The Myth of a Color-Blind Society. Berkeley, Los Angeles, and London: University of California Press.

Buchheit, Ezekiel, 1997 People Even More Ignorant Than I. Arizona Daily Wildcat, Friday, October 10:5.

Bucholtz, Mary, 1999 You Da Man: Narrating the Racial Other in the Production of White Masculinity. Journal of Sociolinguistics 3/4:443–460.

Bumiller, Elisabeth and Carl Hulse, 2002 Lott Vows Fight to Retain His Post as Senate Leader. New York Times, December 18:A1, A22.

Bush: Anthem Should Be Sung in English, 2006 Electronic document. www.msnbc.msn.com/id/12520667/.

Butler, Judith, 1997 Excitable Speech: A Politics of the Performative. New York and London: Routledge.

Cameron, Deborah, 1995 Verbal Hygiene. London: Routledge.

Campbell, Lyle, and Martha Muntzel, 1989 The Structural Consequences of Language Death. *In* Investigating Obsolescence: Studies in Language Contraction and Death. Nancy Dorian, ed., pp. 181–196. Cambridge: Cambridge University Press.

Candidate Bush Would Sing the Star-Spangled Banner in Spanish at Hispanic Festivals, 2006 Electronic document. thinkprogress.org/2006/05/02/bush-sing-spanish/.

Carr, David, 2003 Gaffes on Hispanics, From 2 Well-Known Mouths. New York Times, February 10:C9.

Cassidy, Frederick G., 1978 Another Look at Buckaroo. American Speech 53:49–51.

Castro, Max J., Margaret Haun, and Ana Roca, 1990 The Official English Movement in Florida. *In* Perspectives on Official English: The Campaign for English as the Official Language of the USA. Karen L. Adams and Daniel Brink, eds., pp. 151–160. New York and Berlin: Mouton de Gruyter.

Chandler, Raymond, 1981[1953] The Long Goodbye. New York: Vintage Books.

Charles, Camille Zubrinsky, 2003 The Dynamics of Racial Segregation. Annual Review of Sociology 29:167–207.

Chun, Elaine W., 2004 Ideologies of Legitimate Mockery: Margaret Cho's Revoicings of Mock Asian. Pragmatics 14:263–290.

Clemetson, Lynnette, 2002 Black Republicans Speak of Their Outrage at Lott. New York Times, December 17:A31.

Clymer, Adam, 2002 30-Year Dream of Leadership is Undone by a Lack of Allies. New York Times, December 21:A17.

Cohen, Richard, 2002a Leadership Requires Empathy. Washington Post, December 12:A45.

Cohen, Richard, 2002b A Record of Racial Intolerance. Washington Post, December 17:A33.

Cohen, Richard, 2002c Empty Vessel. Washington Post, December 19:A41.

Cohen, Stanley, 1972 Folk Devils and Moral Panics. London: McGibbon & Kee.

Coleman, Linda, and Paul Kay, 1981 Prototype Semantics: The English Verb "Lie." Language 57:26–44.

Collins, Jim, 1998 Understanding Tolowa History. New York: Routledge.

Consent of the Governed, 2007 Press "One" for English. Wednesday, July 18. Electronic document. yedies.blogspot.com/2007/07/press-one-for-english.html/.

Crapanzano, Vincent, 1985 Waiting: The Whites of South Africa. New York: Random House.

Crawford, James, 1992a Language Loyalties: A Source Book on the Official English Controversy. Chicago: University of Chicago Press.

Crawford, James, 1992b Hold Your Tongue: Bilingualism and the Politics of English Only. Reading, MA: Addison-Wesley.

Crawford, James, 2000 At War with Diversity: US Language Policy in an Age of Anxiety. Clevedon: Multilingual Matters.

Crawford, James, 2004 Educating English Learners: Language Diversity in the Classroom. Los Angeles: Bilingual Education Services.

Crehan, Kate, 2002 Gramsci, Culture and Anthropology. Berkeley and Los Angeles: University of California Press.

Crenshaw, Kimberlé, Neil Gotanda, Gary Peller, and Kendall Thomas, eds., 1995 Critical Race Theory: The Key Writings that Formed the Movement. New York: New Press.

Crenshaw, Kimberlé, Neil Gotanda, Gary Peller, and Kendall Thomas, 1995 Introduction. *In* Critical Race Theory: The Key Writings that Formed the Movement. Kimberlé Crenshaw, Neil Gotanda, Gary Peller, and Kendall Thomas, eds., pp. xiii–xxxii. New York: New Press.

Cutler, Cecilia, 2003 "Keepin' it Real": White Hip-hoppers' Discourses of Language, Race and Ethnicity. Journal of Linguistic Anthropology 13:211–233.

Cutler, Charles, 1994 O Brave New Words! Native American Loanwords in Current English. Norman and London: University of Oklahoma Press.

Damron, Joseph R., 2007 Education is Not a Cultural Value for Latinos. Tucson Weekly, July 5. Electronic document. www.tucsonweekly.com/gbase/Opinion/Content?oid=97993/.

D'Andrade, Roy, 1995 The Development of Cognitive Anthropology. New York and Cambridge: Cambridge University Press.

DARE I: Dictionary of American Regional English, Volume I, Introduction and A–C. Frederick G. Cassidy, ed. Cambridge, MA: Harvard University Press.

DARE II: Dictionary of American Regional English, Volume II, D–H. Frederick G. Cassidy, ed. Cambridge, MA: Harvard University Press.

DARE III: Dictionary of American Regional English, Volume III, I–O. Frederick G. Cassidy, ed. Cambridge, MA: Harvard University Press.

Davis, Peggy C., 2000 Law as Microaggression. *In* Critical Race Theory: The Cutting Edge. 2nd edition. Richard Delgado and Jean Stefancic, eds., pp. 141–151. Philadelphia: Temple University Press.

Davis, Tony, 2002 Clean Air Fiesta Loses Party Hat. Arizona Daily Star, March 29: A1.

Delgado, Richard, and Jean Stefancic, eds., 1997 Critical White Studies: Looking Behind the Mirror. Philadelphia: Temple University Press.

Delgado, Richard, and Jean Stefancic, eds., 2000 Critical Race Theory: The Cutting Edge. 2nd edition. Philadelphia: Temple University Press.

Delgado, Richard, and Jean Stefancic, 2000 Images of the Outsider in American Law and Culture. *In* Critical Race Theory: The Cutting Edge. 2nd edition. Richard Delgado and Jean Stefancic, eds., pp. 223–235. Philadelphia: Temple University Press.

Deloria, Philip, 1998 Playing Indian. New Haven: Yale University Press.

Derrida, Jacques, 1988 Limited, Inc. Evanston, IL: Northwestern University Press.

Diaz, Elva, 2004 Measure Would Change Makeup of Panel in Piestewa Peak Flap. Arizona Republic, February 24. Electronic document. www.azcentral.com/arizonarepublic/local/articles/0224nameboard24.html/.

Dominguez, Virginia, 1986 White by Definition: Social Classification in Creole Louisiana. New Brunswick, NJ: Rutgers University Press.

Douglas, William, 2003 A Case of Race? One POW Acclaimed, Another Ignored. Seattle Times, November 9. Electronic document. seattletimes.nwsource.com/html/nationworld/2001786800_shoshana09.html/.

Dowd, Maureen, 2001 I Have a Nickname!!! New York Times, April 29:D17.

Dowd, Maureen, 2002 Ghosts and Mississippi. New York Times, December 18: A33.

Du Bois, W. E. B., 1986 Selected Writings. New York: Library of America.

Ducote, Richard, 1993 Airline's Pullout Aren't Tucson's Fault, Officials Say. Arizona Daily Star, February 1:D1.

Duranti, Alexander, 1993 Intentions, Self, and Responsibility: An Essay in Samoan Ethnopragmatics. *In* Responsibility and Evidence in Oral Discourse. Jane H. Hill and Judith T. Irvine, eds., pp. 24–47. Cambridge: Cambridge University Press.

Edsall, Thomas B., 2002a Lott Decried for Part of Salute to Thurmond, GOP Senate Leader Hails Colleague's Run as Segregationist. Washington Post, December 7. Electronic document. www.washingtonpost.com/articles/A207630–2002Dec6. html/.

Edsall, Thomas B., 2002b "Poor Choice of Words," Lott Says. Washington Post, December 10:A13.

Edsall, Thomas B., and Darryl Fears, 2002 Lott Has Moved Little on Civil Rights; Analysts Say Remarks, Record Consistent. Washington Post, December 13:A01.

Eliasoph, Nina, 1999 "Everyday Racism" in a Culture of Political Avoidance: Civil Society, Speech, and Taboo. Social Problems 46:479–502.

¡El Gato Negro! 2006 ¡El Gato Negro! Says. April 15. Electronic document. www. actblue.com/page/gatoblue.

Entman, Robert M., and Andrew Rojecki, 2000 The Black Image in the White Mind. Chicago: University of Chicago Press.

Epps, Garrett, 2007 Let's Abolish the Electoral College. Electronic document. www. salon.com/opinion/feature/2007/10/12/electoral_college/.

Errington, J. Joseph, 2003 Getting Language Rights: The Rhetorics of Language Endangerment and Loss. American Anthropologist 105:723–732.

Espinoza, Leslie, and Angela P. Harris, 2000 Embracing the Tar Baby: LatCrit Theory and the Sticky Mess of Race. *In* Critical Race Theory: The Cutting Edge. 2nd edition. Richard Delgado and Jean Stefancic, eds., pp. 440–447. Philadelphia: Temple University Press.

Excerpts from News Conference Held by Senator Lott in Mississippi, 2002 New York Times, December 14:A14.

Excerpts from an Interview with Trent Lott, 2002 New York Times, December 14: A14.

Ezekiel, Raphael S., 1995 The Racist Mind: Portraits of American Neo-Nazis and Clansmen. New York and London: Penguin Books.

Feagin, Joe R., 2006 Systemic Racism. New York and London: Routledge.

Feagin, Joe R., and Melvin P. Sykes, 1994 Living with Racism: The Black Middle-Class Experience. Boston: Beacon Press.

Feagin, Joe R., and Hernán Vera, 1995 White Racism: The Basics. New York and London: Routledge.

Feinstein, John, 1999 The Majors: In Pursuit of Golf's Holy Grail. New York: Little, Brown.

Finnerty, Megan, 2006 Suggestive Name Puts Eatery, City At Odds. Arizona Republic, April 22. Electronic document. www.azcentral.com/ent/dining/articles/0422pinktaco.html/.

Fire Trent Lott (Editorial), 2002 New York Times, December 12:A38.

Fischer, Claude S., 1996 Inequality by Design: Cracking the Bell Curve. Princeton: Princeton University Press.

Fluehr-Lobban, Carolyn, 2006 Race and Racism: An Introduction. Lanham, New York, Toronto, and Oxford: Rowman & Littlefield.

Foucault, Michel, 1972 The Archaeology of Knowledge. New York: Pantheon Books.

Frankenberg, Ruth, 1992 The Social Construction of Whiteness: White Women, Race Matters. New York and London: Routledge.

Fredrickson, George M., 2002 Racism: A Short History. Princeton and Oxford: Princeton University Press.

Freedman, Samuel G., 2007 On Education: Calling the Folks About Campus Drinking. New York Times, September 12:A6.

Friedman, Samantha, and Gregory D. Squires, 2005 Does the Community Reinvestment Act Help Minorities Access Traditionally Inaccessible Neighborhoods? *Social Problems* 52:209–231.

Fuzzy, 1997. Electronic document (Video). www.cnn.com/US/9704/21/fuzzy/.

Gal, Susan, and Judith T. Irvine, 1995 The Boundaries of Languages and Disciplines: How Ideologies Construct Differences. Social Research 62(4):967–1001.

Gates, Henry Louis, ed., 1986 Race, Writing and Difference. Chicago: University of Chicago Press.

Gibbs, Nancy, 1996 An American Voice. Time 149(1):32–33.

Goddard, Ives, 1997 Since the Word Squaw Continues to be of Interest. News from Indian Country, Mid-April:19A.

Goffman, Erving, 1974 Frame Analysis: An Essay on the Organization of Experience. Cambridge, MA: Harvard University Press.

Goldberg, David Theo, 1990 The Social Formation of Racist Discourse. *In* Anatomy of Racism. David Theo Goldberg, ed., pp. 295–317. Minneapolis: University of Minnesota Press.

Goldberg, David Theo, 1993 Racist Culture: Philosophy and the Politics of Meaning. Cambridge, MA: Blackwell Publishing.

Goldberg, David Theo, 1997 Racial Subjects: Writing on Race in America. New York and London: Routledge.

Goldberg, David Theo, 1999 Racism and Rationality: The Need for a New Critique. *In* Racism. Leonard Harris, ed., pp. 369–397. Amherst, NY: Humanity Books.

Goldstein, Donna M., 2003 Laughter Out of Place: Race, Class, Violence and Sexuality in a Rio Shantytown. Berkeley and Los Angeles: University of California Press.

Goldstein, Richard, 2004 Marge Schott, Eccentric Owner of the Reds, Dies at 75. Electronic document. www.nytimes.com/2004/03/03/sports/baseball/003SCHO.html/.

Gonzalez, David, 2007 Risky Loans Help Build Ghost Town of New Homes. New York Times, September 24. Electronic document. www.nytimes.com/2007/09/24/nyregion/24citywide.html/.

Gonzalez, Juan, and Rafael Olmeda, 2003 NAHJ Criticizes Dame Edna, Vanity Fair. Electronic document. www.nahj.org/president/gonzalez_vanityfair.html/.

Goodman, Ellen, 2006 Hillary and Barack for Real, Despite Sexism and Racism. Arizona Daily Star, December 29:A11.

Gootman, Elissa, and Al Baker, 2007 Noose on Door at Columbia Prompts Campus Protest. New York Times, October 11:A24.

Gouskova, Elena, and Frank Stafford, 2007 Trends in Household Wealth Dynamics 2003–2005. Electronic document. psidonline.isr.umich.edu/Data/Documentation/wlth2005_Report.pdf/.

Gravlee, Clarence C., H. Russell Bernard, and William R. Leonard, 2003 Heredity, Environment, and Cranial Form: A Reanalysis of Boas's Immigrant Data. American Anthropologist 105(1):125–138.

Gray, Hollis, Virginia Jones, Patricia Parker, Alex Smith, and Klonda Lynn, 1949 Gringoisms in Arizona. American Speech 24:234–236.

Gregory, Steven, and Roger Sanjek, eds., 1994 Race. New Brunswick, NJ: Rutgers University Press.

Grice, H. P., 1975 Logic and Conversation. *In* Syntax and Semantics 3: Speech Acts. Peter Cole and Jerry Morgan, eds., pp. 41–58. New York: Academic Press.

Grutter v. Bollinger et al., 2003 Syllabus. Electronic document. a257.g.akamaitech. net/7/257/2422/23jun20030800/www.supremecourtus.gov/opinions/02pdf/02–241.pdf/.

Gubar, Susan, 1997 Racechanges: White Skin, Black Face in American Culture. New York and Oxford: Oxford University Press.

Gutiérrez, Ramón, 1989 Aztlán, Montezuma, and New Mexico: The Political Uses of American Indian Mythology. *In* Aztlán: Essays on the Chicano Homeland. Rudolfo A. Anaya and Francisco Lomelí, eds, pp. 172–190. Albuquerque: Academia/El Norte Publications.

Hall, Perry A., 1997 African-American Music: Dynamics of Appropriation and Innovation. *In* Borrowed Power: Essays on Cultural Appropriation. Bruce Ziff and Pratima V. Rao, eds., pp. 31–51. New Brunswick, NJ: Rutgers University Press.

Haney Lopez , Ian F., 2000 The Social Construction of Race. *In* Critical Race Theory: The Cutting Edge. 2nd edition. Richard Delgado and Jean Stefancic, eds., pp. 164–175. Philadelphia, PA: Temple University Press.

Hargraves v. Capital City Mortgage Corp. C.A. No. 98–1021 (US District Court, D. D. C.). Electronic document. www.usdoj.gov/crt/housing/documents/hargraves1. htm/.

Harris, Cheryl, 1995 Whiteness as Property. *In* Critical Race Theory: The Key Writings that Formed the Movement. Kimberlé Crenshaw, Neil Gotanda, Gary Peller, and Kendall Thomas, eds., pp. 276–291. New York: New Press.

Harris, Marvin, 1964 Patterns of Race in the Americas. New York: Walker.

Harrison, Faye V., 1995 The Persistent Power of "Race" in the Cultural and Political Economy of Racism. Annual Review of Anthropology 24:47–74.

Hartigan, John, 1999 Racial Situations: Class Predicaments of Whiteness in Detroit. Princeton: Princeton University Press.

Hartigan, John, 2005 Odd Tribes: Toward a Cultural Analysis of White People. Durham, NC: Duke University Press.

Hartman, Saidiya V., 1997 Scenes of Subjection: Terror, Slavery and Self-Making in Nineteenth-Century America. New York and Oxford: Oxford University Press.

Health, United States, 2006 US Department of Health and Human Services, Center for Disease Control and Prevention, National Center for Health Statistics. Electronic document. www.cdc.gov/nchs/data/hus/hus06.pdf#133/.

Herrnstein, Richard, and Charles A. Murray, 1994 The Bell Curve: Intelligence and Class Structure in American Life. New York: Free Press.

Hesman, Tina, 2003 Genetically Speaking, There's No Such Thing As Race. St. Louis Post Dispatch May 11:A1. Electronic document. Lexis Nexis Academic.

Heumann, Milton, Thomas W. Church, with David P. Redlawsk, 1997 Hate Speech on Campus: Cases, Case Studies, and Commentary. Boston: Northeastern University Press.

Hill, Jane H., 1993a Hasta La Vista, Baby: Anglo Spanish in the American Southwest. Critique of Anthropology 13:145–176.

Hill, Jane H., 1993b Is it Really "No Problemo"? *In* SALSA I: Proceedings of the First Annual Symposium about Language and Society at Austin. Robin Queen and Rusty Barrett, eds. Texas Linguistic Forum 33:1–12.

Hill, Jane H., 1998 Language, Race and White Public Space. American Anthropologist 100:680–689.

Hill, Jane H., 2000 Read My Article: Language Ideology and the Over-Determination of "Promising" in American Presidential Politics. *In* Regimes of Language. Paul V. Kroskrity, ed., pp. 259–292. Santa Fe: SAR Press.

Hill, Jane H., 2001 Mock Spanish, Covert Racism, and the (Leaky) Boundary Between Public and Private Spheres. *In* Languages and Publics: The Making of Authority. Susan Gal and Kathryn Woolard, eds., pp. 83–102. Manchester and Northampton, MA: St. Jerome Publishing.

Hill, Jane H., 2002 "Expert Rhetorics" in Advocacy for Endangered Languages: Who is Listening, and What Do They Hear? Journal of Linguistic Anthropology 12(2):119–133.

Hill, Jane H., 2005a A Grammar of Cupeño. University of California Publications in Linguistics. Volume 136. Berkeley and Los Angeles: University of California Press.

Hill, Jane H., 2005b Intertextuality as Source and Evidence for indirect indexical meanings. Journal of Linguistic Anthropology 15:113–124.

Hill, Jane H. and Daniel Goldstein, 2001 Mock Spanish, Cultural Competence, and Complex Inference. Textus. English Studies in Italy 14(2):243–262.

Hill, Kenneth C., 2002 On Publishing the Hopi Dictionary. *In* Making Dictionaries: Preserving Indigenous Languages of the Americas. William Frawley, Kenneth C. Hill, and Pamela Munro, eds., pp. 299–311. Berkeley: University of California Press.

Hilton Hotels, 2007 Electronic document. www1.hilton.com/en_US/hi/hotel/PHXSPPR-Pointe-Hilton-Squaw-Peak-Resort-Arizona/index.do/.

Hirschfeld, Lawrence A., 1996 Race in the Making: Cognition, Culture, and the Child's Construction of Human Kinds. Cambridge, MA: MIT Press.

Hockstader, Lee, 2002 In Miss. Home, Reaction Mimics Racial Divide. Washington Post, December 15:A28.

Hockstader, Lee, and Helen Dewar, 2002 Sen. Lott Fights to Save Post as Leader. Washington Post, December 14:A1.

Home Ownership by Race and Ethnicity of Householder, 2007 Infoplease.com (US Census Bureau). Electronic document. www.infoplease.com/ipa/A0883976.html/.

Hopi Dictionary Project, 1998 Hopi Dictionary/Hopìikwa Lavàytutuveni: A Hopi – English Dictionary of the Third Mesa Dialect. Tucson: University of Arizona Press.

Horowitz, David, 1997 An Academic Lynching: Why a Veteran Professor of Law is Being Strung Up for Saying the Obvious. Electronic document. www.salon.com/sept97/columnists/horowitz2970922.html/.

Housing Patterns, 2000 US Census Bureau, Electronic document. www.census.gov/hhes/www/housing/resseg/ch1.html.

Hoyt, Clark, 2007 The Public Editor: The Truth and Alberto Gonzales. New York Times, September 9:A14.

Hulse, Carl, 2002 Lott Apologizes Again on Words about Race. New York Times, December 12:A1, A27.

Hulse, Carl, 2007 Senator to Quit Over Sex Sting, Republicans Say. New York Times, September 1:A1.

Hulse, Carl, with Elisabeth Bumiller, 2002 Republicans Say Lott Lacks Bush's Support. New York Times, December 17:A1.

Ignatiev, Noel, 1995 How the Irish Became White. New York: Routledge.

Illegalimmigrationbumperstickers.com, 2006 Electronic document (images). www.illegalimmigrationbumperstickers.com/illegal_t_shirts/.

Indian Country Today, 2004 Report on Arizona Legislature Debate on "Squaw" Place Names. Electronic document. www.indiancountry.com/?1074890583/.

Irvine, Judith, 1989 When Talk Isn't Cheap: Language and Political Economy. American Ethnologist 16:248–267.

Is it Fixed Yet? (Editorial), 2007 New York Times, September 9:A13.

Izumi, Lance, 2002 University of California Shuts Out Asian Achievers. Electronic document. www.bizjournals.com/sanfrancisco/stories/2002/09/02/editorial2.html/.

Jacobson, Matthew Frye, 1998 Whiteness of a Different Color: European Immigrants and the Alchemy of Race. Cambridge, MA: Harvard University Press.

Jakobson, Roman, 1971 Shifters, Verbal Categories and the Russian Verb. In Selected Writings of Roman Jakobson. Volume 2, pp. 130–147. The Hague: Mouton Press.

Jamieson, Kathleen Hall, and Carolyn Kohrs Campbell, 1992 The Interplay of Influence: News, Advertising, Politics and the Mass Media. Belmont, CA: Wadsworth Publishing.

Kahn, Jonathan, 2005 Misreading Race and Genomics after BiDil. Nature Genetics 37(7):655–656.

Katel, Peter, 2001 Don't Stop Thinking About Mañana. Time, Monday, June 11. Electronic document. www.time.com/time/magazine/article/0,9171,1000102,00.html/.

Keane, Webb, 2002 Sincerity, "Modernity," and the Protestants. Cultural Anthropology 17:65–92.

Keane, Webb, 2007 Christian Moderns. Berkeley and Los Angeles: University of California Press.

Keller, Bill, 2003 Fear on the Home Front. New York Times, February 22:A35.

Kelley, Jack, 2001 Are You Sure It's a Bandido? USA Today, April 27:A1.

Kennedy, Randall, 2002 Nigger: The Strange Career of a Troublesome Word. New York: Pantheon Books.

Kennicott, Philip, 2002 A "Sorry" Spectacle. Washington Post, December 13:C1.

Kerr, Dave, 2002 For Fun, a Mucho Macho Black Hero. New York Times, May 26: AR11.

Konigsberg, Eric, 2007 Summer Rituals: Grilling at "Da Crib." A Simple Hamptons Barbecue, Aglow with a Little Star Power. New York Times, August 11: A1–11.

Kornmiller, Debbie, 2007a My Opinion: Join Us on the Pages of ¡Vamos!. Arizona Daily Star, March 24:A7.

Kornmiller, Debbie, 2007b My Opinion: TV Listings' Headaches Fixed Today. Arizona Daily Star, March 18:A7.

Kovel, Joel, 1970 White Racism: A Psychohistory. New York: Pantheon Books.

Krauthammer, Charles, 2002 A Clear Choice of Words. Washington Post, December 12:A45.

Kripke, Sol, 1972 Naming and Necessity. Cambridge, MA: Harvard University Press.

Krugman, Paul, 2002a All These Problems. New York Times, December 10:A31.

Krugman, Paul, 2002b The Other Face. New York Times, December 13:A33.

Kurtz, Howard, 2002a Why So Late On Lott. Media Watch. Washington Post, December 10:C1.

Kurtz, Howard, 2002b Lott's "Sorry" Doesn't Cut It. Media Watch. Washington Post, December 11:C1.

Kurtz, Howard, 2002c A Hundred-Candle Story and How To Blow It. Washington Post, December 16:C1.

Labov, William, 1972 Language in the Inner City. Philadelphia: University of Pennsylvania Press.

Labov, William, 2007 Unendangered Dialects, Endangered People: The Case of African American Vernacular English. Paper presented to the Annual Meeting of the American Anthropological Association, Washington, DC, November 29.

Lakoff, George, 1987 Women, Fire and Dangerous Things: What Categories Reveal about the Mind. Chicago: University of Chicago Press.

Lakoff, George, 1993 The Contemporary Theory of Metaphor. *In* Metaphor and Thought. Anthony Ortony, ed., pp. 202–251. Cambridge: Cambridge University Press.

Lakoff, George, 2004 Don't Think of an Elephant! – Know Your Values and Frame the Debate: An Essential Guide for Progressives. White River Junction, VT: Chelsea Green.

Lakoff, George, and Mark Johnson, 1980 Metaphors We Live By. Chicago: University of Chicago Press.

Lancaster, Roger N., 1991 Skin Color, Race, and Racism in Nicaragua. Ethnology 30:339–353.

Lawrence, Charles R. III, 1993 If He Hollers Let Him Go: Regulating Racist Speech on Campus. *In* Words that Wound: Critical Race Theory, Assaultive Speech, and the First Amendment. Mari J. Matsuda, Charles R. Lawrence III, Richard Delgado, and Kimberlé Williams Crenshaw, eds., pp. 53–88. Boulder, CO: Westview.

Lee, Cynthia Kwei Yung, 2000 Race and Self-Defense: Toward a Normative Conception of Reasonableness. *In* Critical Race Theory: The Cutting Edge. 2nd edition. Richard Delgado and Jean Stefancic, eds., pp. 204–210. Philadelphia: Temple University Press.

LeStrade, Patricia, 2002 The Continuing Decline of Isleño Spanish in Louisiana. Southwest Journal of Linguistics 21(1): 99–118.

Lieberson, Stanley, 1985 Stereotypes: Their Consequences for Race and Ethnic Interaction. *In* Research in Race and Ethnic Relations: A Research Annual. Volume 4. C. Marrett and C. Leggon, eds., pp. 113–137. Greenwich, CT: JAI Press.

Limbaugh, David, 2003 Targeting Campus Speech Codes. Worldnetdaily.com, August 16. Electronic document. www.worldnetdaily.com/news/article.asp?ARTICLE_ID=34138/.

Lippi-Green, Rosina, 1997 English with an Accent: Language, Ideology and Discrimination in the United States. London and New York: Routledge.

Lipsitz, George, 1998 The Possessive Investment in Whiteness: How White People Profit from Identity Politics. Revised and expanded edition. Philadelphia: Temple University Press.

Louisor-White, Dominique, and Dolores Valencia Tanno, 1994 Code-Switching in the Public Forum: New Expressions of Cultural Identity and Persuasion. Paper presented to the Conference on Hispanic Language and Social Identity, University of New Mexico, Albuquerque, February 10–12.

Loury, Glenn C., 2002 The Anatomy of Racial Inequality. Cambridge, MA: Harvard University Press.

Luksa, 1997 Electronic document at www.tigertales.com/'tiger/luksa0412.html/.

Lyke, M. L., 2006 No Crowds? No Rush? In Mexico, No Problemo. Washington Post, December 3:P1.

Maldonado, Wendy, 2003 Dame Edna. Electronic document. urbanlegends.miningco.com/library/bl-dame-edna.htm/.

Mann, Juan, 2005 Chertoff's "Catch-and-Release" Trick Reveals Bush's Secret Agenda. Electronic document. www.vdare.com/mann/051024_chertoff.htm (October 25, 2005).

Marable, Manning, 1995 Beyond Black and White: Transforming African-American Politics. London and New York: Verso.

Maricopa Residents Not Offended by Word "Squaw," Poll Finds (AP), 1993 Arizona Daily Star, February 9:D5.

Marshall, Joshua Michael, 2002a Talking Points Memo. December 6. Electronic document. www.talkingpointsmemo.com/archives/week_2002_12_01.php/.

Marshall, Joshua Michael, 2002b Talking Points Memo. December 9. Electronic document. www.talkingpointsmemo.com.

Marshall, Joshua Michael, 2002c Talking Points Memo. December 10. Electronic document. www.talkingpointsmemo/dec0202.html/.

Marshall, Joshua Michael, 2002d Talking Points Memo. December 12, 2002. Electronic document. www.talkingpointsmemo.com/archives/week_2002_12_01.php/.

Marshall, Joshua Michael, 2005 Aqua-Duke. Talking Points Memo. July 6. Electronic document. www.talkingpointsmemo.com.

Marshall, Joshua Michael, 2006 Talking Points Memo. Electronic document. www.talkingpointsmemo.com/archives/week_2006_10_08.php/.

Martínez, Glenn A., 2006 Mexican Americans and Language: Del Dicho al Hecho. Tucson: University of Arizona Press.

Massey, Douglas S., 2005 Racial Discrimination in Housing: A Moving Target. Social Problems 52:148–151.

Matsuda, Mari J., 1993 Public Response to Racist Speech: Considering the Victim's Story. In Words that Wound: Critical Race Theory, Assaultive Speech, and the First Amendment. Mari J. Matsuda, Charles R. Lawrence III, Richard Delgado, and Kimberlé Williams Crenshaw, eds., pp. 17–52. Boulder, CO: Westview.

Matsuda, Mari J., 1996 Where is Your Body? and Other Essays on Race, Gender, and the Law. Boston: Beacon Press.

Matsuda, Mari J., Charles R. Lawrence III, Richard Delgado, and Kimberlé Williams Crenshaw, eds., 1993 Words that Wound: Critical Race Theory, Assaultive Speech, and the First Amendment. Boulder, CO: Westview.

McDermott, Monica, 2004 Varieties of White Racial Identity. Presentation to the Department of Cultural and Social Anthropology, Stanford University, January 12.

McDermott, Monica, and Frank L. Samson, 2005 White Racial and Ethnic Identity in the United States. Annual Review of Sociology 31:245–261.

McIntosh, Peggy, 1989 White Privilege: Unpacking the Invisible Knapsack. Electronic document. seamonkey.ed.asu.edu/~mcisaac/emc598ge/Unpacking.html/.

McWilliams, Carey, 1943 Brothers Under the Skin. Boston: Little, Brown.

Meek, Barbara, 2004 Icons, Images and Everyday Interaction. Paper presented to Invited Session of the Society for Linguistic Anthropology: Language, Discourse and Racism. American Anthropological Association Annual Meetings, Atlanta, December.

Meek, Barbara, 2006 And the Injun Goes "How": Representations of American Indian English in White Public Space. Language in Society 35:93–128.

Memmi, Albert, 2000 Racisme. Minneapolis: University of Minnesota Press.

Menchaca, Martha, 1993 Chicano Indianism: A Historical Account of Racial Repression in the United States. American Ethnologist 20:583–603.

Menchaca, Martha, 1995 The Mexican Outsiders: A Community History of Marginalization and Discrimination in California. Austin: University of Texas Press.

Menchaca, Martha, 2001 Recovering History, Constructing Race: The Indian, Black and White Roots of Mexican Americans. Austin: University of Texas Press.

Milbank, Dana, and Jim VandeHei, 2002 President Decries Lott's Comments. Washington Post, December 13:A1.

Miles, Robert, 1989 Racism. London and New York: Routledge.

Milroy, James, and Leslie Milroy, 1999 Authority in Language: Investigating Standard English. New York and London: Routledge.

Miniño, Arialdi M., Melanie P. Heron, and Betty L. Smith, 2006 Deaths: Preliminary Data for 2004. National Vital Statistics Reports 54(19). Electronic document. www.cdc.gov/nchs/data/nvsr/nvsr54/nvsr54_19.pdf/.

Mitchell-Kernan, Claudia, 1972 Signifying and Marking: Two African-American Speech Acts. In Directions in Sociolinguistics: The Ethnography of Communication. Dell H. Hymes and John Gumperz, eds., pp. 161–179. New York: Holt, Rinehart & Winston.

Montini, E. J., 2003 Who Would Call a Warrior "Squaw"? Here's a Chance to Right a Wrong. Arizona Republic, April 8:B3.

Morgan, Marcyliena, 1994 The African-American Speech Community: Reality and Sociolinguistics. In Language and the Social Construction of Identity in Creole Situations. Marcyliena Morgan, ed., pp. 121–148. Los Angeles: Center for Afro-American Studies, UCLA.

Morgan, Marcyliena, 1999 "No Woman No Cry": Claiming African American Women's Place. In Reinventing Identities: From Category to Practice in Language and Gender. Mary Bucholtz, A. C. Liang, and Lauren A. Sutton, eds., pp. 27–45. Oxford: Oxford University Press.

Morgan, Marcyliena, 2001 "Ain't Nothin' but a G Thang": Grammar, Variation and Language Ideology in Hip Hop Identity. In African American Vernacular English. Sonja Lanehart, ed., pp. 185–207. Philadelphia and Amsterdam: John Benjamins.

Morgan, Marcyliena, 2007 The Real Hiphop: Battling for Knowledge, Power, and Respect in the Underground. Durham, NC: Duke University Press.

Morin, Richard, 2002 Majority Say Lott Should Not Lead. Washington Post, December 17:n.p. Accessed May 10, 2003.

Morrison, Toni, 1992 Playing in the Dark: Whiteness and the Literary Imagination. Cambridge, MA: Harvard University Press.

Morsy, Soheir, 1994 Beyond the Honorary "White" Classification of Egyptians: Societal Identity in Historical Context. *In* Race. Steven Gregory and Roger Sanjek, eds., pp. 175–198. New Brunswick, NJ: Rutgers University Press.

Mr. Lott Steps Down (Editorial), 2002 Washington Post, December 22: A22.

Myrdal, Gunnar, 1944 An American Dilemma (with the assistance of Richard M. E. Sterner and Arnold Rose). New York and London: Harper & Brothers.

Myers, Kristen, 2005 Racetalk: Racism Hiding in Plain Sight. Lanham, MD: Rowman & Littlefield.

Nagourney, Adam and Carl Hulse, 2002 Bush Rebukes Lott Over Remarks on Thurmond. New York Times, December 13:A15.

Napolitano Also Seeking Veterans' Memorial (AP), 2003 Electronic document. www.azcentral.com/news/articles/o416napolitanomemorial-ON.html/.

Navarro, Meyra, 2007 The Mexican Will See You Now. New York Times, June 24: B1.

9-in-10 School-Age Children Have Computer Access; Internet Use Pervasive, 2001. United States Department of Commerce News, Census Bureau Reports. Electronic document. www.census.gov/Press-Release/www/2001/cb01–147.html.

Ochs, Elinor, 1996 Linguistic Resources for Socializing Humanity. *In* Rethinking Linguistic Relativity. John J. Gumperz and Stephen C. Levinson, eds., pp. 407–487. Cambridge: Cambridge University Press.

Ochs, Elinor, and Bambi Schieffelin, 1984 Language Acquisition and Socialization: Three Developmental Stories and Their Implications. *In* Culture Theory: Essays on Mind, Self, and Emotion. R. A. Shweder and R. A. LeVine, eds., pp. 276–320. Cambridge: Cambridge University Press.

Omi, Michael, and Howard Winant, 1994 Racial Formation in the United States: From the 1960s to the 1990s. 2nd edition. New York: Routledge.

Orzechowski, Shawna, and Peter Sepielli, 2003 Net Worth and Asset Ownership of Households: 1998 and 2000. Household Economic Studies. Current Population Reports. US Census Bureau. Electronic document. www.census.gov/prod/2003pubs/p70–88.pdf/.

Parker, Basil G., 1902 The Life and Adventures of Basil G. Parker: An Autobiography. Plano, CA: Fred W. Reed, American Printer (cited in Bagley 2002).

Parmentier, Richard J., 1994 Peirce Divested for Nonintimates. *In* Signs in Society: Studies in Semiotic Anthropology, pp. 3–22. Bloomington: Indiana University Press.

Peñalosa, Fernando, 1981 Chicano Sociolinguistics. Rowley, MA: Newbury House Press.

Perea, Juan F., 1998 The Black/White Binary Paradigm of Race. *In* The Latino/a Condition: A Critical Reader. Richard Delgado and Jean Stefancic, eds., pp. 359–368. New York: New York University Press.

Philips, Susan, 2004 The Organization of Ideological Diversity in Discourse: Modern and Neotraditional Visions of the Tongan State. American Ethnologist 31(2):231–250.

Picca, Leslie Houts, and Joe R. Feagin, 2007 Two-Faced Racism: Whites in the Backstage and Frontstage. New York: Routledge.

Pierce, Charles H., 1997 The Coming of Tiger Woods. GQ, April:196–202, 248–249.

Piestewa Peak! Our Stand: Rename Squaw Peak to Honor Soldier from Tuba City (Editorial), 2003 Arizona Republic, April 8:B10.

Piestewa Peak: Our Stand: Board Rights a Wrong in Renaming Phoenix Mountain (Editorial), 2003 Arizona Republic, April 18: B10.

Portillo, Ernesto, 2002 Stereotypical Images Should Be Shunned By Government. Arizona Daily Star, March 30:B1.

Purdom, Todd S., 2002 A Nixon-Era Distraction Steps out of the Limelight. New York Times, December 21:A16.

Putnam, Hillary, 1975 The Meaning of "Meaning." In Mind, Language and Reality. Philosophical Papers. Volume 2, pp. 215–271. Cambridge: Cambridge University Press.

Rasmussen, Birgit Brander, Eric Klinenberg, Irene J. Nexica, and Matt Wray, eds., 2001 The Making and Unmaking of Whiteness. Durham, NC: Duke University Press.

R.A.V. v. City of St. Paul, 2002 Syllabus. Electronic document. supct.law.cornell. edu/supct/html/90–7675.ZS.html/.

Readers' Response, 2003 Electronic document. www.hispaniconline.com/pol&opi/ readers_response_vc_oped_edna.htm.

Reddy, Michael, 1979 The Conduit Metaphor, a Case of Frame Conflict in Our Language About Language. In Metaphor and Thought. Anthony Ortony, ed., pp. 164–201. Cambridge: Cambridge University Press.

Reid, Betty, 2003 Piestewa Family Says Snow Was Message. Arizona Republic, April 8:A8.

Reid, T. R., 2005 Spanish at School Translates to Suspension. Washington Post, December 9:A03.

Reisigl, Martin, and Ruth Wodak, 2001 Discourse and Discrimination: Rhetorics of Racism and Antisemitism. London and New York: Routledge.

Rhodes, Richard, and John Lawler, 1981 Athematic Metaphors. Proceedings of the Annual Meeting of the Chicago Linguistic Society 17:318–342.

Rich, Frank, 2002 Bonfire of the Vanities. New York Times, December 21:A35.

Rieff, David, 2006 Nuevo Catholics. New York Times Magazine, December 24:40.

Rodríguez, Clara E., 1994 Challenging Racial Hegemony: Puerto Ricans in the United States. In Race. Steven Gregory and Roger Sanjek, eds., pp. 131–145. New Brunswick, NJ: Rutgers University Press.

Rodríguez, Clara E., ed., 1997 Latin Looks: Images of Latinos and Latinas in the US Media. Boulder, CO: Westview Press.

Rodríguez, Clara E., 1997 The Silver Screen: Stories and Stereotypes. In Latin Looks: Images of Latinos and Latinas in the US Media. Clara E. Rodríguez, ed., pp. 73–79. Boulder, CO: Westview Press.

Rodríguez, Sylvia, 1987 Land, Water, and Ethnic Identity in Taos. In Land, Water, and Culture: New Perspectives on Hispanic Land Grants. Charles Briggs and John R. Van Ness, eds., pp. 313–403. Albuquerque: University of New Mexico Press.

Rodríguez González, Félix, 1995 Spanish Influence on English Word-Formation: The Suffix -ista. American Speech 70:421–429.

Roediger, David, 1991 The Wages of Whiteness: Race and the Making of the American Working Class. London and New York: Verso.

Rogers, Will, 2002 Comment is Lott's to Think About. Los Angeles Times, December 18, 2002: n.p. Accessed May 10, 2003.

Rogin, Michael, 1995 Blackface, White Noise. Berkeley: University of California Press.

Ronkin, Maggie, and Helen Karn, 1999 Mock Ebonics: Linguistic Racism in Parodies of Ebonics on the Internet. Journal of Sociolinguistics 3:360–380.

Rosaldo, Michelle, 1981 The Things We Do With Words: Ilongot Speech Acts and Speech Act Theory in Philosophy. Language in Society 11:203–237.

Ross, Stephen L., and Margery Austin Turner, 2005 Housing Discrimination in Metropolitan America: Explaining Changes between 1989 and 2000. Social Problems 52:152–180.

Roston, Michael, 2007 McCain Takes Aim at Romney Over Immigration. Raw Story, May 21. Electronic document. rawstory.com/news/2007/McCain_takes_aim_at_Romney_over_0521.html/.

Rubin, D. L., 1992 Nonlanguage Factors Affecting Undergraduates' Judgements of Nonnative English-Speaking Teaching Assistants. Research in Higher Education 33:511–531.

Rubin, D. L., and K. A. Smith, 1990 Effects of Accent, Ethnicity, and Lecture Topic on Undergraduates' Perceptions of Non-native English-Speaking Teaching Assistants. International Journal of Intercultural Relations 14:337–353.

Rumsey, Allan, 1990 Wording, Meaning, and Linguistic Ideology. American Anthropologist 92:346–361.

Rutenberg, Jim, and Felicity Barringer, 2002 Attack on Lott's Remarks Has Come From Variety of Voices on the Right. New York Times, December 17:A25.

Samuels, David, 2001 Indeterminacy and History in Britton Goode's Western Apache Placenames: Ambiguous Identity on the San Carlos Apache Reservation. American Ethnologist 28:277–302.

Sanders, Thomas E., and Walter W. Peek, 1973 Literature of the American Indian. New York: Glencoe Press.

Sands, Dan, 2003 Piestewa Deserves More. Letter to the Editor. Arizona Republic, April 12:B11.

Sanjek, Roger, 1994 Intermarriage and the Future of Races in the United States. *In* Race. Steven Gregory and Roger Sanjek, eds., pp. 103–130. New Brunswick, NJ: Rutgers University Press.

Santa Ana, Otto, 1999 "Like an Animal I was Treated": Anti-Immigrant Metaphor in US Public Discourse. Discourse in Society 10:191–224.

Santa Ana, Otto, 2002 Brown Tide Rising: Metaphors of Latinos in Contemporary American Public Discourse. Austin: University of Texas Press.

Sawyer, Janet B., 1959 Aloofness from Spanish Influence in Texas English. Word 15:270–281.

Sawyer, Janet B., 1975 Spanish–English Bilingualism in San Antonio, Texas. *In* El Lenguaje de los Chicanos. Eduardo Hernández-Chavez, Andrew D. Cohen, and Anthony F. Beltramo, eds., pp. 77–98. Arlington, VA: Center for Applied Linguistics.

Schechter, Maya, 2000 Chicano/Hispano Students Host Speaker. Arizona Daily Wildcat, February 28. Electronic document. wc.arizona.edu/papers/93/107/01_5_m.html.

Schiffrin, Deborah, Deborah Tannen, and Heidi Hamilton, eds., 2001 The Handbook of Discourse Analysis. Malden, MA: Blackwell Publishing.

Schwartz, Adam, 2006 The Teaching and Culture of Household Spanish: Understanding Racist Reproduction in "Domestic" Discourse. Critical Discourse Studies 3:107–121.

Searle, John, 1969 Speech Acts: An Essay in the Philosophy of Language. Cambridge: Cambridge University Press.

Sentencing Project. Statistics State by State, 2007 Electronic document. www.sentencingproject.org/StatsByState.aspx/.

Sheridan, Thomas, 1986 Los Tucsonenses: The Mexican Community in Tucson, 1854–1941. Tucson: University of Arizona Press.

Sheridan, Thomas, 2006 Landscapes of Fraud: Mission Tumacacori, the Baca Float, and the Betrayal of the O'odham. Tucson: University of Arizona Press.

Sheriff, Robin E., 2001 Dreaming Equality: Color, Race, and Racism in Urban Brazil. New Brunswick, NJ, and London: Rutgers University Press.

Sherzer, Joel, 1987 A Discourse-Centered Approach to the Study of Language and Culture. American Anthropologist 89:295–309.

Shiell, Timothy C., 1998 Campus Hate Speech on Trial. Lawrence: University Press of Kansas.

Shuck, Gail, 2004 Conversational Performance and the Poetic Construction of an Ideology. Language in Society 33:195–222.

Silverstein, Michael, 1976 Shifters, Linguistic Categories, and Cultural Description. *In* Meaning in Anthropology. Keith Basso and Henry Selby, eds., pp. 11–55. Albuquerque: University of New Mexico Press.

Silverstein, Michael, 1979 Language Structure and Linguistic Ideology. *In* The Elements: A Parasession on Linguistic Units and Levels. Paul R. Clyne, William F. Hanks, and Carol F. Hofbauer, eds., pp. 193–247. Chicago: Chicago Linguistic Society.

Silverstein, Michael, 1996 Monoglot "Standard" in America: Standardization and Metaphors of Linguistic Hegemony. *In* The Matrix of Language: Contemporary Linguistic Anthropology. Donald Brenneis and Ronald Macaulay, eds., pp. 284–306. Boulder, CO: Westview Press.

Silverstein, Michael, 2001[1981] The Limits of Awareness. In Linguistic Anthropology: A Reader. Alessandro Duranti, ed., pp. 382–401. Malden, MA, and Oxford: Blackwell Publishing.

Sims, Christine, and Hilaire Valiquette, 2000 Miller's Acoma Keresan Work: An Assessment. *In* Uto-Aztecan: Structural, Temporal and Geographic Perspectives. Papers in Memory of Wick R. Miller by the Friends of Uto-Aztecan. Eugene H. Casad and Thomas L. Willet, eds., pp. 19–32. Hermosillo, Sonora: Editorial UniSon.

Smedley, Audrey, 1993 Race in North America: Origin and Evolution of a World View. Boulder, CO: Westview Press.

Smelser, Neil J., ed., 2001 America Becoming: Racial Trends and Their Consequences. Washington, DC: National Academies Press.

Smith, Courtney, 2007 "Black" Theme Party Elicits Concerned Response. Arizona Daily Wildcat, February 6. Electronic document. media.wildcat.arizona.edu/media/storage/paper997/news/2007/02/06/News/black.Theme.Party.Elicits.Concerned.Response-2701102.shtml/.

Smith, David P., and Benjamin S. Bradshaw, 2006 Rethinking the Hispanic Paradox: Death Rates and Life Expectancy for US Non-Hispanic White and Hispanic Populations. American Journal of Public Health 96:1686–1692.

Smitherman, Geneva, 1994 Black Talk: Words and Phrases from the Hood to the Amen Corner. Boston: Houghton Mifflin.

Smitherman, Geneva, 1998 Word from the Hood: The Lexicon of African-American Vernacular English. *In* African-American English: Structure, History and Use. Salikoko S. Mufwene, John R. Rickford, Guy Bailey, and John Baugh, eds., pp. 203–225. London and New York: Routledge.

Sparks, Corey S., and Richard L. Jantz, 2002 A Reassessment of Human Cranial Plasticity: Boas Revisited. Proceedings of the National Academy of Sciences (US) 99(23):14636–146369.

Spears, Arthur K., ed., 1999 Race and Ideology: Language, Symbolism, and Popular Culture. Detroit: Wayne State University Press.

Stearns, Peter N., 1994 American Cool: Constructing a Twentieth-Century Emotional Style. New York and London: New York University Press.

Steele, Claude, 1997 A Threat in the Air: How Stereotypes Shape Intellectual Identity and Performance. American Psychologist 52:613–629.

Stolcke, Verena, 1995 Talking Culture: New Boundaries, New Rhetorics of Exclusion in Europe. Current Anthropology 36(1):1–24.

Stoler, Ann, 1995 Race and the Education of Desire: Foucault's *History of Sexuality* and the Colonial Order of Things. Durham: Duke University Press.

Stoler, Ann, 1997 Racial Histories and their Regimes of Truth. *In* Political Power and Social Theory. Diane E. Davis, ed., Volume 11, pp. 183–206. Greenwich, CT: JAI Press.

Stoler, Ann, 2002 Carnal Knowledge and Imperial Power: Race and the Intimate in Colonial Rule. Berkeley and London: University of California Press.

Strom, Stephanie, 2005 Summer Weekends: Every Friday a Reunion. New York Times, August 12:D1, D12.

Strassman, Paul, 1992 Does CIM Stand For "Consider It Mañana"? Lecture presented to Department of Defense, September 22, 1992. Electronic document. www.c3i.osd.mil.

Sweetser, Eve, 1987 The Definition of Lie. *In* Cultural Models in Language and Thought. Dorothy Holland and Naomi Quinn, eds., pp. 43–66. Cambridge and New York: Cambridge University Press.

Templeton, Alan R., 1998 Human Races: A Genetic and Evolutionary Perspective. American Anthropologist 100: 632–650.

Thai, Xuan, and Ted Barrett, 2007 Biden's Description of Obama Draws Scrutiny. Electronic document. www.cnn.com/2007/POLITICS/01/31/biden.obama/.

Thomas, David Hurst, 1991 Harvesting Ramona's Garden: Life in California's Mythical Mission Past. *In* Columbian Consequences. Volume 3. The Spanish Borderlands in Pan-American Perspective. David Hurst Thomas, ed., pp. 119–156. Washington, DC: Smithsonian Institution Press.

US Census, 2001 Electronic document. www.census.gov/prod/2001pubs/c2kbr01–1.pdf/.

Urban, Greg, 1991 A Discourse-Centered Approach to Culture: Native South American Myths and Rituals. Austin: University of Texas Press.

Urban, Greg, 2001 Metaculture: How Culture Moves Through the World. Minneapolis: University of Minnesota Press.

Urbinas, Helen, 2003 Dame Edna. Hartford Courant, February 11. Electronic document. www.ctnow.com/templates/misc/printstory.jsp?slug=hc%2Dubinas0211%Eartfeb11/.

Urciuoli, Bonnie, 1996 Exposing Prejudice: Puerto Rican Experiences of Language, Race and Class. Boulder, CO: Westview Press.

Urciuoli, Bonnie, 2003 Excellence, Leadership, Skills, Diversity: Marketing Liberal Arts Education. Language and Communication 23:385–408.

US Census Bureau, 2007 Statistical Abstract: National Data Book. Electronic document. www.census.gov/compendia/statab/.

Van den Berghe, Pierre, 1978 Race and Racism: A Comparative Perspective. New York: Wiley.

van Dijk, Teun A., 1987 Communicating Racism: Ethnic Prejudice in Thought and Talk. Newbury Park, CA: Sage Publications.

van Dijk, Teun A., 1991 Racism and the Press. London and New York: Routledge.

van Dijk, Teun A., 1993 Elite Discourse and Racism. Newbury Park, CA: Sage Publications.

van Dijk, Teun A., 1996 Discourse, Racism, and Ideology. Tenerife, Spain: RCEI Editions.

van Dijk, Teun A., 1999 Discourse and Racism. Discourse and Society 10:147–148.

Vanity Fair, 2003 Electronic document. www.latina.com/v3/203/feb/vanityfair.htm/.

Vanity Fair Apology, 2003. Electronic document. www.imdiversity.com/Villages/Hispanic/arts_culture_media/hav_vanity_fair_apology.asp/.

Village of Arlington Heights v. Metropolitan Housing Development Corp., No. 75–616 Supreme Court of the United States 429 US 252; 97 S. Ct. 555; 1977 US LEXIS 28; 50 L. Ed. 2d 450. Electronic document. www.hrcr.org/safrica/equality/arlington_housing.html/.

Villott, Kyle, 2000 The Ethnic Geography of Spanish Street Names in Tucson. Senior Honors Thesis, University of Arizona.

Virginia v. Black 2002. Syllabus. Electronic document. supct.law.cornell.edu/supct/html/01–1107.ZS.html.

Warner, Michael, 1990 The Letters of the Republic: Publication and the Public Sphere in Eighteenth-Century America. Cambridge, MA: Harvard University Press.

Webster, Antony, 2000 The Politics of Apache Place Names: Or Why "Dripping Springs" Does Not Equal "Tónoogah." In SALSA VII: Proceedings of the Seventh Annual Symposium about Language and Society at Austin. Nisha Merchant Goss, Amanda R. Doran, and Anastasia Coles, eds. Texas Linguistic Forum 43:223–232. Austin: University of Texas, Department of Linguistics.

Wentworth, Harold, 1942 The Neo-Pseudo-Suffix "-eroo." American Speech 17:10–15.

Weston, Mary Ann, 1996 Native Americans in the News: Images of Indians in the Twentieth Century Press. London and Westport, CT: Greenwood Press.

Whiteley, Peter, 1992 Hopitutungwi: "Hopi names" as Literature. In On the Translation of Native American Literatures. Brian Swann, ed., pp. 208–226. Washington, DC: Smithsonian Institution Press.

Whiteley, Peter, 2003 Do "Language Rights" Serve Indigenous Interests? Some Hopi and Other Queries. American Anthropologist 105(4):712–722.

Wides-Múñoz, Laura, 2006 Newspapers Struggle with Name Accents. Electronic document. news.yahoo.com/s/ap/20061021/ap_on_bi_ge/accents_please/.

Will, George, 2002 Apologies Are Not Enough. Washington Post, December 17: A33.

Williams, Brackette, 1989 A Class Act: The Race to Nation Across Ethnic Terrain. Annual Review of Anthropology 18:401–444.

Williams, Patricia J., 1995 Metro Broadcasting, Inc. v FCC: Regrouping in Singular Times. *In* Critical Race Theory: The Key Writings that Formed the Movement. Kimberlé Crenshaw, Neil Gotanda, Gary Peller, and Kendall Thomas, eds., pp. 191–200. New York: New Press.

Williams, Raymond, 1977 Marxism and Literature. Oxford: Oxford University Press.

Williams, Richard, Reynold Nesiba, and Eileen Díaz McConnell, 2005 The Changing Face of Inequality in Home Mortgage Lending. Social Problems 52:181–208.

Wilson, Chris, 1997 The Myth of Santa Fe: Creating a Modern Regional Tradition. Albuquerque: University of New Mexico Press.

Wise, Brian, 2003 On Shoshana Johnson, Jessica Lynch, and Disability. American Daily, October 10. Electronic document. www.americandaily.com/item/3255/.

Woolard, Kathryn, 1989 Sentences in the Language Prison: The Rhetorical Structuring of an American Language Policy Debate. American Ethnologist 16:268–278.

Woolard, Kathryn, 1998 Introduction: Language Ideology as a Field of Inquiry. *In* Language Ideologies: Practice and Theory. Bambi B. Schieffelin, Kathryn A. Woolard, and Paul V. Kroskrity, eds., pp. 3–47. Oxford: Oxford University Press.

Zentella, Ana Celia, 1995 The "Chiquita-fication" of US Latinos and their Languages, or Why We Need an Anthro-political linguistics. *In* SALSA III: Proceedings of the Symposium about Language and Society at Austin, pp. 1–18. Austin: University of Texas, Department of Linguistics.

Zentella, Ana Celia, 2002 Latin@ Languages and Identities. *In* Latinos: Remaking America. Marcelo M. Suárez-Orozco and Mariela M. Páez, eds., pp. 321–338. Berkeley and London: University of California Press.

# Index

Printed in the USA/Agawam, MA
April 9, 2010

540663.042